Lecture Notes of the Institute for Computer Sciences, Social Informatics and Telecommunications Engineering 475

The LNICST series publishes ICST's conferences, symposia and workshops. It reports state-of-the-art results in areas related to the scope of the Institute.

LNICST reports state-of-the-art results in areas related to the scope of the Institute. The type of material published includes

- Proceedings (published in time for the respective event)
- Other edited monographs (such as project reports or invited volumes)

LNICST topics span the following areas:

- General Computer Science
- E-Economy
- E-Medicine
- Knowledge Management
- Multimedia
- Operations, Management and Policy
- Social Informatics
- Systems

Cong Vinh Phan · Thanh Dung Nguyen
Editors

Context-Aware Systems and Applications

11th EAI International Conference, ICCASA 2022
Vinh Long, Vietnam, October 27–28, 2022
Proceedings

Springer

Editors
Cong Vinh Phan 🔴
Nguyen Tat Thanh University
Ho Chi Minh City, Vietnam

Thanh Dung Nguyen
Mekong University
Vinh Long Province, Vietnam

ISSN 1867-8211 ISSN 1867-822X (electronic)
Lecture Notes of the Institute for Computer Sciences, Social Informatics
and Telecommunications Engineering
ISBN 978-3-031-28815-9 ISBN 978-3-031-28816-6 (eBook)
https://doi.org/10.1007/978-3-031-28816-6

This Springer imprint is published by the registered company Springer Nature Switzerland AG
The registered company address is: Gewerbestrasse 11, 6330 Cham, Switzerland

Preface

ICCASA 2022 (the 11th EAI International Conference on Context-Aware Systems and Applications), was held during October 27–28, 2022 at Mekong University in Vinh Long province, Vietnam, in hybrid style, due to the travel restrictions caused by the worldwide COVID-19 pandemic. The aim of the conference is to provide an internationally respected forum for scientific research in the technologies and applications of smart computing and communication. ICCASA provides an excellent opportunity for researchers to discuss modern approaches and techniques for smart computing systems and their applications.

For this eleventh edition of ICCASA, and repeating the success of the previous year, the Program Committee received submissions from authors in six countries and each paper was reviewed by at least three expert reviewers. We chose 14 papers after intensive discussions held among the Program Committee members. We really appreciate the excellent reviews and lively discussions of the Program Committee members and external reviewers in the review process. This year we had three prominent invited speakers, Giacomo Cabri from the University of Modena and Reggio Emilia in Italy, Hafiz Mahfooz Ul Haque from the University of Central Punjab in Pakistan and Dang Thanh Tin from Ho Chi Minh City University of Technology, HCM-VNU in Vietnam. ICCASA 2022 was jointly organized by the European Alliance for Innovation (EAI), Mekong University (MKU), and Nguyen Tat Thanh University (NTTU). This conference could not have been organized without the strong support of the staff members of the three organizations. We would especially like to thank Imrich Chlamtac (University of Trento), Patricia Gabajova (EAI), and Martin Vojtek (EAI) for their great help in organizing the conference. We also appreciate the gentle guidance and help of Luong Minh Cu, Rector of MKU.

October 2022
Cong Vinh Phan
Thanh Dung Nguyen

Organization

Steering Committee

Imrich Chlamtac   Bruno Kessler Professor, University of Trento, Italy

Phan Cong Vinh   Nguyen Tat Thanh University, Vietnam

Organizing Committee

General Chair

Phan Cong Vinh   Nguyen Tat Thanh University, Vietnam

Honorary General Chair

Luong Minh Cu   Mekong University, Vietnam

Technical Program Committee Chairs

Abdur Rakib   Coventry University, UK

Nguyen Thanh Dung   Mekong University, Vietnam

Web Chairs

Do Nguyen Anh Thu   Nguyen Tat Thanh University, Vietnam

Nguyen Huu The   Mekong University, Vietnam

Publicity and Social Media Chairs

Ijaz Uddin   City University of Science and Information Technology, Peshawar, Pakistan

Dang Thi Ngoc Lan   Mekong University, Vietnam

Workshops Chairs

Pham Van Dang   Nguyen Tat Thanh University, Vietnam
Tran Van Than   Mekong University, Vietnam

Sponsorship and Exhibits Chair

Vu Tuan Anh   Industrial University of Ho Chi Minh City,
                                       Vietnam

Publications Chair

Phan Cong Vinh   Nguyen Tat Thanh University, Vietnam

Local Chairs

Nguyen Thanh Dung   Mekong University, Vietnam
Tran Thi Hong Lan   State Agency of Technology Innovation, Ministry
                                       of Science and Technology, Vietnam

Technical Program Committee

Technical Program Committee Members

Anh Dinh   University of Saskatchewan, Canada
Ashish Khare   University of Allahabad, India
Bui Cong Giao   Saigon University, Vietnam
Cao Van Kien   Nguyen Tat Thanh University, Vietnam
Chernyi Sergei   Admiral Makarov State University of Maritime
                                       and Inland Shipping, Russia
Chien-Chih Yu   National ChengChi University, Taiwan
Dang Thanh Tin   Ho Chi Minh City University of Technology,
                                       Vietnam
David Sundaram   University of Auckland, New Zealand
Do Van Thanh   Nguyen Tat Thanh University, Vietnam
Gabrielle Peko   University of Auckland, New Zealand
Giacomo Cabri   University of Modena and Reggio Emilia, Italy
Hafiz Mahfooz Ul Haque   University of Central Punjab, Pakistan
Harun Baraki   University of Kassel, Germany
Hiroshi Fujita   Gifu University, Japan

Huynh Xuan Hiep	Can Tho University, Vietnam
Hyungchul Yoon	Chungbuk National University, South Korea
Issam Damaj	Beirut Arab University, Lebanon
Kurt Geihs	University of Kassel, Germany
Le Hoang Thai	Ho Chi Minh City University of Science, Vietnam
Le Hong Anh	University of Mining and Geology, Vietnam
Le Xuan Truong	Ho Chi Minh City Open University, Vietnam
Manish Khare	Dhirubhai Ambani Institute of Information and Communication Technology, India
Muhammad Athar Javed Sethi	University of Engineering and Technology (UET) Peshawar, Pakistan
Ngo Ha Quang Thinh	Ho Chi Minh City University of Technology, Vietnam
Nguyen Ha Huy Cuong	Da Nang University, Vietnam
Nguyen Huu Nhan	Nguyen Tat Thanh University, Vietnam
Nguyen Manh Duc	University of Ulsan, South Korea
Nguyen Thanh Binh	Ho Chi Minh City University of Technology, Vietnam
Nguyen Thanh Hai	Can Tho University, Vietnam
Om Prakash	Hemvati Nandan Bahuguna Garhwal University, India
Pham Quoc Cuong	Ho Chi Minh City University of Technology, Vietnam
Rajiv Tewari	University of Allahabad, India
Shahzad Ashraf	Hohai University, China
Tran Huu Tam	University of Kassel, Germany
Truong Cong Doan	International School, VNU, Vietnam
Vu Tuan Anh	Industrial University of Ho Chi Minh City, Vietnam
Waralak V. Siricharoen	Silpakorn University, Thailand

Contents

Foundation of Context-awareness

Context-Awareness in Internet of Mobile Things

Vu Tuan Anh[1,2], Phan Cong Vinh[3(✉)], and Pham Quoc Cuong[1]

[1] Ho Chi Minh City University of Technology (HCMUT), VNU-HCM,
Ho Chi Minh City, Vietnam
{vtanh.sdh19,cuongpham}@hcmut.edu.vn
[2] Faculty of Electronics Technology, Industrial University of Ho Chi Minh City,
Ho Chi Minh City, Vietnam
vutuananh@iuh.edu.vn
[3] Faculty of Information Technology, Nguyen Tat Thanh University,
Ho Chi Minh City, Vietnam
pcvinh@ntt.edu.vn

Abstract. A new cognitive paradigm in internet of mobile things (IOMT) is currently on spot: Context-Awareness (CA), which is inspired by the activity of the human autonomous nervous system. The comprehensive target of CA is to realize IOMT, that can self-govern without direct human interventions. To solve this enormous challenge of CA requires a basic solution for CA concept. For this purpose, in this paper, the categorical approach is used to establish a strong formal basis for modeling CA in order to achieve the formal aspects of CA.

Keywords: Context-Awareness (CA) · IOMT · DIOMT · NIOMT · Formal aspects · Categorical language

1 Introduction

CA is an important property of IOMT and implies an increased complexity of IOMT behavior management. CA is the primary way for OMT to be manageable [8]. Indeed, a difficulty is that IOMT cannot be centrally managed. For instance, the information needs to make decisions cannot be centralized in IOMT. In such the IOMT, CA is only possible when processing entities in IOMT respond and harmonize with each other autonomously to enable to continue correctly the required processing in IOMT. Therefore, in the context of IOMT, CA is specified as cognitive paradigm in IOMT. In other words, when CA mechanism is implemented in the IOMT then the cognitive paradigm is determined. The intrinsic nature of CA is to allow autonomous networked processing entities in IOMT to self-manage the set of services and resources distributed at any given time while interacting and coordinating with each other. Therefore, for IOMT, one of the main challenges is how to support CA in the face of changes in computational goals, user needs and environmental conditions. In other words,

© ICST Institute for Computer Sciences, Social Informatics and Telecommunications Engineering 2023
Published by Springer Nature Switzerland AG 2023. All Rights Reserved
C. V. Phan and T. D. Nguyen (Eds.): ICCASA 2022, LNICST 475, pp. 3–15, 2023.
https://doi.org/10.1007/978-3-031-28816-6_1

how does the IOMT make sense of the involved contextual data, change with it, and tailor the services and resources it provides, in line with the target-driven processing mechanisms?

Responding to this major IOMT challenge requires a well-founded model and in-depth analysis of the CA concept. With this goal in mind, we develop a solid formal approach in which autonomous networked processing entities in IOMT can detect, diagnose, and repair failures, as well as adjust configurations and optimize their performance as environmental conditions and user needs change. All the things here must be completed while self-protecting and self-healing in the face of natural difficulties and malevolent assaults.

In view of this, we find that a rigorous approach to CA requires fundamental study of all aspects of CA. As a new development for CA, aspects of CA are formalized using categorical language [18], the content of which is reported in the paper.

2   Outline

The content of the paper is useful for readers who already have a basic knowledge of IOMT and are now looking to learn a new approach to formalizing CA in IOMT using a categorical language.

The content of the paper related to formalization is presented in a straight-forward manner with a detailed approach to the required components and a brief expansion of the more advanced components. A number of corollaries explaining the use of formal aspects, including the arguments necessary to achieve a specific result, are presented.

We try to make the presentation as self-contained as possible, despite the fact that assuming you are familiar with the concept of CA in IOMT. Familiarity with algebra and related concepts in the categorical language [9] is helpful for realizing the consequences, but is not absolutely necessary most places.

The rest of this paper is organized as follows: Sects. 3 and 4 present the notions of CA and IOMT, respectively. Section 5 presents models of CA in IOMT. Finally, a short summary is given in Sect. 6.

3   Notion of CA

In IOMT, CA mentions the idea that processing entities can perceive and respond based on their environment. The entities can have information about the circumstances under which they can take action and respond accordingly based on rules. The general term of the entities' context perception in pervasive networks is introduced in [4,15] where context-aware entities can also attempt to make suppositions about the user's current situation. In [11] context is defined as "any information that can be used to describe an entity's situation."

While the IOMT community initially viewed context as a user location mat-ter, as discussed in [11] over the past few years, the concept has come to be regarded not only as a state, but as part of the process in which the user partic-ipates; therefore, generic and complex context models have been proposed [10] to support context-aware applications that use them to

- tune the interface,
- modify the application-related data set,
- augment the accuracy of information retrieval,
- find services,
- make user interaction invisible, or
- establish intelligent environment

For instance, a context-aware mobile phone can recognize if the user is currently in the gathering room and that the user is standing up or sitting down. The context-aware mobile phone can induce if the user is currently in a gathering and dismiss any insignificant calls [10].

Context-aware systems involve [2]

- acquiring context (e.g., using sensors to perceive a situation),
- abstracting, and understanding context (e.g. matching a perceived sensory stimulus with a context) and
- perceived context-based application behavior (e.g. triggering a context-based action)

Since user activity and location are so important to many applications, context awareness has received more attention in the research areas of location perception and activity awareness.

Context awareness is considered a technology that enables pervasive net-works. Context awareness is used to design innovative user interfaces and is often used as part of ubiquitous and wearable computing. It also began to be felt on the internet with the advent of hybrid search engines. [25] identifies the human factor and the physical environment as two significant characteristics related to computer science. Recently, much work has also been completed to easily distribute context information; [23] investigated a number of middleware solutions arranged to apply straightforward context administration and supply-ing in mobile systems. Several context-aware location-based service systems were evaluated [14] using data by analyzing developer practice and method choices. Their development occurs during the major stages of context perception (i.e. context acquisition, context representation, reasoning, and context adjustment). [6] conducted a general overview of context-aware computing from the point of view of the Internet of Things, reviewed more than 50 leading projects in the field. Furthermore, [7] also examined a large number of industrial products cur-rently on the IoT market from a context-aware computing standpoint. Their overview aims to serve as a guide and a conceptual structure for contextual product research and development in the IoT model. Evaluation was performed using framework theory developed by [1] over a decade ago. The composition of emerging technologies and the Internet turns everyday objects into intelligent objects that can be aware of and respond to their context [13].

Context related to human factors is constructed into the following three types:

- the user's social environment (location of others, social interactions, group dynamics),
- user tasks (spontaneous activity, engaged tasks, shared goals) and
- information about the user (knowledge of habits, emotional state, biophysical conditions).

Context related to the physical environment is organized into the following three classes [3,5]:

- infrastructure (the surrounding resources to computing, communication, task performance),
- physical conditions (noise, light, pressure, air quality) and
- location (absolute location, relative location, co-location).

In many practical situations, it is essential to use wearable sensors, embedded in mobile devices such as smart phones and smart watches, to measure the emotional state of the user [21]. This will help to understand how emotions affect processes such as decision making and reasoning [19]. Moreover, emotion recognition is still a complex and challenging task, mainly related to the following aspects:

- mode of sensing [21] –that is, what to sense and what kind of sensor can be used? Physical sensors in mobile devices or biosensors in wearables and pervasive sensors (e.g. RF sensors) are now available.
- data analysis [16] – that is, different approaches to emotional recognition are based on different types of collected data.
- application in real life [12,20,24] – that is, effective use of emotional information in pervasive computing and context-aware applications.

4   Internet of Mobile Things (IOMT)

Recently, the idea of connecting all mobile things (MT) has given rise to the emergence of the "Internet of Mobile Things" (IOMT), which can be used as a mobile device to collect data from remotely deployed IOMT devices or can act as a communication bridge [17]. In other words, the IOMT is fundamentally changing the world by allowing multiple mobile devices to communicate and exchange data with each other. Alternatively, persons equipped with their wearable can be considered as another type of movable object providing/receiving services to/from IOMT [22]. A set of MT can form a special mobile wireless network and provide services. Such networks can cover a larger area while devices connected to the network collaborate with each other to perform complex tasks [27].

However, there are several issues that need to be addressed in order to use multiple MT for IOMT applications [17,22,27] efficiently, including:

- dynamic and intelligent management of sensors and devices terrestrial IOMT devices,
- limited power of IOMT and MT,
- privacy and security in IOMT and
- communication between IOMT devices and MT, communication between MT, connectivity of MT

Due to the dynamic nature of the aforementioned issues, supporting these stakeholders becomes a challenging task. Therefore, it is necessary to develop new techniques to manage and optimize the real-time operation of these communication platforms [26].

5   CA in IOMT

As known that CA is attained when IOMT is built. In this way, for shaping IOMT, we begin to observe *deterministic internet of mobile things* (DIOMT) and then extend to *nondeterministic internet of mobile things* (NIOMT) by an approach using categorical language in this section.

5.1   CA in DIOMT

CA in DIOMT we want abstraction to be multiple partial morphism applications in intuition, such as

$$\phi_0 \xrightarrow{\gamma_0} \phi_1 \xrightarrow{\gamma_1} \phi_2 \xrightarrow{\gamma_2} \phi_3 \cdots \tag{1}$$

in which

- All indexes $i \in T \ (= \mathbb{N} \cup \{0\})$ mention to times,
- ϕ is a state of DIOMT in the set, denoted by *IOMT*, of states. ϕ_i indicates the state ϕ at the time i,
- γ is a contextual data in the set, denoted by *Context*, of contextual data. γ_i indicates the contextual data γ at the time i, which makes change of the state ϕ_i to begin to be ϕ_{i+1}.

The adaptation process in (1) is meant by

$$\cdots \phi_2(\phi_1(\phi_0())) = \cdots \phi_2(\phi_1(\gamma_0)) = \cdots \phi_2(\gamma_1) = \cdots \gamma_2 \tag{2}$$

The meaning of (1) can also be descriptively understood as

$$\phi_0() \ \gamma_0 \ \gamma_1 \ \gamma_2 \ \cdots \longmapsto \phi_1(\gamma_0) \ \gamma_1 \ \gamma_2 \ \cdots \longmapsto \gamma_0 \ \phi_2(\gamma_1) \ \gamma_2 \ \cdots \tag{3}$$

or, in another representation

$$\xrightarrow{\phi_0} \gamma_0 \ \gamma_1 \ \gamma_2 \ \cdots \longmapsto \gamma_0 \xrightarrow{\phi_1} \gamma_1 \ \gamma_2 \ \cdots \longmapsto \gamma_0 \ \gamma_1 \xrightarrow{\phi_2} \gamma_2 \ \cdots \tag{4}$$

Note that in (3) and (4), we want to represent the above-mentioned adjustment process of DIOMT based on context where each step of the process is an application of unary partial morphism $1 \xrightarrow{\phi_i} IOMT$ on $1 \xrightarrow{\gamma_{i-1}} Context$, for all i in T.

The tuning process, in (3) and (4), describes the CA concept in DIOMT including the adjustment steps to change the *configurations* of the DIOMT.

Definition 1 (Configuration of DIOMT). *A configuration of DIOMT at an adjustment step is defined as an element of the set* $IOMT \times Context^{i \in T}$*, in which* $Context^{i \in T}$ *stands for*

$$Context^{i \in T} = \underbrace{Context \times Context \times \ldots \times Context}_{i \ times} \tag{5}$$

As we know, when we combine sets by multiplication, each set is *factor* and the resulting set is *product*. Therefore, each set $Context$ is a factor of the result set $Context^{i \in T}$, $IOMT$ and $Context^{i \in T}$ are two factors of the set $IOMT \times Context^{i \in T}$. The multiplication of sets is defined very naturally. Just recall that a product is not just a set, but a set that comes in two morphisms as in

– When i = 2 then $Context^2 = \{< \gamma_1, \gamma_2 > | \gamma_1, \gamma_2 \in Context\}$ is obtained by

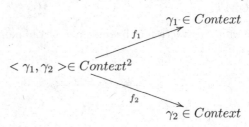

– When i=3 then $Context^3 = \{<< \gamma_1, \gamma_2 >, \gamma_3 > | \gamma_1, \gamma_2, \gamma_3 \in Context\}$ is obtained by

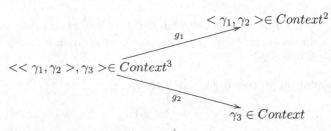

In particular, we have

– If i = 0 then $Context^0 = \{\}$
– If i = 1 then $Context^1 = Context = \{\gamma_1 | \gamma_1 \in Context\}$

The CA is based on mapping one configuration to another. Let's consider the following situations. A particular CA can be specified by the following morphism:

$$CA : (IOMT \times Context) \longrightarrow IOMT \tag{6}$$

(i.e., $CA : (IOMT \times Context^1) \longrightarrow (IOMT \times Context^0)$ or denoted by CA ($IOMT \times Context, IOMT$))

Another specific CA can be specified by

$$CA : (IOMT \times Context) \longrightarrow (IOMT \times Context) \qquad (7)$$

(i.e., $CA : (IOMT \times Context^1) \longrightarrow (IOMT \times Context^1)$ or denoted by CA ($IOMT \times Context, IOMT \times Context$))

Again, we can also specify another specific CA as

$$CA : (IOMT \times Context^n) \longrightarrow (IOMT \times Context) \qquad (8)$$

(i.e., $CA : (IOMT \times Context^n) \longrightarrow (IOMT \times Context^1)$ or denoted by CA ($IOMT \times Context^n, IOMT \times Context$))

and in exactly the same way, any other specific CA can be specified as in.

Definition 2. *In general, an arbitrary context-awareness in DIOMT is specified by*

$$CA : (IOMT \times Context^{i \in T}) \longrightarrow (IOMT \times Context^{j \in T}) \qquad (9)$$

Now, we can prove the following corollaries.

Corollary 1 (CA in DIOMT). *The morphism CA in* (9) *defines context-awareness in* DIOMT

Proof. This comes from (9) and the actuality that CA is described as context-awareness in DIOMT.   Q.E.D.

CA is often described as self-*. Formally, think of self-* as the set of self-_. Each self-_ becoming an element in self-* is called *self-* aspect*. That is,

$$\text{self-*} = \{\text{self-\_} \mid \text{self-\_ is a self-* aspect}\} \qquad (10)$$

We found that self-CHOP includes four self-* aspects which are self-configuration, self-healing, self-optimization and self-protection. Therefore, self-CHOP is a subset of self- *, i.e. self CHOP = { self-configuring, self-healing, self-optimizing, self-protecting} ⊂ self-* [8].

A set $\{CA_{k \in \mathbb{N}}\}$ of mappings is defined by morphism CA in (9) such that

$$\{CA_{k \in \mathbb{N}}\} : (IOMT \times Context^{i \in T}) \longrightarrow (IOMT \times Context^{j \in T}) \qquad (11)$$

Hence, we have the corollary as the following.

Corollary 2 (CA aspects in DIOMT). *The set* $\{CA_{k \in \mathbb{N}}\}$ *in* (11) *defines context-awareness aspects in* DIOMT. *Each mapping* $CA_{k \in \mathbb{N}}$ *is called a context-awareness aspect.*

Proof. This originates from the result of the fact that CA is the set of context-awareness aspects.   Q.E.D.

To investigate more clearly, we can build a category of DIOMT configurations sets and set up CA-algebras as specified in the following corollaries.

Corollary 3 (Category of the sets of DIOMT configurations). *A category is determined by The* DIOMT *configurations sets as in Definition 1.*

Proof. Indeed, as in [18], let **Cat(DIOMT)** be such a category of the DIOMT configurations sets, whose structure is built as follows:

- Each configurations set $IOMT \times Context^{i \in T}$ specifies an object. That is, $Obj(\mathbf{Cat(DIOMT)}) = \{IOMT \times Context^{i \in T}\}$.
- Each CA determines a morphism. That is, $Arc(\mathbf{Cat(DIOMT)}) = \{CA : (IOMT \times Context^{i \in T}) \longrightarrow (IOMT \times Context^{j \in T})\}$.

Easily check that the identity and associativity properties on all CAs are satisfied.   Q.E.D.

Corollary 4 (CA-algebra(DIOMT)). *Each morphism CA in the category* **Cat(DIOMT)** *determines an algebra, aka CA-algebra(DIOMT).*

Proof. This originates as the result of the truth that definition of T-algebra [18], where functor T is determined such that $\mathsf{T} = \biguplus \{CA\}$. Note that the notation $\biguplus$ stands for *disjoint union* or *coproduct*.   Q.E.D.

As a result originates from of Corollary 4, a formal definition of DIOMT is attained as follows.

Definition 3 (DIOMT).   *Each*   DIOMT*is*   *determined*   *by*   *a* CA-*algebra*(DIOMT)

5.2   CA in NIOMT

CA in NIOMT we want model to be multiple partial morphism applications in intuition, such as

$$\phi_0 \xrightarrow{\gamma_0 | x_0} \phi_1 \xrightarrow{\gamma_1 | x_1} \phi_2 \xrightarrow{\gamma_2 | x_2} \phi_3 \cdots \tag{12}$$

in which

- All indexes i in T, ϕ_i and γ_i have the same meaning as those mentioned in (1)
- x_i is a real number that can be thought of as *multiplcity* (or *weight*) where the adjustment from ϕ_i to ϕ_{i+1} appears.

Adjustment process of CA in NIOMT in diagram (12) can be split into two complementary parts as follows:

$$\phi_0 \xrightarrow{\gamma_0} \phi_1 \xrightarrow{\gamma_1} \phi_2 \xrightarrow{\gamma_2} \phi_3 \cdots \tag{13}$$

and

$$\phi_0 \xrightarrow{x_0} \phi_1 \xrightarrow{x_1} \phi_2 \xrightarrow{x_2} \phi_3 \cdots \tag{14}$$

On the one hand, diagram (13) stresses $1 \xrightarrow{\gamma_i} Context$, for all i in T, in the adjustment process. This allows us to conveniently explore the γ_i series as contextual data series. On the other hand, diagram (14) gives rise to $1 \xrightarrow{x_i} \mathbb{R}$, for all i in T, as the weight of the context data series during tuning to support the evaluation of quantitative behaviors based on the weight of the context data series.

Some of the first steps of the tuning process in (12) can also be described as

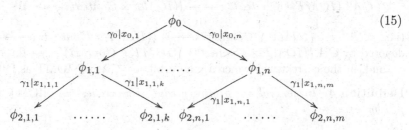

$$(15)$$

Diagram (15) is thought of as

– For the first step,
$$\phi_1 \in \{\phi_{1,1}, \ldots, \phi_{1,n}\} \subset IOMT$$
and
$$x_0 \in \{x_{0,1}, \ldots, x_{0,n}\} \subset \mathbb{R}$$

– For the second step,
$$\phi_2 \in \{\phi_{2,1,1}, \ldots, \phi_{2,1,k}\} \cup \ldots \cup \{\phi_{2,n,1}, \ldots, \phi_{2,n,m}\} \subset IOMT$$
and
$$x_1 \in \{x_{1,1,1}, \ldots, x_{1,1,k}\} \cup \ldots \cup \{x_{1,n,1}, \ldots, x_{1,n,m}\} \subset \mathbb{R}$$

and the meaning of (12) is seen as a following morphism.

$$CA : (IOMT \times Context) \longrightarrow (IOMT \longrightarrow \mathbb{R}) \qquad (16)$$

The adjustment morphism CA in (16) is nondeterministic and this can be explained as follows: CA specifies for each configuration in $IOMT \times Context$ a morphism $IOMT \longrightarrow \mathbb{R}$ that can be seen as a kind of *nondeterministic configuration* (aka *distribution configuration*) and assigns each state ϕ' in $IOMT$ a multiplicity (or weight) $CA(<\phi, \gamma>)(\phi')$ in $\mathbb{R}$.

This nondeterminism of CA in NIOMT extends the ability to represent the categorical models mentioned in Subsect. 5.1. Let's consider the following situations.

A specific CA in NIOMT, indicated by the following morphism, is an extension of (6):

$$CA : (IOMT \times Context) \longrightarrow (IOMT \longrightarrow \mathbb{R}) \qquad (17)$$

(i.e., $CA : (IOMT \times Context^1) \longrightarrow ((IOMT \times Context^0) \longrightarrow \mathbb{R})$ or denoted by $CA \, ((IOMT \times Context), (IOMT \longrightarrow \mathbb{R})))$

The model in (7) is extended to the CA in the NIOMT determined by

$$CA : (IOMT \times Context) \longrightarrow ((IOMT \times Context) \longrightarrow \mathbb{R}) \qquad (18)$$

(i.e., $CA : (IOMT \times Context^1) \longrightarrow ((IOMT \times Context^1) \longrightarrow \mathbb{R})$ or denoted by $CA\,((IOMT \times Context), ((IOMT \times Context) \longrightarrow \mathbb{R})))$

Again, we determine another specific CA in NIOMT as an extension of (8) in

$$CA : (IOMT \times Context^n) \longrightarrow ((IOMT \times Context) \longrightarrow \mathbb{R}) \qquad (19)$$

(i.e., $CA : (IOMT \times Context^n) \longrightarrow ((IOMT \times Context^1) \longrightarrow \mathbb{R})$ or denoted by $CA\,((IOMT \times Context^n), ((IOMT \times Context) \longrightarrow \mathbb{R})))$

and, in the correct way we create an arbitrary CA in NIOMT as follows.

Definition 4. *In general, an arbitrary context-awareness in NIOMT is specified by*

$$CA : (IOMT \times Context^{i \in T}) \longrightarrow ((IOMT \times Context^{j \in T}) \longrightarrow \mathbb{R}) \quad (20)$$

There is a corollary as described below.

Corollary 5 (CA in NIOMT). *The morphism CA in (20) defines context-awareness in NIOMT*

Proof. This originates from (20) as the result of the truth that CA is described as context-awareness in NIOMT.   Q.E.D.

A set $\{CA_{k \in \mathbb{N}}\}$ of mappings is defined by morphism CA in (20) such that

$$\{CA_{k \in \mathbb{N}}\} : (IOMT \times Context^{i \in T}) \longrightarrow ((IOMT \times Context^{j \in T}) \longrightarrow \mathbb{R}) \qquad (21)$$

Thus, there are the following corollaries.

Corollary 6 (CA aspects in NIOMT). *The set $\{CA_{k \in \mathbb{N}}\}$ in (21) defines context-awareness aspects in NIOMT. Each mapping $CA_{k \in \mathbb{N}}$ is called a context-awareness aspect.*

Proof. This originates from the result of the fact that context-awareness is the set of context-awareness aspects.   Q.E.D.

Corollary 7 (Category of the sets of NIOMT configurations). *A category* **Cat(NIOMT)** *of the sets of NIOMT configurations is determined by the category* **Cat(DIOMT)** *equipped with structure* $(IOMT \times Context^{i \in T}) \longrightarrow ((IOMT \times Context^{j \in T}) \longrightarrow \mathbb{R})$.

Proof. This stems immediately from the result of Corollary 3.   Q.E.D.

Corollary 8 (CA-algebra(NIOMT)).   *The structure* $(IOMT \times Context^{i \in T}) \longrightarrow ((IOMT \times Context^{j \in T}) \longrightarrow \mathbb{R})$ *in the category* **Cat(NIOMT)** *determines an algebra, aka CA-algebra(NIOMT).*

Proof. This stems from definition on T-algebra [18], in which functor T is determined such that $T = \uplus\{CA\}$ (similar to Corollary 4) with CA determined in (20).   Q.E.D.

As a result originates from the Corollary 8, a formal definition of NIOMT is attained as follows.

Definition 5 (NIOMT). *Each   NIOMT   is   determined   by   a* CA-*algebra*(NIOMT)

Furthermore, we have the following theorem to get a meaningful relationship between DIOMT and NIOMT.

Theorem 1 (Relationship between DIOMT and NIOMT). DIOMT *is just of a specific NIOMT. In other words, using categorical language,* DIOMT $\xrightarrow{\subseteq}$ NIOMT

Proof. Indeed, by the adjustment morphism in (20) of NIOMT, let f be the morphism $f : (IOMT \times Context^{j \in T}) \longrightarrow \mathbb{R}$, $Config$ be $IOMT \times Context^{j \in T}$ and the finite set $\mathbb{R}(Config) = \{1 \xrightarrow{c} Config | f(c) \neq 0\} \xrightarrow{\subseteq} Config$. So it follows that when
$\exists! 1 \xrightarrow{c} Config : f(c) = 1$ but $\forall c' \neq c : f(c') = 0$ (i.e., the set $\mathbb{R}(Config)$ is a singleton set of configuration with weight of 1. Note that the notation $\exists!$ is understood as "exist only") then (20) begins to be the adjustment morphism of DIOMT as in (9). In other words, in the case, NIOMT will begin to be DIOMT. Q.E.D.

6   Conclusions

In the content of the paper, the concept of CA in IOMT has rigorously been established from which formal features of the CA become visible. CA in deterministic and nondeterministic IOMT (DIOMT and NIOMT) have been considered , in which configuration of IOMT at every adjustment step has been specified as an element in the set $IOMT \times Context^{i \in T}$, then CA as a morphism from a configuration to another for finding the important properties of CA.

Acknowledgement. We acknowledge Ho Chi Minh City University of Technology (HCMUT), VNU-HCM for supporting this study.

References

1. Abowd, G.D., Dey, A.K., Brown, P.J., Davies, N., Smith, M., Steggles, P.: Towards a better understanding of context and context-awareness. In: Gellersen, H.-W. (ed.) HUC 1999. LNCS, vol. 1707, pp. 304–307. Springer, Heidelberg (1999). https://doi.org/10.1007/3-540-48157-5_29
2. Schmidt, A.: Ubiquitous Computing - Computing in Context. PhD thesis, Lancaster University, UK, Computing Department (2002)

3. Chihani, B., Bertin, E., Crespi, N.: A comprehensive framework for context-aware communication services. In: 2011 15th International Conference on Intelligence in Next Generation Networks, pp. 52–57 (2011)
4. Schilit, B.N., Theimer, M.M.: Disseminating active map information to mobile hosts. IEEE Netw. **8**(5), 22–32 (1994)
5. Nicolas, C., Marot, M., Becker, M.: A self-organization mechanism for a cold chain monitoring system. In: 2011 IEEE 73rd Vehicular Technology Conference (VTC Spring), pp. 1–5 (2011)
6. Perera, C., Zaslavsky, A., Christen, P., Georgakopoulos, D.: Context aware computing for the internet of things: a survey. IEEE Commun. Surv. Tutorials **16**(1), 414–454 (2014)
7. Perera, C., Liu, C.H., Jayawardena, S., Chen, M.: A survey on internet of things from industrial market perspective. IEEE Access **2**, 1660–1679 (2014)
8. Cong-Vinh, P.: Formal Aspects of Self-* in Autonomic Networked Computing Systems, pp. 381–410. Springer, Boston (2009)
9. Vinh, P.C.: Parallel programming and applications in grid, P2P and network-based systems, chapter formalizing parallel programming in large scale distributed networks: from tasks parallel and data parallel to applied categorical structures. Advances in Parallel Computing. IOS Press, 1st edition (2009)
10. Bolchini, C., Curino, C.A., Quintarelli, E., Schreiber, F.A., Tanca, L.: A data-oriented survey of context models. ACM SIGMOD Rec. **34**(4), 19–26 (2007)
11. Dey, A.K.: Understanding and using context. Pers. Ubiquitous Comput. **5**(1), 4–7 (2001)
12. Sarmiento-Calisaya, E., Ccori, P.C., Parari, A.C.: An emotion-aware persuasive architecture to support challenging classroom situations. In: 2022 IEEE International Conference on Consumer Electronics (ICCE), pp. 1–2 (2022)
13. Kortuem, G., Kawsar, F., Sundramoorthy, V., Fitton, D.: Smart objects as building blocks for the Internet of things. IEEE Internet Comput. **14**(1), 44–51 (2010)
14. Grifoni, P., D'Ulizia, A., Ferri, F.: Context-awareness in location based services in the big data era. In: Skourletopoulos, G., Mastorakis, G., Mavromoustakis, C.X., Dobre, C., Pallis, E. (eds.) Mobile Big Data. LNDECT, vol. 10, pp. 85–127. Springer, Cham (2018). https://doi.org/10.1007/978-3-319-67925-9_5
15. Mcheick, H.: Ubiquitous computing and context-aware applications: survey and contributions. In: 2016 IEEE First International Conference on Connected Health: Applications, Systems and Engineering Technologies (CHASE), pp. 394–397 (2016)
16. Lin, K., Xia, F., Wang, W., Tian, D., Song, J.: System design for big data application in emotion-aware healthcare. IEEE Access **4**, 6901–6909 (2016)
17. Kamilaris, A., Pitsillides, A.: Mobile phone computing and the internet of things: a survey. IEEE Internet Things J. **3**(6), 885–898 (2016)
18. Lawvere, F.W., Schanuel, S.H.: Conceptual Mathematics: A First Introduction to Categories, 1st edn., p. 376. Cambridge University Press, Cambridge (1997)
19. Chen, M., Zhang, Y., Li, Y., Mao, S., Leung, V.C.M.: EMC: emotion-aware mobile cloud computing in 5g. IEEE Netw. **29**(2), 32–38 (2015)
20. Shanmugam, M., Singh, M.: Analysis on emotion-aware healthcare and Google cloud messaging. In: 2017 International Conference on Innovative Mechanisms for Industry Applications (ICIMIA), pp. 667–670 (2017)
21. Sugaya, M.: Emotion aware robot by emotion estimation using biological sensors. In: 2019 IEEE International Conference on Pervasive Computing and Communications Workshops (PerCom Workshops), pp. 541–541 (2019)

22.) Nahrstedt, K., Li, H., Nguyen, P., Chang, S., Vu, L.: Internet of mobile things: mobility-driven challenges, designs and implementations. In: 2016 IEEE First International Conference on Internet-of-Things Design and Implementation (IoTDI), pp. 25–36 (2016)
23. Bellavista, P., Corradi, A., Fanelli, M., Foschini, L.: A survey of context data distribution for mobile ubiquitous systems. ACM Comput. Surv. **44**(4), 1–45 (2012)
24. Mahmud, R., Toosi, A.N., Ramamohanarao, K., Buyya, R.: Context-aware placement of industry 4.0 applications in fog computing environments. IEEE Trans. Ind. Inf. **16**(11), 7004–7013 (2020)
25. Schmidt, A., Beigl, M., Gellersen, H.-W.: There is more to context than location. Comput. Graph. **23**(6), 893–901 (1999)
26. Talavera, L.E., Endler, M., Vasconcelos, I., Vasconcelos, R., Cunha, M., e Silva, F.J.D.S.: The mobile hub concept: enabling applications for the internet of mobile things. In: 2015 IEEE International Conference on Pervasive Computing and Communication Workshops (PerCom Workshops), pp. 123–128 (2015)
27. Tcarenko, I., et al.: Smart energy efficient gateway for internet of mobile things. In: 2017 14th IEEE Annual Consumer Communications & Networking Conference (CCNC), pp. 1016–1017 (2017)

Context-Aware Systems

Collaborative Recommendation with Energy Distance Correlation

Mun Van Dong[1], Trong Van Nguyen[2] ⓘ, Nhung Cam Thi Mai[3] ⓘ,
Tu Cam Thi Tran[4] ⓘ, and Hiep Xuan Huynh[3]([✉]) ⓘ

[1] Hau Giang Public Administration Service Center, Vi Thanh, Hau Giang, Vietnam
[2] Bac Lieu University, Bac Lieu, Vietnam
nvtrong@blu.edu.vn
[3] Can Tho University, Can Tho, Vietnam
{mtcnhung,hxhiep}@ctu.edu.vn
[4] Vinh Long University of Technology Education, Vinh Long, Vietnam
tuttc@vlute.edu.vn

Abstract. The recommendation systems are applied to many fields of the social life. In which, the measure of the similarity, and the measure of the distance are the core problems of the recommender systems, there are many proposals with the different approaches, it shows the characteristics of each recommendation system, commonly used measures such as: the measure Cosine, the measure Pearson, the measure Jaccard, etc. However, there have not been many studies on the energy dependence to determine the correlation of the objects in the process of building a recommendation system. In this article, we mainly focus on determining the correlation/compatibility of the energy-based objects in building a recommendation model. The experimental results are evaluated on two datasets, that are MSWeb datasets and Learning from Sets of Items 2019 datasets, the results show that the proposed model has higher accuracy than the traditional model.

Keywords: Energy distance · Energy dependence measures · Collaborative filtering · Recommendation system · Distance correlation

1 Introduction

With the continuous development of the science and technology, the amount of the information in each field has increased, so the exploitation and using of the information has been studied and they are applied by many scientists in the practice. In particular, the recommendation system [1–4] uses data based on user's feedback about the items, based on the similarity of product characteristics and based on knowledge forms. The different methods to give suggestions for the users according to the level of interest from high to low.

There are many different proposed methods to solve the recommendation problem, the choice of method, it depends on the type of the information, the learning model, predicting new products for the users [5, 6]. Basically, there are main groups/formations

© ICST Institute for Computer Sciences, Social Informatics and Telecommunications Engineering 2023
Published by Springer Nature Switzerland AG 2023. All Rights Reserved
C. V. Phan and T. D. Nguyen (Eds.): ICCASA 2022, LNICST 475, pp. 19–32, 2023.
https://doi.org/10.1007/978-3-031-28816-6_2

of the recommendation model that are divided as follows: Content-Based Recommender Systems [2, 4, 7, [8]; Collaborative Filtering Systems [2, 4, 7, 9]; Knowledge-Based Recommender Systems [4, 7]; Context-Based Recommender Systems [4, 7]; Hybrid Recommender System [4, 7, 10]. The most approaches to building recommendation systems today are based on a measure of similarity such as: cosine, Pearson, Jaccard, etc. Each model has its own advantages in using the measures, it is suitable for the type of information applied in the model, so there are many recommendation models that have been successfully applied in the various fields, especially in the field of e-commerce [11, 12].

In addition to the traditional similarity measures, the energy distance [13] is a measure used to determine the distance correlation between the vectors (the vectors have arbitrary size), which is a powerful tool in multivariate analysis, opens a new direction in building the recommendation systems. Currently, there are not many studies on applying this measure in building a recommendation system model. In this article, we present a collaborative filtering model that predicts for the users who are missing ratings at specific products and recommends the best products (the most relevant products) based on the distance correlation measures/energy distances [14].

The structure of the article is divided into 5 parts: Sect. 1 introduces the basic issues in the recommender system and the proposes energy measures in building a recommendation model, Part 2 presents an overview of the collaborative filtering model, Part 3 proposes a collaborative filtering model with the distance correlation, Part 4 presents the experimental results and the evaluations, and finally a conclusion presents a summary of the obtained results.

2   Collaborative Filtering

Collaborative filtering [2, 7] uses the user's ratings dataset to rate products liked by users, so it makes the missing rating predictions for the items (the unreviewed product) or recommend a specific number of products considered best to a user who needs recommendations.

Given a list of m users $U = \{u_0, u_1,..., u_m\}$ and a list of n items $I = \{i_0, i_1,..., i_n\}$. Where $R = r_{jk}$ is the rating stored in the user rating matrix m x n where each row represents user u_j (with $1 \leq j \leq m$)) and each column represents a item i_k (with $1 \leq k \leq n$). R_{jk} represents the rating of the user u_j for the item i_k, all is shown in Table 1.

Let $u_a \in U$ be the user who needs to be suggested or the active users, and $I_a = I\backslash\{i_l \in I | r_{al} = 1\}$ is the set of the items unknown to user u_a.

The task is to predict the ratings for all items I_a or create a list (top N) of the best recommendations for u_a. The missing ranked values are predicted on each row of matrix r_a, where the missing values are estimated from other data in R, on the basis of ratings for all unknown items I_a, select the N highest predictions in ranking order.

For example, a set of 7 users $U = \{u_0, u_1, u_2, u_3, u_4, u_5, u_6\}$ and 5 items $I = \{i_0, i_1, i_2, i_3, i_4\}$. Each user gives their rating of the products on a rating scale of $\{?, 1, 2, 3, 4, 5\}$. Table 2 represents the user's rating matrix with items, where the intersection of the user (column) and item (row) is the user's rating value corresponding to that item, the cells represent "?" are products that have not been rated by users.

Table 1. The general matrix of users and items.

	i_0	i_1	$i...$	i_{n-1}	i_n
u_0	$r_{0,0}$	$r_{0,1}$	$r_{0,.}$	$r_{0,n-1}$	$r_{0,n}$
u_1	$r_{1,0}$	$r_{1,1}$	$r_{1,.}$	$r_{1,n-1}$	$r_{1,n}$
$u...$	$r_{.,0}$	$r_{.,1}$	$r_{.,.}$	$r_{.,n-1}$	$r_{.,n}$
u_{m-1}	$r_{m-1,0}$	$r_{m-1,1}$	$r_{m-1,.}$	$r_{m-1,n-1}$	$r_{m-1,n}$
u_m	$r_{m,0}$	$r_{m,1}$	$r_{m,.}$	$r_{m,n-1}$	$r_{m,n}$

Table 2. The rating matrix for users and items.

	i_0	i_1	i_2	i_3	i_4
u_0	5	4	?	2	2
u_1	5	?	4	2	0
u_2	2	?	1	3	4
u_3	0	0	?	4	?
u_4	1	?	?	4	?
u_5	?	2	1	?	?
u_6	?	?	1	4	5

To predict missing ratings, the system recommends using distance correlation to calculate the values. The way to determine the value is to predict each pair of users against each other, for example, if we want to predict the rating value for product i_2 by user u_0 ($u_{0,2}$), we will calculate the correlation between the user pair $\{u_{0,1}; u_{0,2}; u_{0,3}; u_{0,4}; u_{0,5}; u_{0,6}\}$, selecting the best compatible value to determine the prediction for user u_0 at item i_2 (Table 3).

Table 3. The matrix predicts the ratings.

	i_0	i_1	i_2	i_3	i_4
u_0	5	4	3.31	2	2
u_1	5	3.04	4	2	0
u_2	2	3.05	1	3	4
u_3	0	0	0.38	4	0.8
u_4	1	1.31	2.36	4	2.64
u_5	0.87	2	1	2.35	2.35
u_6	4.18	3.75	1	4	5

However, in practice we don't need to predict all the rating values for a user, we just find the most suitable item to suggest to that user or suggest the user to match the item, that is called nearest neighbor (Table 4).

Table 4. The correlation of user pairs.

u_i	u_0
u_1	0.71
u_2	0.24
u_3	0.94
u_4	0.86
u_5	0.38
u_6	0.12

Assuming u_0 is the user to suggest, we will determine the similarity of user u_0 with previous users, choose k = 2 then the nearest neighbor of u_0 {u_3, u_4}.

3   Recommendation with Distance Correlation

3.1   Distance Covariance

Distance covariance measures the dependence between random vectors with an arbitrary dimension, these dimensions are not necessarily equal [15, 17] and they are adjustable [16], specifically:

Assume there are the random observation vector samples $(X_i, Y_i) \in R$ (i = 1, 2, ...n).

Convention:

$$a_{ij} = |X_i - X_j| (i, j = 1, 2, \ldots, n)$$

$$a_{i.} = \sum_{k=1}^{n} a_{ik} \quad a_{.j} = \sum_{k=1}^{n} a_{kj} \quad \bar{a}_i = \bar{a}_{i.} = \frac{1}{n} a_{i.}$$

$$a_{..} = \sum_{i,j=1}^{n} a_{ij} \quad \bar{a} = \frac{1}{n^2} \sum_{i,j=1}^{n} a_{ij}$$

$$b_{ij} = |Y_i - Y_j| (i, j = 1, 2, \ldots, n)$$

$$b_{i.} = \sum_{k=1}^{n} b_{ik} \quad b_{.j} = \sum_{k=1}^{n} b_{kj}$$

$$b_{..} = \sum_{i,j=1}^{n} b_{ij} \quad \bar{b} = \frac{1}{n^2} \sum_{i,j=1}^{n} b_{ij}$$

$$A_{i,j} = a_{ij} - \overline{a}_i - \overline{a}_j + \overline{a} \quad B_{i,j} = b_{ij} - \overline{b}_i - \overline{b}_j + \overline{b}$$

$$A_{i,j}^* = \begin{cases} \frac{n}{n-1}\left(A_{i,j} - \frac{a_{ij}}{n}\right), & i \neq j \\ \frac{n}{n-1}(\overline{a}_i - \overline{a}), & i = j \end{cases}$$

$$B_{i,j}^* = \begin{cases} \frac{n}{n-1}\left(B_{i,j} - \frac{b_{ij}}{n}\right), & i \neq j \\ \frac{n}{n-1}(\overline{b}_i - \overline{b}), & i = j \end{cases}$$

Then, the modified distance covariance statistical formula is [16]:

$$v_n^*(X, Y) = \frac{1}{n(n-3)}\left\{ \sum_{i,j=1}^{n} A_{i,j}^* B_{i,j}^* - \frac{n}{n-2} \sum_{i=1}^{n} A_{i,i}^* B_{i,i}^* \right\} \tag{1}$$

With $n \geq 3$.

3.2 Distance Correlation

The statistics on distance correlation dcorT [14] were proposed by G. J. Székely, M. L. Rizzo, and N.K. Bakirov in 2013.

The statistical operation of distance correlation dcorT is formed base on the transformed parameter t of dCor [14] of G.J. Szekely, M.L. Rizzo, N.K. Bakirov. The advantage of dcorT checks the independence between vectors (the size of the vector is arbitrary), this approach is applied to replace the traditional analysis.

The adjusted distance covariance statistical formula [16] is:

$$R_n^*(X, Y) = \frac{v_n^*(X, Y)}{\sqrt{v_n^*(X, X)v_n^*(Y, Y)}} \tag{2}$$

With:

X, Y are random vectors.

$v_n^*(X, Y)$, $v_n^*(X, X)$, $v_n^*(Y, Y)$ are modified distance covariance statistics.

3.3 Recommendation

The calculation to determine the rating matrix similarity using the distance correlation statistic dcorT [14] is built as follows:

Algorithm1.1. recommendation with distance correlation

Input: User set U, item set I, and the rating matrix of the users U for the items I

New user (ux)

Output: Recommend items $I_{ux}=\{i_1, i_2,...,i_k\}$ for ux users with item by preference level from high to low;

Begin

Step 1: Determine k nearest neighbors of new user u_x

For user $u_i \in U_n$ perform

<Calculate the similarity of each pair of users u_i, u_x using the distance correlation in energy>

<Sort the list of the users in order of similarity from highest to lowest>

<Select a list of k users closest to user u_x>

Step 2: Predictions and recommend the items to the users u_x

Step 3: Evaluation of the proposed model

End.

In this section, we build a collaborative filtering model with user-based energy distance correlation. This is a method of analyzing data that evaluates users' ratings based on the favorite items of many individuals. If two users have the same interests, they will like similar items. Therefore, the first works is to fill in the missing predictions of the users by finding the k users with the most similar preferences (nearest neighbors) and then perform calculations to rank their ratings for these users go to the best most relevant recommendations (Fig. 1).

The determination of the k users with the closest preferences is done using the dcorT statistic [14], which tests the energy distance correlation between the ratings of each user.

This collaborative filtering model is built with input data of two variables: (1) The matrix of the user reviews of the previous products; (2) the user needs to be referred to the item.

3.4   Training and Testing for Model

To evaluate the models, we split the dataset into 2 parts: the training data set called "Train" and test them on some test data called "Test".

In this article, we use the k-fold cross-validation method [22] to divide the dataset to evaluate the recommender model. The k-fold cross-validation method is a method that divides the data into a number of parts (k parts of the same size), performs k evaluations, each time it evaluates the system, it takes one part as the test training set, the remaining

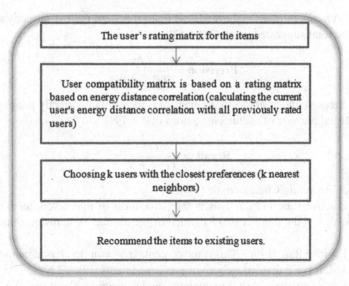

Fig. 1. Collaborative filtering model with distance correlation.

parts (k-1) serve as the training set and we proceed similarly, the result is determined by the average of the evaluations. With this method, make sure each user thing appears in the test suite at least once, then we can measure more accurately.

3.5 Evaluating of the Model

The overall performance of the model is evaluated by several evaluation metrics, we can evaluate the rating based on the confusion matrix and ROC curve (Table 5):

Table 5. Evaluation of the recommendation system.

	Practical class	
Prediction class	True Positive (TP)	False Positive (FP)
	False Negative (FN)	True Negative (TN)

In there:

+True Positive (TP): These are the recommended items that have been purchased.

+False Positive (FP): These are suggested but not purchased items.

+False Negative (FN): These are not recommended items purchased.

+True Negative (TN): These are not recommended items that have not been purchased.

Precision: A measure/index of the model accuracy that is the ratio of correctly suggested items (TP) to total suggested items (TP + FP).

$$Precision = \frac{TP}{TP + FP} \tag{3}$$

Recall: A measure/index of model accuracy, it is the ratio of correctly suggested items (TP) to the total number of useful suggestions (TP + FN).

$$Recall = \frac{TP}{TP + FN} \tag{4}$$

Receiver Operating Characteristic (ROC):

+True Positive Rate (TPR): This is the percentage of purchased items that were recommended. It is the number of TP divided by the number of items purchased (TP + FN).

+False Positive Rate (FPR): This is the percentage of non-purchased items that were recommended. It is FP divided by zero of purchased items (FP + TN).

Area Under the Curve (AUC) to quantify model accuracy based on calculating the area under the curve. The area AUC is the area from the horizontal axis that is bounded by the curve. If the ROC is closer to the left corner, the AUC area will be larger, the accuracy of the model will be higher.

4 Experiment

4.1 Data

The MSWeb [18] and Learning from Sets of Items 2019 [19] datasets are used to evaluated for the propose model.

MSWeb is a sampled dataset of anonymous users visiting www.microsoft.com on a one-week timeframe in February 1998. This dataset is sampled from 32710 anonymous users visiting over 285 original web address. User ratings in this dataset are binaryRatingMatrix.

Learning from Sets of Items 2019 is a user-rated dataset of movies rated on [phimmoi.org] (https://movielens.org/) from February to April 2016 with 45897 ratings of 854 person for 13012 movies, rated movies from 1 to 5, real data type is realRatingMatrix.

4.2 Tool

To implement the experiment, we have updated and added the recommended packages arules_1.7-3 [21] and recommenderlab_1.0.0 [22] in R language.

In addition, we used the recommended package energy_1.7-10 [20] to build a user-based collaborative filtering model, writing a function to measure the distance correlation in RStudio, and we named the function is ebms_energy_dcorT (in R language).

4.3   Scenario 1: Recommendation on Learning from Sets of Items 2019

To compare the performance of the built model, we test two models with three measures: Collaborative filtering model on users with the ebms_energy_dcorT measure we built; Additive filtering model on UBCF users with measures of cosine and pearson respectively on the Learning from Sets of Items 2019 dataset.

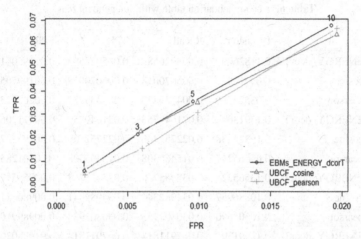

Fig. 2. The graph of ROC curve on Learning from Sets of Items 2019 with 3 measures.

Experimental results in Fig. 2 shows that the predictive accuracy of the model with the ebms_energy_dcorT measure is higher than that of the UBCF model with the cosine and pearson measures, the area under the AUC curve of our proposed model is the largest. The prediction accuracy of UBCF_cosine is the lowest about 0.062, while the prediction accuracy of EBMS_ENERGY_dcorT is the highest, about 0.068 (Fig. 3).

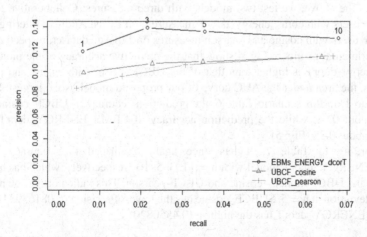

Fig. 3. The recall chart on Learning from Sets of Items 2019 with three measures.

The precision evaluation performance of the model based on the ebms_energy_dcorT tool has a higher rate than the UBCF-cosine and UBCF-pearson models shown in Table 6. With n = 1 precision index of $ The lowest UBCF_pearson (0.08521739) and the highest $EBMs_ENERGY_dcorT (0.1182609). Similar to n = {3, 5, 10}, the Precision of ebms_energy_dcorT is higher than $UBCF_cosine and $UBCF_pearson.

Table 6. Recommendation table with independent bias.

	Precision	Recall	TPR	FPR	n
$EBMs_ENERGY_dcorT	0.1182609	0.005926583	0.005926583	0.001950615	1
$UBCF_cosine	0.09913043	0.006070018	0.006070018	0.001995051	1
$UBCF_pearson	0.08521739	0.004339777	0.004339777	0.002027737	1
$EBMs_ENERGY_dcorT	0.1391304	0.021649753	0.021649753	0.005712064	3
$UBCF_cosine	0.10724638	0.022752706	0.022752706	0.005934277	3
$UBCF_pearson	0.09565217	0.015465308	0.015465308	0.006012859	3
$EBMs_ENERGY_dcorT	0.1356522	0.035455768	0.035455768	0.009555129	5
$UBCF_cosine	0.10886957	0.034982341	0.034982341	0.009866516	5
$UBCF_pearson	0.10608696	0.030807933	0.030807933	0.009899105	5
$EBMs_ENERGY_dcorT	0.1299130	0.067911814	0.067911814	0.019240201	10
$UBCF_cosine	0.11339130	0.063980242	0.063980242	0.019616993	10
$UBCF_pearson	0.11426087	0.066532646	0.066532646	0.019602998	10

4.4 Scenario 2: Recommendation on MSWeb Dataset

Similar to the above, we test two models with three measures: Collaborative filtering model on users with ebms_energy_dcorT measure built by us; Additive filtering model on UBCF users with cosine and pearson measures on MSWeb dataset, respectively.

Experimental results in Fig. 4 show that the predictive accuracy of the model with ebms_energy_dcorT is higher than that of the UBCF model with cosine and pearson measures, the area under the AUC curve of our proposed model. is the largest. Similar to scenario 1, in this scenario Table 6, the prediction accuracy of UBCF_cosine is the lowest about 0.08, while the prediction accuracy of EBMS_ENERGY_dcorT is the highest, about 0.28 (Fig. 5).

According to Table 7, it has once again confirmed the accuracy of the EBMs_ENERGY_dcorT model with n = {1, 3, 5, 10} respectively, which has a higher rate than the UBCF models- cosine and UBCF-pearson. This indicator is shown on the highest deviation at n = 5, $UBCF_cosine has the lowest Precision (0.08163934), while $EBMs_ENERGY_dcorT has the highest (0.4550820).

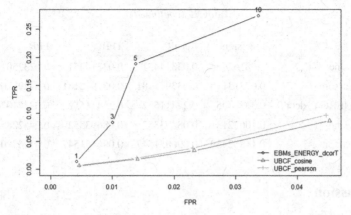

Fig. 4. The graph of ROC curves on MSWeb dataset with three measures.

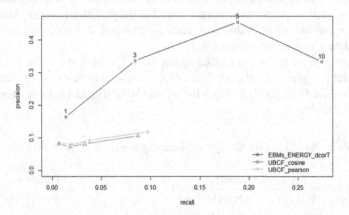

Fig. 5. The recall chart on MSWeb dataset with three measures.

Table 7. Recommendation table with independent bias.

	Precision	Recall	TPR	FPR	n
$EBMs_ENERGY_dcorT	0.1639344	0.01373053	0.01373053	0.00423476	1
$UBCF_cosine	0.08196721	0.00659319	0.00659319	0.004647951	1
$UBCF_pearson	0.08360656	0.006767633	0.006767633	0.004639796	1
$EBMs_ENERGY_dcorT	0.3366120	0.08419550	0.08419550	0.01007666	3
$UBCF_cosine	0.07322404	0.01791563	0.01791563	0.014079057	3
$UBCF_pearson	0.08087432	0.020058621	0.020058621	0.013963848	3
$EBMs_ENERGY_dcorT	0.4550820	0.18833600	0.18833600	0.01378538	5

(continued)

Table 7. (*continued*)

	Precision	Recall	TPR	FPR	n
$UBCF_cosine	0.08163934	0.03314451	0.03314451	0.023250781	5
$UBCF_pearson	0.09213115	0.037918181	0.037918181	0.022987034	5
$EBMs_ENERGY_dcorT	0.3337705	0.27411552	0.27411552	0.03371074	10
$UBCF_cosine	0.10672131	0.08693352	0.08693352	0.045228540	10
$UBCF_pearson	0.11852459	0.096851547	0.096851547	0.044632079	10

5 Discussion

With two scenarios, the experiment results show that with two different datasets (MSWeb (binaryRatingMatrix) and Learning from Sets of Items 2019 (realRatingMatrix), The precision rating of the proposed model is higher than the precision rating of the traditional model, even the number of evaluations (and) are changed. The proposed model works well on datasets with different data types.

With the type of dataset is realRatingMatrix, the results show that the precision of the model is higher than the precision of the model with the type of dataset to be binaryRatingMatrix in Table 8. Precision of the MSWeb and Learning from Sets of Items 2019 dataset.

Table 8. Precision of the MSWeb and Learning from Sets of Items 2019 dataset.

	Dataset	Precision	n
$EBMs_ENERGY_dcorT	**MSWeb**	0.1182609	1
		0.1391304	3
		0.1356522	5
		0.1299130	10
	Learning from Sets of Items 2019	0.1639344	1
		0.3366120	3
		0.4550820	5
		0.3337705	10

6 Conclusion

In this paper, we proposed a collaborative filtering model based on energy distance correlation. We used the energy distance correlation algorithm between users to recomend for user, who need of advice. In order to have a new direction in using energy in the recommender system.

To evaluate the model's effectiveness, we have experimented on the MSWeb and Learning from Sets of Items 2019 datasets with three measures: the model with the dcorT measure (EBMs_ENERGY_dcorT); UBCF user-based collabora-tive filtering model with the Cosine measures (UBCF_cosine) and Pearson measures (UBCF_pearson). The experimental results show that the proposed model is more accurate than the traditional model and the proposed model runs well on both binaryRatingMatrix and realRatingMatrix.

References

1. Woerndl, W., Schlichter, J.: Introducing context into recommender systems. In: AAAI - Workshops, pp. 138–140 (2007)
2. Felfernig, A., Jeran, M., Ninaus, G., Reinfrank, F., Reiterer, S., Stettinger, M.: Basic approaches in recommendation systems. In: Robillard, M., Maalej, W., Walker, R., Zimmermann, T. (eds.) Recommendation Systems in Software Engineering, pp. 15–38. Springer, Berlin, Heidelberg (2014). https://doi.org/10.1007/978-3-642-45135-5_2
3. Mpela, M.D., Zuva, T.: A mobile proximity job employment recommender system. In: 2020 International Conference on Artificial Intelligence, Big Data, Computing and Data Communication Systems (icABCD), pp. 1–6, (2020)
4. Ricci, F., Rokach, L., Shapira, B. (eds.): Recommender Systems Handbook. Springer, Boston, MA (2015). https://doi.org/10.1007/978-1-4899-7637-6
5. Lu, J., Wu, D., Mao, M., Wang, W., Zhang, G.: Recommender system application developments: a survey. Decis. Support Syst. (2015)
6. Sindhwani, P.M.V.: Recommender systems. Commun. ACM 1–21 (2010)
7. Adomavicius, G., Tuzhilin, A.: Toward the next generation of recommender systems: a survey of the state-of-the-art and possible extensions. IEEE Trans. Knowl. Data Eng. 17(6), 734–749 (2005)
8. Pazzani, M.J., Billsus, D.: Content-based recommendation systems. In: Brusilovsky, P., Kobsa, A., Nejdl, W. (eds.) The Adaptive Web. LNCS, vol. 4321, pp. 325–341. Springer, Heidelberg (2007). https://doi.org/10.1007/978-3-540-72079-9_10
9. Schafer, J.B., Frankowski, D., Herlocker, J., Sen, S.: Collaborative filtering recommender systems. In: Brusilovsky, P., Kobsa, A., Nejdl, W. (eds.) The Adaptive Web. LNCS, vol. 4321, pp. 291–324. Springer, Heidelberg (2007). https://doi.org/10.1007/978-3-540-72079-9_9
10. Cai, Y., Leung, H., Li, Q., Min, H., Tang, J., Li, J.: Typicality-based collaborative filtering recommendation. Knowl. Data Eng. IEEE Trans. 26(3), 766–779 (2013)
11. Hussien, F.T.A., Rahma, A.M.S., Wahab, H.B.A.: Recommendation systems for e-commerce systems an overview. J. Phys. Conf. Ser. 1897, 1–14. IOP Publishing (2021)
12. Tang, J., et al.: Recommendation with social dimensions. In: Proceedings of the Thirtieth AAAI Conference on Artificial Intelligence (AAAI-16), pp. 251–257 (2016)
13. Rizzo, M.L., Szekely, G.J.: Energy distance. WIRES Comput. Stat. 8(1), 27–38. Wiley (2016)
14. https://github.com/mariarizzo/energy
15. Székely, G.J., Rizzo, M.L.: Brownian distance covariance. Ann. Appl. Stat. 3(4), 1236–1265 (2009)
16. Szekely, G.J., Rizzo, M.L.: The distance correlation t-test of independence in high dimension. J. Multivar. Anal. 117, 193–213 (2013)
17. Székely, G.J., Rizzo, M.L., Bakirov, N.K.: Measuring and testing independence by correlation of distances. Ann. Stat. 35(6), 2769–2794 (2007)
18. Breese, J.S., David, H., Carl, M.K.: Anonymous web data from. Microsoft Research, Redmond WA, 98052–6399, USA, (1998). https://www.microsoft.com/en-in/

19. Sharma, M., Harper, F.M., Karypis, G.: Learning from sets of items in recommender systems. In: Proceedings of the ACM Transactions on Interactive Intelligent Systems (TiiS) (2019)
20. https://cran.r-project.org/web/packages/energy/index.html
21. https://cran.r-project.org/web/packages/arules/index.html
22. https://cran.r-project.org/web/packages/recommenderlab/index.html

Blockchain Model in Industrial Pangasius Farming

Cuong Ngoc Duong[1], Linh Thuy Thi Nguyen[2] (ID), Tu Cam Thi Tran[3] (ID), and Hiep Xuan Huynh[2(✉)] (ID)

[1] VNPT Dong Thap, Cao Lãnh, Dong Thap, Vietnam
cuongdn.dtp@vnpt.vn
[2] Can Tho University, Can Tho, Vietnam
{nttlinh,hxhiep}@ctu.edu.vn
[3] Vinh Long University of Technology Education, Vinh Long, Vietnam
tuttc@vlute.edu.vn

Abstract. Today, the problem of counterfeit goods, counterfeit goods, circulating goods, they have no origin, products such as seafood containing banned substances, toxic substances are negatively affecting consumers' health, the solution of the traceability of manufactured products acts as an essential quality management tool to ensure the safety of providing complete information for products. However, current solutions data is stored centrally on a group of servers, this information can be edited and deleted by the administrator and by hackers; leading to low reliability of the data. In this article, we propose a blockchain model in industrial pangasius farming, one of the current solutions is to switch to a distributed model, data will be distributed to different physical servers, they are not data can be added, removed, edited or deleted without the consent of the parties involved. The proposed solution focuses on controlling all interactions and transactions between all involved participants in the production process, all transactions are recorded and stored in the ledger (immutability) of the blockchain. The experimental results are the transactions, all transactions are recorded and stored in the ledger of the blockchain. In addition, the data can be retrieved as needed.

Keywords: Blockchain · Pangasius · Traceability · Smart Contracts · Supply Chain

1 Introduction

Pangasius in particular is a food that plays an important role in providing nutrition for the people in the world. However, the food hygiene and safety have caused businesses to suffer heavy financial and reputational losses. The main cause of the above situation is that the production stage is not satisfactory, the hatchery cannot trace the origin of the seed, such as: where did the broodfish come from? what year did the fish spawn? Where is the place to supply the food? how is it processed? how is it tranported?. Besides, the demand for safe and quality food is increasingly important. The market mixes the safe

C. V. Phan and T. D. Nguyen (Eds.): ICCASA 2022, LNICST 475, pp. 33–44, 2023.
https://doi.org/10.1007/978-3-031-28816-6_3

and unsafe foods, the clean and dirty foods, the real and fake foods. The consumers need information to check and to use food safely, to improve health, and to reduce disease.

In recent years, the traceability of the products, the fish foods, the seafoods has received much attention in the scientific research community in the country and on the world. Aly Farag El Sheikha et al. [1] presented a study on Traceability as a Key to Fisheries Safety using the DGGE PCR technique. However, this technique cannot clearly trace the history of fish and other aquatic products. Iñigo Cuiñas et al. [2] presented an RFID-based Traceability study. Ganjar Alfian et al. [3] presented the studies to improve the efficiency of RFID-based Traceability System, data is stored centrally in one or a group of servers. Thus, due to the centralized nature, and it dependents on people, so the current solutions have very low reliability and transparency.

One of the solutions today is to switch to a distributed model. Data will be distributed to different physical servers, it is not possible to add, edit or delete data without the consent of the participants. Essentially, a blockchain is an immutable and decentralized [11], the ledger is shared public to allow the participants, who can track the transactions. Each block is hashed and they are linked to the next block, which becomes a secure chain of immutable and tamper-proof records. In this article, we propose a blockchain model in industrial pangasius farming. The proposed solution focuses on controlling all interactions and transactions between all involved participants in the production process. All transactions are recorded and stored in the blockchain's immutable ledger. The purpose of this study is that it has contributed to the development of a supply chain [12] to ensure the safety, quality of the product and the reliability of the users.

The article layout is divided into six parts: Sect. 1 introduces the basics of traceability and proposes a blockchain model in industrial pangasius farming, Sect. 2 presents the blockchain concept and analyzes transactions in the block. Section 3 describes how to connect to Ethereum, Sect. 4 presents the process of raising pangasius on the farm and a blockchain-based pangasius farming model, Sect. 5 presents experimental results, and finally the conclusion, it presents a summary of the results obtained.

2   Blockchain and Transactions

2.1   Blockchain

Blockchain is a database system that allows the storage and transmission of blocks of information. They are linked together by encryption. Basically, each block contains the following key information: Data (The data in each block depends on the type of blockchain); Hash (to identify a block and the data in it). The hash is unique, any change in the block will change the hash; The matching hash (which is the hash of the previous block) will form the chain. With any change, one block will cause the next blocks to not fit and some other additional information like Index, Nonce, Timestamp.

Hashing alone is not enough to prevent tampering [4], as hashes can be quickly computed by computers. The Proof-of-Work (PoW) algorithm controls the difficulty of generating a new block. For blockchains like BitCoin or Ethereum, blocks are created (mined) by people called miners. When a new block must be generated, a computational difficulty is sent to the network. Miners will generate new blocks and be rewarded with cryptocurrency.

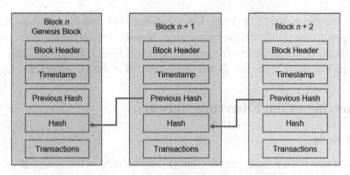

Fig. 1. Illustrated diagram of a chain of blocks linked together to form a blockchain.

In Fig. 1 illustrated a blockchain consisting of 3 blocks: block n, block $n + 1$, bolck $n + 2$ linked together to form a chain of blocks. The hash of block n is the previous hash of block $n + 1$, the hash of block $n + 1$ is the previous hash of block $n + 2$, the hash of block $n + 2$ continues to be the hash of the next block.

2.2 Transaction in Block

A transaction [5] represents an interaction between the parties. With cryptocurrencies, a transaction represents the transfer of coins between Blockchain users. For a business environment, a transaction can be a way of recording activities that occur on a digital or physical asset (Fig. 2).

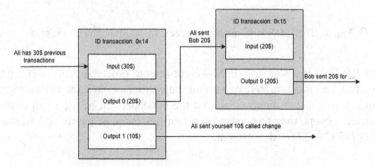

Fig. 2. Illustrated example of cryptocurrency trading.

Each block in the Blockchain may contain no transactions or it may contain multiple transactions. A user submits information to the Blockchain network. The information sent may include the person's address, the sender's public key, digital signatures, and transaction inputs and outputs.

The internal transaction [6] is the result of the smart contract [7, 13], the transaction is transmitted from the EOA to the smart contract. Smart contracts are one of the most important aspects of the Ethereum blockchain. They are digital contracts, it does business automation. In addition, Ethereum smart contracts are programs, they are installed on the blockchain to manage Ether balance [14], and transactions. Smart contracts are open to the public on the blockchain. Smart contract transactions are tracked and sent through externally owned accounts (known as EOA). These transactions appear as internal transactions in the transaction history ETH and they are not displayed.

3 Connecting to the Ethereum Network

3.1 Local Node

To run a local node, we need to install Geth [8]. With Geth on the computer, it synchronizes with the network. The local node requires a machine with strong configuration, large storage capacity, takes a lot of time to create a local node. Use the Json RPC method to interact with the Ethereum network. By default, the Ethereum package will connect to port 8545 on localhost (Fig. 3).

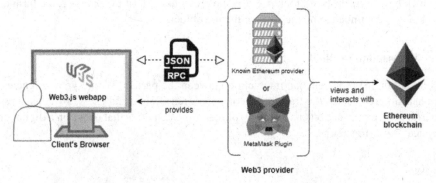

Fig. 3. The JSON RPC method connects to the Ethereum blockchain.

JSON-RPC [9] is a stateless, light-weight remote procedure call (RPC) protocol. Primarily, this specification defines several data structures and the rules around their processing. It is transport agnostic in that the concepts can be used within the same process, over sockets, over http, or in many various message passing environments. It uses JSON (RFC 4627) as data format.

3.2 Public Node

To interact with the Ethereum network via a public node using the public RPC provided by Infura [9], it is the best choice.

Infura is a Web3-enabled service delivery project focused on Ethereum [10] Infura provides tools and infrastructure that allow developers to easily connect their applications to platform blockchains such as Ethereum. Essentially, Infura provides the necessary tools for any application to start developing anything on Ethereum right away, without having to run complex infrastructure yourself. Infura provides connectivity for all developers using the Ethereum blockchain. The highlight of the Infura infrastructure is the network hosted on Ethereum: Mainnet, Ropsten, Rinkeby, Kovan (See Fig. 4).

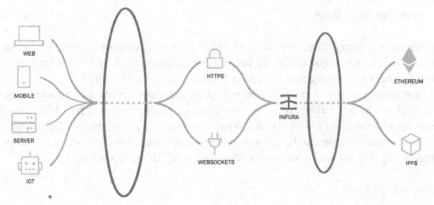

Fig. 4. RPC Infura model. Using the Infura's PROJECT ID KEYS to point the Ethereum packet to the Infura RPC interface.

4 The Process of Raising Pangasius

4.1 Processing of the Raising Pangasius at the Farm

Processing of the raising pangasius at a farm is carried out as follows:

- Preparing the pond

Before stocking fish, the pond must be renovated according to the technical process, such as: with an area of at least 500 m^2 or more, the pond edge is compacted firmly to avoid water leakage. Ponds should be near motorways or near rivers, canals and canals to transport food, seed, and commercial fish more conveniently. Ponds need to have separate supply and drainage drains; the size depends on the pond area. The location of the pond should be near a clean, unpolluted water source, so that it can actively supply water to the pond during the farming period.

- Water supply

All types of ponds must have a sewer system, and set up drains so that when pumping, the water falls into the pond to create a lot of foam to provide more oxygen for the fish. If possible, it is advisable to dig more ponds to store water and treat settling ponds before pumping into the pond, because it will make the pond to limit pathogens. It is necessary to build and install a large-diameter discharge culvert, which can discharge from 1/3 to 1/2 of the water in the pond in two hours to promptly prevent risks from occurring. The water must be taken from clean water sources that are less polluted, water is taken through a drain with a mesh filter to prevent harmful fish and predators. When the pond has been filled with water about 50–70 cm, then pausing for 3–5 days, then getting enough water.

- Provide fingerlings

On the market today, there are many types of pangasius of poor quality, so farmers must follow the technique of raising pangasius for export carefully from selecting and carefully checking the origin and situation. Disease…to ensure healthy fish, no scratches, uniform size from 10–12 cm/fish. Depending on the water quality as well as the area and depth of the pond along with the experience of raising fish, it is possible to stock different densities from 15–60 fish/m^2. When new fingerlings are purchased, fish should be released into the pond in the early morning or cool afternoon (mild weather), before releasing the fish should be bathed for 15–20 min with dilute salt water.

- Provide fish food

Homemade food: The downside of this type of food is that if you don't add minerals and vitamins, the fish will be slow to grow, so it takes a long time, about 6 months, for the fingerlings to have a size of 2.5 cm. However, if fed with enough nutrients, it only takes 4.5 months to harvest. Besides, the production of homemade food also pollutes the water very quickly, causing for fish to get sick.

- Supply of medicine

This is an indispensable step in the catfish farming process. It is necessary to pay attention to the weather to have a suitable way to feed the fish, when it is too hot to feed the fish vitamin C and change the water regularly. If the fish is sick, use antibiotics at a dose of 0.1%. Antibiotics will work if the pond environment is clean. However, if antibiotics are abused, fish will slow down and reduce weight gain.

- Harvest

The most reasonable time to harvest is after 9–10 months of rearing, when the fish reaches 0.7–1.2 kg/fish. We can base on the market situation to harvest in the most efficient way, avoiding the case that the fish has not reached the size, reducing the selling price and waste food. After the harvest, the pond needs to be drained and the pond needs to be renovated to prepare for the next crop.

4.2   Blockchain Model in the Farming Process of the Pangasius

In the farming process chain of the pangasius, the participant is the farmer (FARMERS) including the following tasks: pond preparation, water supply, seed supply, food supply, medicine supply and harvesting (in Fig. 5). Each subject has its own task function. Subjects interacting with the farmer generate a transaction. Transactions are permanently stored on the blockchain. When needed, information can be retrieved at any time.

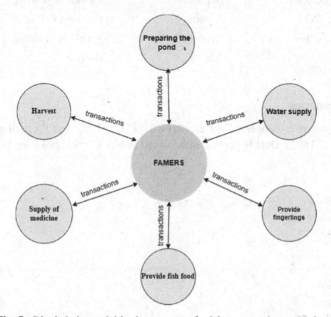

Fig. 5. Blockchain model in the process of raising pangasius at the farm.

5   Experiment

5.1   Assign Accounts to Subjects

Identifying the objects involved in the production process, then select the Address code and assign a management label in Table 1. In this experiment, the authors used Metamask (an add-on utility on Chrome browser, helping to manage accounts and interact with Blockchain).

Determining the data to be stored on the Blockchain, the data must be useful, clearly and accurately. In this article, we choose the Rinkeby Testnet (https://rinkeby.ethers can.io), where we can search for all recorded transactions for future tracing.

Table 1. List of accounts used to participate in the pangasius farming process.

Address	Name	Subjects
0xF8B86C3...c1d5	Account 2	Farmers
0xBe8B4ce...1802	Account 3	Preparing the pond
0xDE8B3c3...6206	Account 4	Water supply
0xDA8a137...CD3e	Account 5	Provide fingerlings
0x6eA0e74...7A30	Account 6	Provide fish food
0x5E0FA1E...c7B6	Account 7	Supply of medicine
0xD754425...9Ad3	Account 8	Harvest

5.2 The Scenarios

Case 1: Transaction between Farmer (0xF8B86C3...c1d5) and Preparing the pond (0xBe8B4ce...1802). Data is permanently stored at block 10933294 (See Fig. 6).

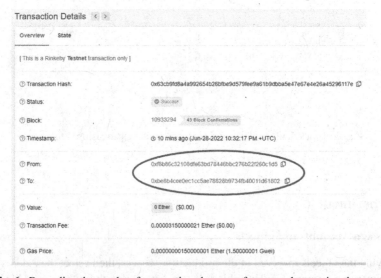

Fig. 6. Recording the results of transactions between farmer and preparing the pond.

Case 2: Transaction between Farmer (0xF8B86C3...c1d5) and Water Supply (0xDE8B3c3...6206). Data is permanently stored at block 10933297 (See Fig. 7).

Case 3: Transaction between Farmer (0xF8B86C3...c1d5) and Provide fingerlings (0xDA8a137...CD3e). Data is permanently stored at block 10933299 (See Fig. 8).

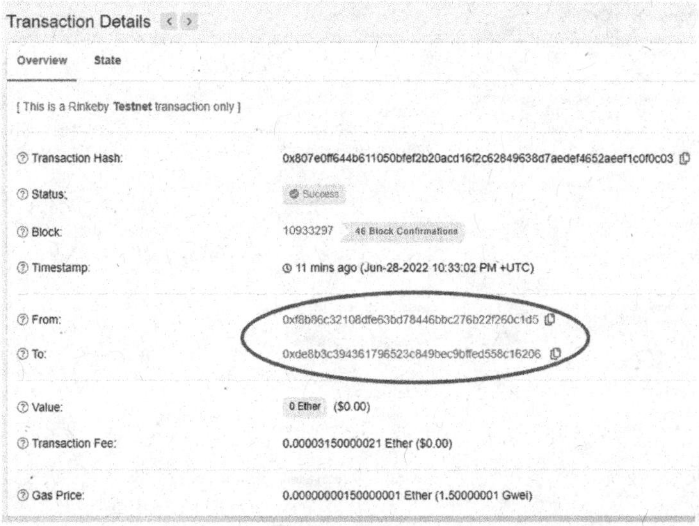

Fig. 7. Recording the results of transactions between farmer and water supply.

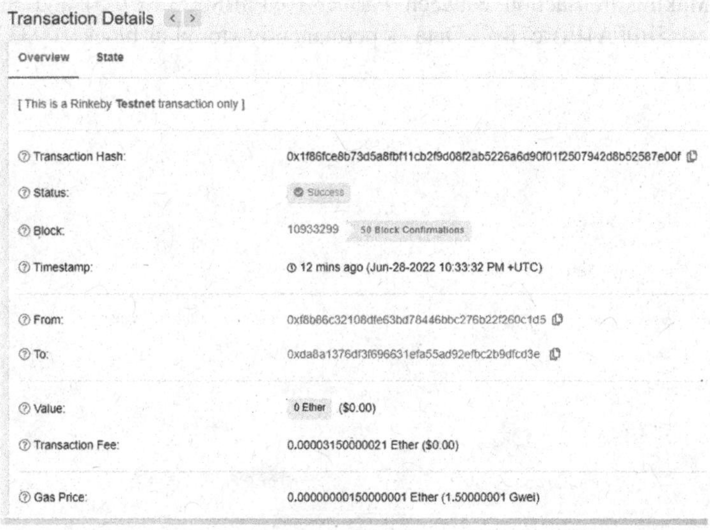

Fig. 8. Recording the results of the transaction between farmer and provide fingerlings.

Case 4: Make a transaction between Farmer (0xF8B86C3…c1d5) and Provide fish food (0x6eA0e74…7A30). Data is permanently stored at block 10933301 (See Fig. 9).

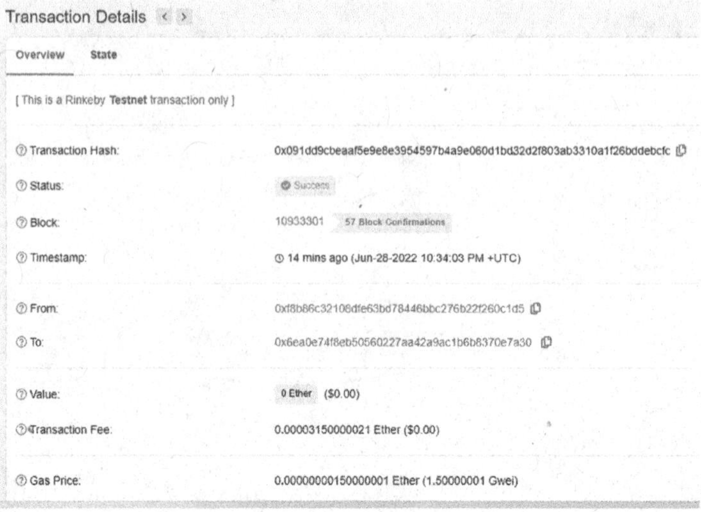

Fig. 9. Recording transaction performance between farmer and provide fish food.

Case 5: Making transaction between Farmer (0xF8B86C3…c1d5) and Supply of medicine (0x5E0FA1E…c7B6). Data is permanently stored at block 10933301 (See Fig. 10).

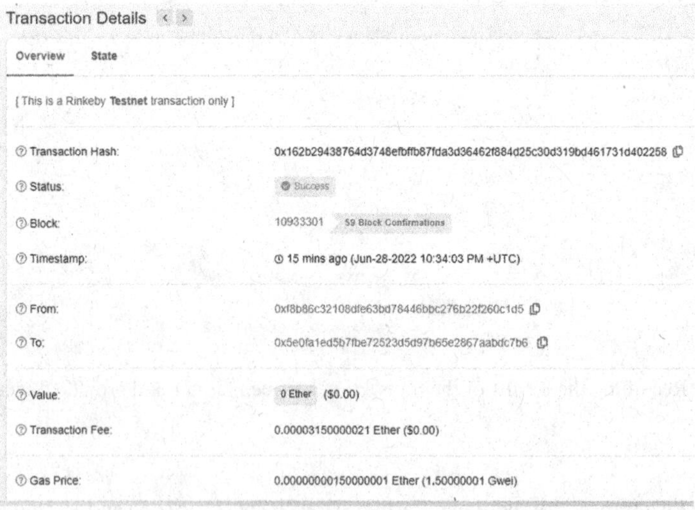

Fig. 10. Recording the results of transactions between farmer and supply of medicine.

Case 6: Make a transaction between Farmer (0xF8B86C3...c1d5) and Harvest (0xD754425...9Ad3). Data is permanently stored at block 10933303 (See Fig. 11).

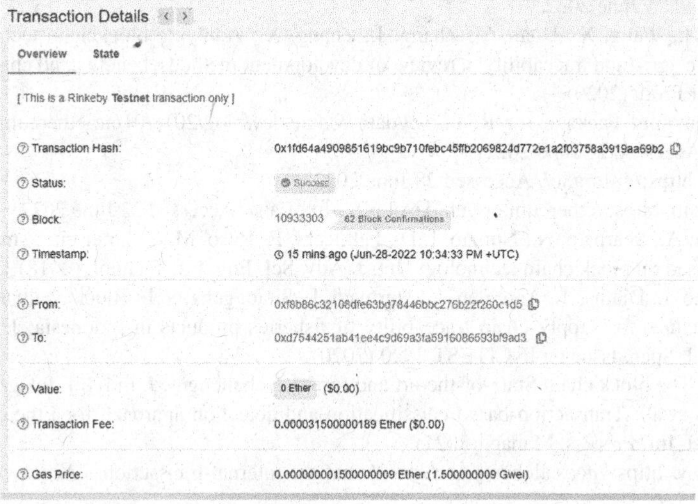

Fig. 11. Recording the results of transactions between farmer and harvest.

6 Conclusion

The blockchain technology has shown great potential, helping industries, agriculture, fisheries, all from the tradition of transformation to develop with Industry 4.0 and it has features such as: decentralization, immutability, decentralization, transparency. It is thanks to these characteristics that Blockchain-based frameworks are very interested and applied by the community in many fields such as finance and banking, economy, politics - society, health, education, etc. smart contract. In this article, we have used the advantages of Blockchain, specifically the Ethereum platform, to put into the industrial pangasius farming model.

References

1. El Sheikha, A.F., Xu, J.: Traceability as a key of seafood safety: reassessment and possible applications. Rev. Fish. Sci. Aquac **25**(2), 158–170 (2017)
2. Cuiñas, I., Newman, R., Trebar, M., Catarinucci, L., Melcón, A.A.: RFID-based traceability along the food-production chain. Departamento de Teoria de la Señal y Comunicaciones University Carlos III of Madrid Despacho 4.3B10 Avenida de la Universidad
3. Alfian, G., et al.: Improving efficiency of RFID-based traceability system for perishable food by utilizing IoT sensors and machin learning model (2019)

4. Building a blockchain in R. http://users.dimi.uniud.it/~massimo.franceschet/HEX0x6C/blockchain/blockchainR.html. Accessed 29 June 2022

5. Ethescan. https://info.etherscan.com/understanding-an-ethereum-transaction/. Accessed 21 June 2022

6. Coinmarketcap.   https://coinmarketcap.com/alexandria/glossary/internal-transaction. Accessed 25 June 2022

7. Feng, H., Wang, X., Duan, Y., Zhang, J., Zhang, X.: Applying blockchain technology to improve agri-food traceability: a review of development methods, benefits and challenges. J. Cleaner Prod. (2020)

8. An Ethereum Package for R. https://datawookie.dev/blog/2018/01/an-ethereum-package-for-r/. Accessed 20 June 2022

9. Infura. https://infura.io/. Accessed 28 June 2022

10. Ethereum. https://ethereum.org/en/developers/tutorials/. Accessed 22 June 2022

11. Pieroni, A., Scarpato, N., Nunzio, L.D., Fallucchi, F., Raso, M.: Smarter city: smart energy grid based on block chain technology. Int. J. Adv. Sci. Eng. Inf. Technol. (2018)

12. Afrianto, I., Djatna, T., Arkeman, Y., Hermadi, I., Sitanggang, S. I.: Block chain technology architecture: for supply chain traceability of fisheries products in Indonesia. J. Eng. Sci. Technol. Spec. Issue on INCITEST 2020 (2020)

13. Lu, Y.: The block chain State-of-the-art and research challenges. J. Ind. Inf. Integr. (2019)

14. Hu, T., et al.: Transaction-based classification and detection approach for Ethereum smart contract. Inf. Process. Manag. (2021)

15. Alchemy. https://docs.alchemy.com/docs/what-are-internal-transactions. Accessed 25 June 2022

Multiple-Criteria Rating Recommendation with Ordered Weighted Averaging Aggregation Operators

Hiep Xuan Huynh[✉], Loi Tan Nguyen, Hai Thanh Nguyen,
and Linh Thuy Thi Nguyen

College of Information and Communication Technology,
Can Tho University, Can Tho 900000, Vietnam
hxhiep@ctu.edu.vn

Abstract. In recent years, the Fourth Industrial Revolution in Industry 4.0 has exploded, along with the increasing development of websites, social networks, and other Internet services, leading to tremendous growth in collected data resources. Therefore, it is becoming more and more challenging to select useful information to make decisions. The recommendation systems are considered a great solution to assist humans in finding helpful information effectively and speedily. Such systems can automatically analyze, classify, select, and provide valuable information to users. Furthermore, they can explore reviews on products and services using artificial intelligence techniques to provide valuable recommendations. Users sometimes give reviews and ratings multiple times on the same products, but they differ depending on the user's mood, context, behavior, etc. Thus, the problem is accurately determining the user's rating when exploring such reviews. This work has proposed a solution for multiple-criteria rating analysis. This study has explored reviews on different criteria and integrated them into one aggregate rating by considering the similar relationship between the ratings, users, or products based on criteria in the collaborative filtering-based recommendation approach. The proposed method has performed better than traditional collaborative filtering-based methods on more than 5000 film reviews from the DePaulMovie dataset.

Keywords: Multiple-criteria ratings · Recommendation systems · Reviews · Context

1 Introduction

The problem of information overload [1] has become popular with the strong development of Internet services. The amount of information that people have access to is expanding. We can access many sources of information via email, articles, posts, advertising on social networks, e-commerce sites, etc. With the

C. V. Phan and T. D. Nguyen (Eds.): ICCASA 2022, LNICST 475, pp. 45–58, 2023.
https://doi.org/10.1007/978-3-031-28816-6_4

current expansion of information from the Internet and social networks, it will be more and more challenging to select useful information for decision-making by computer and savvy device users. A recommender system is a field of machine learning that is considered a solution to help users select information effectively and is widely applied in many fields such as science, health, education, e-commerce, entertainment, etc. The system tries to predict the "products" for the appropriate "users". In e-commerce, the recommendation system helps buyers find suitable goods, helps sellers find potential customers and boosts sales. The system recommends items according to the user's interests in entertainment and education. The recommendation system opens up the research potential of building natural systems, supporting users in decision-making.

The recommendation system is capable of automatically analyzing information, classifying, selecting, and providing users with products, goods, and services of interest through the application of statistical and artificial intelligence techniques in which machine learning algorithms play an essential role [2,3]. People divide the recommender model into many different types based on calculating the suggested results from the data. For example, the recommendation approach based on collaborative filtering is widely used in commercial fields [4–6], recommending products to users based on the similarity between users and communities. The users with the same similarity in a context can be commended for the same product. In addition, users are also suggested to use the product when most users have the same preferences on those products.

In contrast, the recommendation approach based on content filtering offers recommended products to the user when that product is similar to other products that the user in the past, which the user made as revealed in [7,8]. Furthermore, the recommendation model based on the demographic characteristics gives the recommended products to the user by using the user's demographic information such as gender, age, nationality [9,10]. The approaches based on knowledge can explore specialized knowledge, determining the product's suitability (based on descriptive attributes) with the needs or preferences of the user use in order to achieve the goal of a product that is useful to users [11–13]. The proposed integrated recommendation model aims to limit the shortcomings of the above methods [10,14,15]. Typically, integrated recommender solutions use two or more different recommendation solutions to overcome the weaknesses of each solution. Many studies prove that integrated recommender models are more accurate than single recommendation models [2]. However, these methods are also more demanding resource costs and computation time. With the diversity of recommendation models and solutions, recommendation models have been deployed and applied practically in many fields (management, commerce, health, education, and entertainment). However, technical problems still need to be further researched and perfected in the current suggested models. The recommender model based on content filtering has several disadvantages: overspecialization, feature extraction problem, and cold-Start problem; The recommendation model based on collaborative filtering suffers from limitations: new user/new product problem (cold-Start), sparsity problem, scalability problem.

problem); The demographic model based on demographic characteristics has several disadvantages: identifying user groups, determining users' preferences, and collecting personal information (demographic of users).); The knowledge-based recommendation model has several disadvantages: the cost of knowledge acquisition, the interaction with users, and the property independence problem depending on users' preferences. Users can rate multiple times. In addition, users can give subjective preference ratings across multiple reviews of an item because it depends on the user's mood, context, behavior, etc. Thus, the problem is determining the user's rating and rating to build the most accurate and appropriate recommendation system for information/products through many reviews and ratings.

2   Related Work

A recommender/recommendation system (RS), as mentioned in [4,15–17], can automatically analyze, classify, predict, and provide helpful recommendations to users with information on products or services. In the recommendation system, the objects that need attention are the user (user), the item (item), and the user's feedback on the item (referred to as reviews or ratings). A recommendation system can predict how a user would rate an item, predicting the order (ranking) of items in a list from most attractive to least attractive to a user, or item (or list) item book) which is suitable for the user. A set of users (users), items (items, data items), and ratings explicitly or implicitly represent how much a user likes or dislikes an item that he or she has viewed. The recommendation system predicts the rating for an item the user has not viewed or provides a list of items the user might like. Recommendation systems are classified into the following main groups: Content-Based Recommendation Systems (CBRS), Collaborative Filtering Systems (CFS), Collaborative Filtering Systems (CFS), and Collaborative Filtering Systems (CFS). Knowledge-Based Recommendation Systems (KBRS), Hybrid Recommender System, and Context-Based Recommendation Systems (CBRS)

2.1   Content-Based Recommendation Systems

The content-based recommendation system [4,8,15,16] suggests to the user items that are similar to items he or she has liked in the past. This system focuses on item-specific attributes (item profile). If people make subjective judgments about some items in the past, they will also make similar judgments on other similar items in the future. So, a content-based recommendation system must learn a user's interest profile. Then, based on the user's profile, similar items that the user has liked or appreciated in the past are suggested to the user. Some techniques commonly used by content-based recommendation systems [4,8,15,17] are clustering, Bayesian classifiers, decision trees, and decision trees. Tree), rule induction, nearest neighbor method, and appropriate feedback. In content-based methods, cosine and term frequency/inverse document frequency (TF-IDF) measurements are used to measure similarity [4,15]. Some limitations of content-based recommendation systems [4,10] are: content analysis is limited because content-based techniques require explicit item descriptions; or the system recommends items whose scores are higher when compared to user profiles, so users will be suggested items that are similar to those they have previously rated, or fail to distinguish two different items represented by the same feature set; The problem is that new users - who have very few reviews - cannot get accurate recommendations.

2.2   Collaborative Filtering Systems

A recommendation system based on collaborative filtering [4,5,15,16] recommends a list of items for a user or predicts the rating for a particular item based on similarity measurement between users/between entries. In collaborative filtering methods, Pearson correlation coefficient, cosine-based similarity, and vector space similarity are widely used in measuring similarity between users (or items). [4,10]. Collaborative filtering is an important and popular technology for recommender systems. Collaborative filtering methods [4,15,16,18] can be grouped into two main classes: memory-based/neighborhood/heuristic (memory-based/ neighborhood-based/ heuristic-based), and model-based. The memory-based collaborative filtering approach requires that information of all ratings, items, and users be stored in the system; and directly used these assessments to make suggestions. This approach is implemented in two ways: user-based collaboration filtering and item-based collaboration filtering. The basic idea of user-based collaborative filtering is to find a set of users whose favorites are similar to a particular user (the "neighbor" of the particular user) and recommend them to others using Users or items that other users in the same group. The item-based collaborative filtering method provides a user with a recommendation for an item based on other highly correlated items ("neighbors" of the item). The techniques commonly used in memory-based collaborative filtering recommender systems [4,5,19] are the nearest neighbor, graph-based, and clustering. Meanwhile, the model-based collaborative filtering approach uses a collection of assessments to learn a model and then uses this model to make recommendations. The techniques commonly used in model-based collaborative filtering recommendation systems [4,5,20] include matrix factorization, association rule, neighbor model, neural network, and probabilistic models. Although without some of the shortcomings of content-based recommendation systems, pure collaborative filtering recommender systems have limitations [4], such as the new user problem (or the item problem). New) - the same problem as the content-based recommendation system; Sparsity problem - the number of estimates obtained is minimal compared to the number of evaluations needed for the prediction.

2.3   Knowledge-Based Recommendation Systems - KBRS

Knowledge-based recommendation system (KBRS) is helpful in cases where items are not frequently used. For example, in e-commerce, products are related to real estate, cars, automobiles, or tourism. In this case, the user rating matrix is not informative enough to recommend. Instead, the system can combine user ratings, product attributes, and relevant historical knowledge of similarities between user requirements to make recommendations accordingly.

3   Methods

3.1   Rating Aggregation

Rating Aggregation is calculated from the total number of ratings averaging the total number of user reviews. The aggregate function (f) represents the relationship between the overall and Multiple-criteria ratings, i.e., $r_0 = f(r_1, ..., r_k)$.

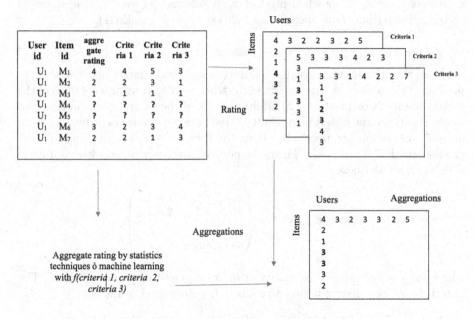

Fig. 1. Average aggregate rating method.

The method consists of three steps. Firstly, we estimate k individual ratings (using any recommendation technique). Then, the k-dimensional Multiple-criteria ranking problem is decomposed into k single-rank recommendation problems. In the second step, the aggregate function f is chosen by rank aggregation, statistical techniques, or machine learning techniques. Finally, the overall rating of each unevaluated data item is calculated based on the predicted k individual criterion ratings and the selected average rating aggregate as shown in Fig. 1. The approach mentioned above has applied multiple criteria ratings instead of single-criteria ratings.

3.2   Recommender Model with Multiple-criteria Rating

In rating evaluation, the criteria of the user or the product are the specific criteria when the user selects the product or the specific condition when the user selects the product. For example, the system suggests that users who wish for a tour booking support system advise choosing a deserved vacation. In that case, the time factor and the person accompanying them will significantly affect the user when determining the destination for the trip. Alternatively, a movie that many users choose to watch in a particular space and time. From the above description, we can see that the information about the user or product criteria depends on each specific consulting problem. However, to model the recommendation problem based on the criteria, the information about the user's or product's criteria is defined as follows: We consider the set $U = \{u_1, u_2, ..., u_n\}$ including of n users while the set of $I = \{i_1, i_2, ..., i_m\}$ being m products; $C = \{c1, c2, ..., ck\}$ is the set of k criteria attributes when the user selects the products. When user u_a selects product i_j, or when product i_j, is selected by user u_a, the values of the criteria attributes are specified as follows (as shown in Eq. 1):

$$C_{a,j} = c1_{a,j}, c2a, j, ..., cka, j \tag{1}$$

From the criteria, we construct a criterion similarity matrix between users or products that is a symmetric matrix with structure, i.e., rows and columns of the matrix are users or products. In addition, cells of the matrix (row and column intersection) are the criterion similarity value between two users or two products on row and column, respectively. Given the user set $U = u_1, u_2, ..., u_n$ and the product set $I = i_1, i_2, ..., i_m$. Then, the criteria similarity matrix between users is determined as Eq. 2.

$$matrix_{sim}(C_u) = \begin{pmatrix} 1 & su_{1,2} & ... & su_{1,n} \\ su_{2,1} & 1 & ... & su_{2,n} \\ ... & & & \\ su_{n,1} & su_{n,2} & ... & 1 \end{pmatrix} \tag{2}$$

where $su_{a,b}$ is the value of similarity criteria between two users u_a and u_b. The criteria similarity matrix between products is determined as Eq. 3.

$$matrix_{sim}(C_u) = \begin{pmatrix} 1 & si_{1,2} & ... & si_{1,m} \\ si_{2,1} & 1 & ... & si_{2,m} \\ ... & & & \\ si_{m,1} & si_{m,2} & ... & 1 \end{pmatrix} \tag{3}$$

where $si_{j,h}$ is the value of similarity criteria between two products i_j and i_h

3.3   Recommendations Based on Similarity Between Users/Items

The similarity-based recommendation model between users is defined as follows.

Let $U = \{u_1, u_2, ..., u_n\}$ be the set of n users; $I = \{i_1, i_2, ..., i_m\}$ is the set of m products; $C = \{c1, c2, ..., ck\}$ denotes the set of k criteria attributes when the user selects the products; $R = r_{c,j}$ exhibits user U's rating matrix for items I in criterion C, with each row representing one user $u_c, (1 \leq c \leq n)$, each column representing for an item $i_j, (1 \leq j \leq m)$, $r(c,j)$ is the rating value of user u_c for product i_j in the criterion C_{cj}. N is the number of products with high similarity and $u_a \in U$ is the user who needs to suggest with criteria: $C_{a,j} = \{c1_{a,j}, c2_{a,j}, ..., ck_{a,j}\}$.

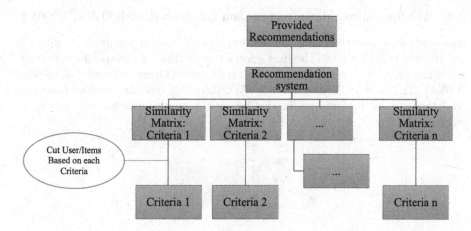

Fig. 2. Recommendation system based on the similarity between users/items.

The recommendation systems are based on the similarity of user criteria as presented in Fig. 2. In the first stage, the criteria are conducted from a user-based ranking matrix using the User splitting technique. Then, based on the criteria attributes, we build the criteria similarity matrix between users; Finally, the user-criteria similarity-based recommendation model is built based on the integration matrix between the User-Based Rating Matrix and the user-criteria similarity matrix. Based on input which includes Rating from users/items;criteria;users/items for recommendations: u_α. To provide N products recommended for u_α, the algorithm based on the similarity between criteria according to the user (in the case of items we present in *brackets*) is exhibited as follows:

- Step 1: Build user-based similarity matrix- SU_R (items-based similarity matrix SI_R in the case we based on items):
    - Handle cutting users (items);
    - Build users-based similarity matrix (items-based similarity matrix);
- Step 2: Build a similarity matrix of criteria according to users: SU_C (similarity matrix of criteria according to items: SI_C):
    - Similarity of criteria between 2 users (2 items);
    - Building similarity matrix based on user criteria (item criteria);
- Step 3: Build the integrated similarity matrix: $SU_I = SU_R + SU_C$ (if we use "item", it will be $SI_I = SI_R + SI_C$);

- Step 4: Build User-Based Collaborative Filtering based on the average integrated similarity matrix of the Criteria: UBCFC (in the case with items, i.e., Item-Based Collaborative Filtering based on the average integrated similarity matrix of the Criteria (IBCFC));
- Step 5: Define a list of similar products for user u_α;
- Step 6: Present the user $u_a N$ with the item with the highest similarity value;

3.4   The Recommendation Approach Integrated with OWA, WOWA

The study evaluates the rating of the criteria of the user or the product, which is the specific criterion when the user selects the product or the specific condition when the product is selected by the user integrating Ordered Weighted Average (OWA) [21,22], and Weighted OWA (WOWA) [23] into the process proposed to estimate user preferences, predicting into a "multi-dimensional" rating as exhibited in Fig. 3.

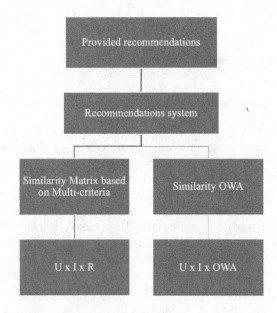

Fig. 3. Recommendation system integrated with OWA.

4   Experiments

4.1   Data Description

We evaluated the proposed method on DePaulMovie dataset. DePaulMovie[1] was updated in 2018 by the Pepoul Center for Data Science, including a survey of

---

[1] https://github.com/JDonini/depaulmovie-recommender-system.

students ranking movies by different time, place, and companions. The dataset consists of 5043 ratings from 97 students of 319 movies based on three context attributes Time, Location, and Companion (each context is a criterion). The rank attribute has a positive integer value ranging from 1 (very unsatisfied) to 5 (very satisfied), in which the value 1 appears in 829 reviews while the value of 2 is in 625 reviews, etc.

4.2 Contextual Data Processing on DePaulMovie Dataset

From students' ratings on movies, we construct a real numeric rating data matrix for the DePaulMovie dataset with a structure of 97 rows (corresponding to 97 users) and 319 columns (corresponding to 319 movies/items) with 5043 rating values. The criteria attributes are used to cut users according to each specific criteria when the user chooses to watch movies to build a similarity matrix of criteria according to users.

There are three considered contexts Time, Location, and Companion (each context is considered as a criterion). Each criterion contributes to a user matrix with 97 rows and 319 columns so that the data has three matrices of the user. In addition, the criteria attribute crop products according to specific criteria when the user selects the movies to watch to build a product-specific criterion similarity matrix.

4.3 Evaluation of Multiple-Criteria-Based Approach

The dataset was divided into 5-fold-cross-validation to evaluate the effectiveness of the recommendation system. The method with a Multiple-criteria ranking was conducted from the traditional collaborative filtering model. For example, if the data is divided by 80% for the training set, and the test set occupies 20%, the results of the training data set can contain 3723 evaluations from 71 users (71 rows × 319 columns). The test set includes 26 users (26 rows × 319 columns) with 1320 reviews. The experiments are done with the support from some libraries in R, such as Recommenderlab [24,25], agop [26], and the performance is measured by Mean Square Error (RMSE), Mean Square Error (MSE), Mean Absolute Error (MAE) on the test set.

Table 1. Comparison between UBCFC and UBCF in various metrics.

Method	RMSE	MSE	MAE
UBCFC	1.409295	1.986112	1.114970
UBCF	1.410167	1.988571	1.114970

Table 1 presents the results and compares UBCFC and the traditional User-Based Collaborative Filtering (UBCF) method in RMSE, MSE, and MAE on the test set. This result shows that the approach that integrated the user-criteria similarity matrix for providing recommendations, UBCFC, has lower error rates than UBCF.

Table 2. Comparison between IBCFC and IBCF in various metrics.

Mô hình	RMSE	MSE	MAE
IBCFC	1.592475	2.535977	1.220261
IBCF	1.598317	2.543797	1.230216

The recommendation model is based on the similarity of user-selected product criteria (IBCFC) and the traditional Product-Based Collaborative Filtering Recommendation Model (IBCF). From the experimental results, measure error parameters: Square root of mean square error (RMSE), mean square error (MSE), mean absolute error (MAE) in Table 2. This result shows that the model that integrates the user-selected product criteria similarity matrix (IBCFC) has lower error parameters than the traditional Product-Based Collaborative Filter Recommendation Model (IBCF).

Table 3. Comparison between IBCF_OWA and IBCF in RMSE, MSE and MAE.

Methods	RMSE	MSE	MAE
IBCF_OWA	1.431843	2.050174	1.179211
IBCF	1.598317	2.543797	1.230216

The OWA Integrated Recommendation method (IBCF_OWA) and the traditional Item-Based Collaborative Filtering Recommendation Model (IBCF) with results in Square root of mean square error (RMSE), mean square error (MSE), mean absolute error (MAE) are revealed in Table 3. In addition, they show that the OWA integration model (IBCF_OWA) has lower error parameters than the traditional Product-Based Collaborative Filtering Recommendation Model (IBCF) running on the same DePaulMovie dataset.

To evaluate the effectiveness of the methods, we compare the proposed method with the traditional collaborative filtering model UBCF and IBCF in the ROC metric based on the Precision/Recall ratio on the DePaulMovie dataset.

The recommendation strategy is based on the similarity of user criteria for products (UBCFC) and the traditional User-Based Collaborative Filtering Recommendation Model (UBCF). The results of comparing the model's accuracy are shown in (Fig. 4) with the number of films introduced to users of the models increasing gradually from 1 to 10. The results show that the Precision/Recall

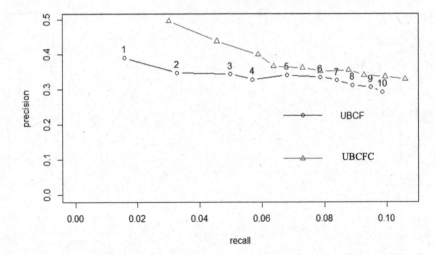

Fig. 4. The comparison results on DePaulMovie dataset between UBCFC and UBCF.

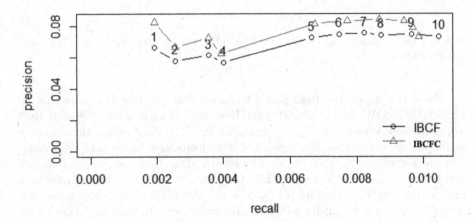

Fig. 5. The comparison results on DePaulMovie dataset between IBCFC and IBCF.

ratio of the models increased gradually from 1 to 10. the UBCFC model is relatively higher than the Precision/Recall ratio of the two UBCF models. Therefore, the recommendation approach based on the similarity of user criteria for products (UBCFC) can improve the accuracy of the recommender system.

The proposed method compares user-selected product criteria (IBCFC) and the traditional Product-Based Collaborative Filtering Recommendation Model (IBCF). The results are presented in Fig. 5 with the number of films introduced to users of the models that increase gradually from 1 to 10. The results show that the Precision/Recall ratio of the models is increased. Furthermore, the IBCFC model is relatively higher than the Precision/Recall ratio of the two IBCF models. As observed, the recommendation methods based on the similarity of selected product criteria (IBCFC) can improve the accuracy of the recommender system.

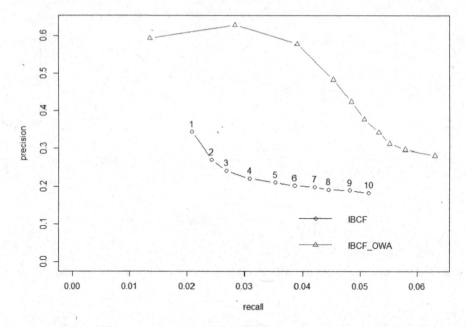

Fig. 6. The comparison results on DePaulMovie dataset between IBCF and IBCF_OWA.

The OWA integrated Item-Based Collaborative Filtering Recommendation Model (IBCF_OWA) and the traditional Item-Based Collaborative Filtering Recommendation Model (IBCF) are compared in Fig. 6. Comparing the accuracy of the model reveals that the number of films introduced to users of the models increased gradually from 1 to 10. The results show that the Precision/Recall ratio of the models is increased. The OWA model (IBCF_OWA) is relatively higher than the Precision/Recall ratio of the two IBCF models. It shows that the OWA integrated Item-Based Collaborative Filtering Recommendation Model can improve the accuracy of the recommender system.

5   Conclusion

Experimental results are evaluated on film reviews of the DePaulMovie dataset with a recommendation system's desired results. The study proposes a method to improve the accuracy of the collaborative filtering recommender model by considering the similar relationship between users or products based on the criteria in building the model. Collaborative filtering consulting. The recommendations are calculated based on the integration of similarity values, i.e., similarity based on user's criteria for products and similarity based on product criteria selected by users. The Selected and matched items/users are based on OWA integration. Experimentation on the DePaulMovie dataset shows that the proposed model has higher accuracy than the traditional collaborative filtering recommender model. From these experimental results, it can be confirmed that the recommendation model based on Multiple-criteria ratings is applicable in practice.

References

1. Toffler, A.: Future Shock. Bantam Books (1970)
2. Nghia, P.Q., Phuong, D.H., Hiep, H.X.: Lua chon mo hinh va tham so cho bai toan tu van loc cong tac dua tren do thi. Can Tho University, Journal of Science, p. 171 (2017). https://doi.org/10.22144/ctu.jsi.2017.023
3. Bobadilla, J., Ortega, F., Hernando, A., GutiéRrez, A.: Recommender systems survey. Know. Based Syst. **46**, 109–132 (2013). https://doi.org/10.1016/j.knosys.2013.03.012
4. Adomavicius, G., Tuzhilin, A.: Toward the next generation of recommender systems: a survey of the state-of-the-art and possible extensions. IEEE Trans. Knowl. Data Eng. **17**(6), 734–749 (2005)
5. Schafer, J.B., Frankowski, D., Herlocker, J., Sen, S.: Collaborative filtering recommender systems. In: Brusilovsky, P., Kobsa, A., Nejdl, W. (eds.) The Adaptive Web. LNCS, vol. 4321, pp. 291–324. Springer, Heidelberg (2007). https://doi.org/10.1007/978-3-540-72079-9_9
6. Ekstrand, M.D., Riedl, J.T., Konstan, J.A.: Collaborative filtering recommender systems. Found. Trends Hum. Comput. Interact. 4(2), 81–173 (2011). https://doi.org/10.1561/1100000009
7. Cantador, I., Bellogín, A., Vallet, D.: Content-based recommendation in social tagging systems. In: Proceedings of the Fourth ACM Conference on Recommender Systems, ser. RecSys 2010, pp. 237–240. New York, NY, USA: Association for Computing Machinery (2010). https://doi.org/10.1145/1864708.1864756
8. Pazzani, M.J., Billsus, D.: Content-based recommendation systems. In: Brusilovsky, P., Kobsa, A., Nejdl, W. (eds.) The Adaptive Web. LNCS, vol. 4321, pp. 325–341. Springer, Heidelberg (2007). https://doi.org/10.1007/978-3-540-72079-9_10
9. Krulwich, B.: Lifestyle finder-intelligent user profiling using large-scale demographic. AI Mag. 10 (1997)
10. Cobos, C., et al.: A hybrid system of pedagogical pattern recommendations based on singular value decomposition and variable data attributes. Inf. Process. Manage. **49**(3), 607–625 (2013). https://doi.org/10.1016/j.ipm.2012.12.002
11. Felfernig, A., Teppan, E., Gula, B.: Knowledge-based Recommender technologies for marketing and sales. Int. J. Pattern Recogn. Artif. Intell. **21**(02), 333–354 (2007). https://doi.org/10.1142/s0218001407005417
12. Shambour, Q., Lu, J.: A trust-semantic fusion-based recommendation approach for e-business applications. Decis. Support Syst. **54**(1), 768–780 (2012). https://doi.org/10.1016/j.dss.2012.09.005
13. Nguyen, T.T.S., Lu, H.Y., Lu, J.: Web-page recommendation based on web usage and domain knowledge. IEEE Trans. Knowl. Data Eng. **26**(10), 2574–2587 (2014)
14. Lucas, J.P., Luz, N., Moreno, M.N., Anacleto, R., Figueiredo, A.A., Martins, C.: A hybrid recommendation approach for a tourism system. Expert Syst. Appl. **40**(9), 3532–3550 (2013). https://doi.org/10.1016/j.eswa.2012.12.061
15. Burke, R.: Hybrid web recommender systems. In: Brusilovsky, P., Kobsa, A., Nejdl, W. (eds.) The Adaptive Web. LNCS, vol. 4321, pp. 377–408. Springer, Heidelberg (2007). https://doi.org/10.1007/978-3-540-72079-9_12

16. Felfernig, A., Jeran, M., Ninaus, G., Reinfrank, F., Reiterer, S., Stettinger, M.: Basic approaches in recommendation systems. In: Robillard, M.P., Maalej, W., Walker, R.J., Zimmermann, T. (eds.) Recommendation Systems in Software Engineering. LNCS, pp. 15–37. Springer, Heidelberg (2014). https://doi.org/10.1007/978-3-642-45135-5_2

17. Leskovec, J., Rajaraman, A., Ullman, J.D.: Mining of Massive Datasets. Cambridge University Press, Cambridge (2014)

18. Breese, J.S., Heckerman, D., Kadie, C.: Empirical analysis of predictive algorithms for collaborative filtering. In: Proceedings of the Fourteenth Conference on Uncertainty in Artificial Intelligence, ser. UAI 1998, pp. 43–52 San Francisco, CA, USA: Morgan Kaufmann Publishers Inc. (1998)

19. Desrosiers, C., Karypis, G.: A comprehensive survey of neighborhood-based recommendation methods. In: Ricci, F., Rokach, L., Shapira, B., Kantor, P.B. (eds.) Recommender Systems Handbook. LNCS, pp. 107–144. Springer, Boston, MA (2011). https://doi.org/10.1007/978-0-387-85820-3_4

20. Koren, Y., Bell, R.: Advances in collaborative filtering. In: Ricci, F., Rokach, L., Shapira, B., Kantor, P.B. (eds.) Recommender Systems Handbook. LNCS, pp. 145–186. Springer, Boston, MA (2011). https://doi.org/10.1007/978-0-387-85820-3_5

21. Yager, R.R., Kacprzyk, J.: The Ordered Weighted Averaging Operators. Springer, Cham (1997)

22. Csiszar, Ò.: Ordered weighted averaging operators: a short review. IEEE Systems, Man Cybern. Mag. **7**(2), 4–12 (2021)

23. Torra, V.: The WOWA operator: a review. In: Yager, R.R., Kacprzyk, J., Beliakov, G. (eds.) Recent Developments in the Ordered Weighted Averaging Operators: Theory and Practice. Studies in Fuzziness and Soft Computing, vol. 265, pp. 17–28. Springer, Heidelberg (2011). https://doi.org/10.1007/978-3-642-17910-5_2

24. Gorakala, S.K., Usuelli, M.: Building a Recommendation System with R. Packt Publishing, Birmingham (2015)

25. Hahsler, M. : recommenderlab: a framework for developing and testing recommendation algorithms (2011)

26. Gagolewski, M., Cena, A.: AGOP: aggregation operators package for R (2014). http://agop.rexamine.com/

A Survey of On-Chip Hybrid Interconnect for Multicore Architectures

Cuong Pham-Quoc[1,2](✉)

[1] Ho Chi Minh City University of Technology (HCMUT),
268 Ly Thuong Kiet Street, District 10, Ho Chi Minh City, Vietnam
cuongpham@hcmut.edu.vn
[2] Vietnam National University - Ho Chi Minh City (VNU-HCM),
Ho Chi Minh City, Vietnam

Abstract. In this paper, we present a survey of hybrid interconnects for multicore architecture proposed in the literature. Before making a survey, we introduce an overview of on-chip hybrid interconnects and the taxonomies to classify them. We also present different architectures of standard interconnects that are frequently used for multi/many-core system in both the academia and industry. Finally, we conduct a survey of hybrid interconnects where we categorize them into two different groups. The first one includes hybrid interconnects that create the interconnects by using different Network-on-Chip topologies. We named this group as *topology-mixture hybrid interconnect*. The second group, named *architecture-mixture hybrid interconnects*, combines different architectures, such as bus and NoC, to form hybrid interconnects.

Keywords: Multicore systems · Hybrid interconnect · FPGA · ASIC

1   Introduction

In the past years, it has become clear that the continued scaling in transistor dimensions can no longer significantly increase processor performance. Factors like the power wall, memory wall, and instruction-level parallelism (ILP) wall have shifted the effort to increase performance towards parallel multicore processing. On the other hand, with the rapid development of technology, more and more transistors are integrated into a single chip. Today, it is possible to integrate more than 30 billion transistors [10] into one system. However, the more transistors are integrated into a system; the more challenges need to be addressed, such as power consumption, thermal emission, and memory access bottleneck. Therefore, homogeneous and heterogeneous multicore systems were introduced to efficiently utilize such large numbers of transistors. Compared to homogeneous multicore systems, heterogeneous multicore systems offer more computation power and efficient energy consumption [24] because of the efficiency of specialized cores for specific tasks.

Interconnect in a multicore system plays an important role because data is exchanged between all components, typically between processing elements (PEs)

C. V. Phan and T. D. Nguyen (Eds.): ICCASA 2022, LNICST 475, pp. 59–75, 2023.
https://doi.org/10.1007/978-3-031-28816-6_5

and memory modules, using the interconnect. However, interconnect design is one of the two open issues along with programming model in multicore system design [32]. During the last decades, many on-chip interconnects, especially hybrid interconnects, have been proposed, along with the rising number of PEs in the systems. Figure 1 (adapted from [26]) summarizes the evolution of on-chip interconnects.

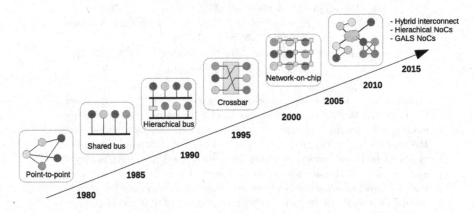

Fig. 1. The evolution of the on-chip interconnects (re-draw from [26])

In this paper, we conduct a survey of hybrid interconnects where we categorize them into two different groups. The first one includes hybrid interconnects that create the interconnects by using different Network-on-Chip topologies. We named this group as *topology-mixture hybrid interconnect*. The second group, named *architecture-mixture hybrid interconnects*, combines different architectures, such as bus and NoC, to form hybrid interconnects.

2   On-Chip Interconnect: An Overview

In modern computing systems, especially for big data processing multi/many-core systems, PEs cannot function independently. Therefore, these systems require communication networks, so-called the interconnection network, to transfer data from PE to PE or memory. System performance is substantially improved when deploying a suitable interconnection network because data communication overhead may take up to 50% processing time of entire applications. Performance, scalability, and cost are fundamental factors in choosing the right interconnection network [8].

As a sub-category of a more comprehensive - data communication network, an on-chip interconnect creates a connection and delivers required data for systems nodes[1] in a system-on-chip (SoC). Many approaches can be used to categorize interconnects into groups. In this paper, we presented five taxonomies for the classifying purpose.

---

[1] A node is any part that joins the network like a PE or a buffer.

2.1   Technique-Based Classification

We can classified on-chip interconnects two groups: shared memory and message passing [30] according the techniques used for transferring data from node to node.

- *Shared memory*: in this technique, a buffer/cache is responsible for exchanging data of PEs. When communicating, PE stores shared data into the buffer/cache in a joint address space so other PEs can load data for further processing. Bus-based communication, cache sharing, and crossbar are famous examples of this technique.
- *Message passing*: in this technique, explicit messages are responsible for conducting data communication among nodes. The source PE encapsulates data into packets according to the interconnect protocols before forwarding them to the destination via a the on-chip interconnect. Network-on-Chips (NoCs) are delegates of this type.

2.2   Topology-Based Classification

Duato et al. categorize interconnects into four groups including shared medium networks, direct networks, indirect networks and hybrid networks. The categories are based on the way PEs connected together [8].

- *Shared medium networks*: all computing nodes are connected to the same physical component for transferring data. Any communication between any pair of nodes will be conducted through the component. This group is similar to the Shared memory classification above.
- *Direct networks*: NoCs illustrate this group where a node is connected to a subset of other nodes in the system through P2P links. Network routers/adapters are attached to every node to encode data according to the NoCs protocol.
- *Indirect networks*: a crossbar is a good instance of this type of network in which one or more switches attach communicating nodes together.
- *Hybrid network*: this type of connection merges more than one type of network to alleviate this type's drawbacks by exploring others' benefits.

2.3   Link-Based Classification

Gama et al. classify interconnect into static and dynamic networks according to the characteristic of links that connect nodes [13].

- *Static networks*: links attaching nodes are fixed for data transferring. A link is dedicated to any pair of nodes. NoCs or buffer/cache sharing are delegates for this type.
- *Dynamic networks*: in contrast with the static one, a dynamic network includes switches and links that are reserved for data communication between two nodes for a while before being updated for the others. Buses and crossbars are instances of this type.

2.4   Routing Technique-Based Classification

El-Rewini et al. use the routing techniques for transferring messages from a source to a destination to classify interconnect into two classes: circuit switching and packet switching [9].

- *Circuit switching networks*: this type creates a physical path from a source node to a destination before transmitting data through the network. The published route exists for an entire communication interval. During this period, no other nodes contend to use the path. Buses, crossbars, and cache/buffer sharing are examples of this type.
- *Packet switching networks*: The networks encapsulate transferred data into fixed-length network packets. These packets are transmitted independently from a source to a destination through various paths. Some well-known examples of this switching technique are wormhole or virtual cut-through routing.

2.5   Architecture-Based Classification

On interconnects can be categorized according to the hardware architectures [11,23]. Below, we discuss shared cache/buffer (or shared memory), buses, crossbars, and network-on-chips because they are primary used in multi/many-core systems.

- *Shared cache/buffer*: in this architecture, as the name mentioned, nodes transfer communication data through a shared cache/buffer as illustrated in Fig. 2(a). Data movement between PEs is conducted with load/store behaviors through memory interfaces.
- *Bus*: The bus is one of the simplest and widely used in both sing core and multi/many-core systems. A bus attaches all system nodes as shown in Fig. 2(b). A bus-protocol [29] with request and granted behaviors is responsible for exchanging data between nodes.
- *Crossbar*: A generic crossbar includes n inputs and m outputs that can create an arbitrary connection between any pair of input and output. Figure 2(c) illustrates a 2×2 crossbar. Crossbars are frequently used to make connection of n computing and m storage (memory) nodes.
- *NoC*: network-on-chip is a generic architecture that is mainly used for transferring in multi/many-core systems. A NoC contains a set of routers connected by dedicated links. Router connections define different network topologies according to the connection patterns. Ring, 2D-mesh, torus or tree are primary network topologies explored in computing systems. Figure 2(d) shows a 3×3 2D-mesh NoC.

Table 1 summarizes and shows relations of categories and hardware architecture of interconnects. Figure 3 presents pros and cons of four primary interconnect architectures mainly used in computing systems. Five parameters including latency, area-efficiency, scalability, system-performance, and power-efficiency are discussed in this comparison. Due to sequentially transferring data [33], buses

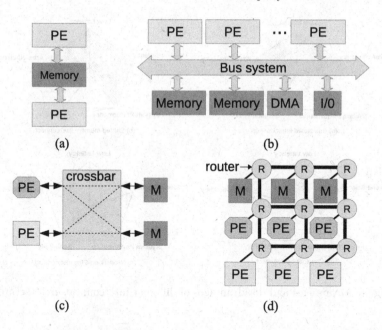

Fig. 2. (a) Shared cache/buffer; (b) Bus; (c) Crossbar; (d) Network-on-Chip

Table 1. Summary and relation of different interconnects

Classification	Shared cache/buffer	Bus	Crossbar	NoC
Technique	SM	SM	SM	MP
Topology	SMed	SMed	Indirect	Direct
Link	Dynamic	Dynamic	Dynamic	Static
Routing	CS	CS	CS	PS

- SM: Shared memory
- MP: Message passing
- SMed: Shared medium
- CS: Circuit switching
- PS: Packet switching

cannot offer high performance and suffer from low scalability. However, because of simplicity, buses are very efficient in terms of power consumption and hardware area. Since the connection is established for a source and a destination, the latency for data transferring is relatively low. Although shared cache/buffer provides an area-efficient, low hardware complex, and power-efficient architecture, it suffers from the worst scalability due to port limitations. However, compared to buses, shared cache/buffer does not introduce any data communication delay because there is no communication competition. Hence, systems with shared cache/buffer can achieve good performance. A crossbar can offer better system performance with low communication latency than a bus because multiple con-

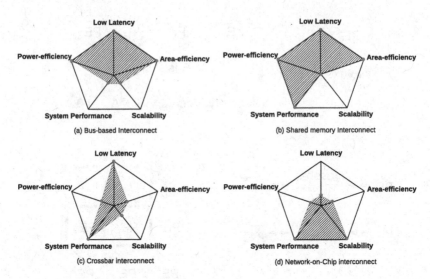

Fig. 3. Advantages and disadvantages of different interconnect architectures

nections between inputs and outputs can be established simultaneously [17]. However, when adding more ports, the resource usage for crossbars expands dramatically. Due to the rapid increase in hardware resource usage, a crossbar has high hardware complexity and power consumption. Finally, although offering absolute advantages such as high system performance and scalability, NoCs consume much power, require a vast amount of resources, and introduce high latency [16]. Therefore, hybrid interconnects taking all advantages of various architectures is a promising approach for multi/many-core systems that require high performance for time-consuming applications.

3   Survey of Hybrid Interconnects

As mentioned above, hybrid interconnect is a promising approach for improving system performance in multi/many-core platforms. In this section, we survey hybrid interconnect designs in the literature. We presented five approaches to categorize standalone on-chip connection networks into groups. Each group provides various advantages but also suffers from many drawbacks. For instance, direct networks are more straightforward than indirect ones in implementation cost. However, the former provides lower system performance and scalability than the latter. Besides, although circuit switching techniques offer higher bandwidth communication channels, packet switching ones will not block any messages because no routers or links are reserved for any physical paths. However,

the encoding and decoding processes of the packet switching techniques introduce overhead that may reduce system performance unawareness. Therefore,
hybrid interconnects are getting accepted and proposed more and more in the
last decades for exploiting the successes of various interconnect architectures and
techniques.

From our perspective, hybrid interconnects can be designed with two different mixtures, including multiple NoC topologies and architectures. The first
approach combines NoCs topologies like the 2D-mesh with the ring to create a
hybrid mesh-ring interconnect. We call this approach as *Topology-mixture hybrid
interconnect*. Meanwhile, the second approach exploits the advantages of various
interconnect architectures. A new hybrid interconnect is designed by combining different architecture like a bus and an NoC. We call this hybrid type as
Architecture-mixture hybrid interconnect. The following sections summarize the
hybrid interconnects of each type.

3.1 Topology-Mixture

Network-on-chip topology [18] defines a structure that connects routers through
physical links so that data can be transferred from a source to a destination.
Some mainly used standard topologies are 2D-mesh, ring, hypercube, tree, and
star, as illustrated in Fig. 4. Although each standard topology offers particular advantages, each has drawbacks that the others can improve. For instance,
communication latency scalability and traffic concentration at center nodes are
the two main obstacles of the 2D-mesh [5]. Meanwhile, ring topology cannot
guarantee consistent latency for all nodes [30]. Therefore, mixture-topology
or application-specific topology interconnects can help solve the drawbacks to
improve advantages further. The following sections present mixture-topology
interconnects in the literature.

CMesh (concentrated mesh) proposed by Balfour et al. in [2] connects every
four nodes by a star topology. A 2D-mesh network links these 4-node groups
at the higher level. The most significant advantage of CMesh compared to the
original mesh is less average hop count. Kim et al. [21] extended the CMesh
network and presented the Flattened Butterfly one where dedicated physical
channels link 4-node groups in a row or a column. Hence, the dedicated P2P
channels reduce the average hop counts to two. The simulated results show that
CMesh improved area efficiency by 24% and reduced energy consumption by
48%. Meanwhile, the Flattened Butterfly used fewer hardware resources than
2D-mesh and CMesh 4× and 2.5×, respectively.

Murali et al. [28] introduced a design method to automatically synthesize a
custom-tailored, application-specific NoC. The automated designed NoCs satisfy
the targeted application domain's design objectives and constraints. The design
framework considers two major minimizations: network power consumption and
hops count. Hence, the framework executes the following step with task graphs
as inputs to achieve the goals: (1) considering multiple topologies with variant
switches number; (2) conducting the topologies floor-planning automatically; (3)

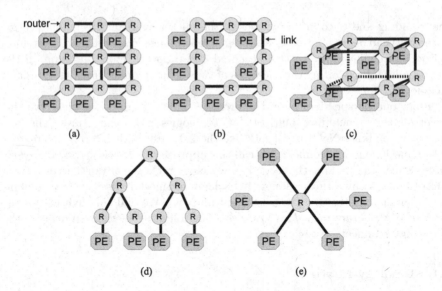

Fig. 4. Examples of NoC topologies: (a) 2D-mesh; (b) ring; (c) hypercube; (d) tree; and (e) star.

selecting the most optimized topologies with all the design objectives and constraints satisfied. An ARM-based embedded platform was used for evaluating the framework. The experimental results show that synthesized topologies automatically improved system performance by 1.73× with 2.78× power consumption reduced on average compared to the standard topologies.

Balkan et al. proposed the Mesh-of-Tree (MoT) [3] interconnection network that connects PEs and memory through two tree-based networks. In contrast to other architectures, the communicating nodes link with the root nodes instead of being connected to the leaf nodes. In this approach, a fan-out tree manages PEs while another fan-in tree handles memory modules. The fan-in and fan-out tree leaf nodes attach through 1-to-1 connecting channels. Two primary characteristics of the MoT network are a unique path between a pair of a source and a destination and not interfering in transferring packets from sources to destinations. The proposed architecture network is simulated for validation. The experimental results show that MoT improved network throughput by 76% and 28% compared to the butterfly and hypercube topologies, respectively.

Extending the MoT network, Balkan et al. presented the hybrid MoT-BF network architecture [4]. The extended version of MoT, MoT-BF, merges the MoT topology with the area-efficient butterfly network (BF). The ultimate target of this extension is to achieve low hardware resource usage for the MoT network implementation. Consequently, 2 × 2 butterfly networks replace the fan-in and fan-out trees' leaf nodes and some intermediate nodes. Furthermore, parameter h, the level of the MoT-h-BF network, was introduced as the number of intermediate nodes was replaced. Based on the simulated results, a 64 node MoT-BF save area overhead by 34% with only 0.5% throughput penalty compared to the original MoT network.

Stensgaard et al. introduced the ReNoC [34] architecture to allow reconfiguring of NoC topologies with different applications' task graphs. ReNoC's nodes comprise traditional NoC routers in the proposed architecture, but topology switches wrap them. These switches can create links between NoC's routers and links or links together to bypass unneeded routers. This ability of switches allows various topologies to be defined according to applications' task graphs. The ultimate results could be a combination of 2D-meshes, P2P links, rings, or stars topologies. The implementation of ReNoC with the 90nm ASIC technology shows that ReNoC requires only 25% hardware resource compared to a static 2D-mesh with a 56% reduction in energy consumption.

G-Star/L-Hybrid proposed by Kim et al. [22] mixes a star topology global network and a star-mesh local network. The proposed network aims to degrade packet-drop rates. After trying different topologies combinations with various application domains, the authors decided that the star and mesh topologies combination is the most optimized approach regarding packet-drop rate. Experimental results show that the proposed architecture saves 45.5% packet-drop rate compared to others. In addition, the architecture also offers better power and area efficiency.

Modarressi presented the VIP hybrid interconnect architecture [27] that exploits the NoCs' scalability and P2P links' superior communication performance. The framework to define VIP's topology follows the below steps with applications' task graphs as a parameter: 1) physically assigning applications' tasks to a 2D-mesh NoC's routers; 2) building numerous P2P links for applications' tasks; 3) routing data packets through P2P links to save the 2D-mesh NoC's energy consumption and latency. The proposed VIP architecture is evaluated by simulation that introduces 20% NoC power consumption on average saved.

Bourduas et al. [5] presented various hierarchical topologies with ring networks. These hierarchies' ultimate goal is to lessen global traffic's hop counts and latencies. Therefore, the approach divides generic 2D meshes into several smallest 2×2 meshes, called sub-meshes. A ring connects every four sub-meshes to create a local mesh. Accordingly, these local meshes are then linked through another ring. A newly designed ring-mesh bridge element transfers packets between mesh and ring nodes. Besides, this approach also designed two new ring architectures. The first one aims for simplicity and low implementation cost. In contrast, the second one exploits the wormhole and virtual channel techniques to guarantee flexibility and performance. The simulated results prove the proposal's goals when outperforming a 2D-mesh if the number of nodes is less than forty-four.

Wang et al. introduced DMesh [38] consisting of E-subnet and W-subnet networks. Each subnet's router includes diagonal links to neighbor ones. These subnet networks transfer data packets separately eastward (E-subnet) and westward (W-subnet). When a source node starts forwarding data, packets are delivered through either E-router or W-router according to the destination's direction. The authors also introduce a new routing technique for the proposal. SystemC-based simulation results show that DMesh is better than other 8 × 8 networks.

An extension of CMesh was proposed by Camacho et al. called PC-Mesh [6]. In PC-Mesh, extra 2D-meshes link batches of four consecutive nodes that the original CMesh network does not attach. With extra links, PC-Mesh offers higher fault tolerance and decreases latency in hops count. Furthermore, the authors propose a new routing algorithm to utilize the extra 2D-mesh networks because of multiple connections from a node to switches. The simulated results indicate that PC-Mesh can improve performance 2× and save 50% energy consumption compared to CMesh.

Yin et al. proposed a hybrid-switch NoC [39] that integrates P2P links with a standard 2D-mesh network. The architecture uses explicit configuration messages to define these P2P channels for often disseminating nodes. In other words, the architecture uses both packet and circuit switching techniques. Packets in the former technique are buffered, routed, and delivered at routers, while the latter uses dedicated channels for transferring data without communication overhead. Experimental results with simulation reveal that the architecture achieves 12% better system performance and saves 24% energy consumption compared NoCs without dedicated links.

Swaminathan et al. [35] introduced a hybrid NoC topology that merges 2D-mesh, torus, and folded. The mesh links attach two neighboring routers. Meanwhile, the folded-like channels connect odd routers or even routers in a row or a column. Finally, the torus-like links unite two border routers in a row/column. Because of extra channels, the authors designed a new routing algorithm for the proposed topology. Under the support of various topologies, the architecture decreases the average hop count compared to a single topology and enhances communication throughput. The experimental results with simulation indicate that the hybrid NoC improves 24% system performance compared to 2D-mesh networks.

Kang et al. [20] introduced an extension of MoT called 3-D MoT that allows topology to be reconfigurable. As a result, packets from nodes to nodes can travel through traditional or user-demand routes with the support of reconfigurable switches modified from the original ones. Experimental results state that 3-D MoT saves 13.34% execution time compared to conventional networks. Besides, the power consumption is also lower than the baseline networks. However, one of the biggest obstacles to this proposal is the lack of a formal approach for application designers.

Table 2 concludes all the aforementioned mixture topologies interconnects. We also summarize the targets of each approach in the last column of the table. According to the goals, most proposals focus on performance (latency or throughput) because it is the most important factor in multi/many-core systems.

Table 2. Topology mixture hybrid interconnects

Research	Mixture topology	Input data[a]	Goals
[2, 21]	Mesh/Star	Static[b]	Area, Power
[28]	Various[c]	User constraints	Performance, Power
[3]	Mesh/Tree	Static	Throughput
[4]	Mesh/Tree/ Butterfly	Static	Throughput
[34]	Various	Task graph	Area, Energy
[22]	Mesh/Star	Static	Packet drop, Area, Power
[27]	Mesh/P2P[d]	Task graph	Power
[5]	Mesh/Ring	Static	Latency
[38]	Mesh/Mesh	Static	Performance
[6]	Several Meshes	Static	Performance, Energy
[39]	Mesh/P2P	Communication rate	Performance, Energy
[35]	Folded/Mesh/ Torus	Static	Performance
[20]	Mesh/Tree	N/A	Performance

[a]Parameters determine the topology.
[b]*Static*: fixed design without any parameters taken into account.
[c]*Various* multiple topologies used.
[d]Point-to-point.

3.2 Architecture-Mixture

Although many computing systems use shared caches/buffers, buses, cross-bars, and NoCs as the primary communication infrastructure, these interconnect architectures still have some drawbacks, as presented in Sect. 2.5. Hence, many researchers have proposed hybrid interconnects exploiting multiple interconnect architectures to alleviate drawbacks of this type with the advantages of the others. In this section, we survey architecture-mixture hybrid interconnects published in recent years.

Richardson introduced dTDMA/NoC [31] hybrid interconnect, including buses and an NoC. The system uses a bus to link more frequent communication nodes to create an affinity group. Meanwhile, nodes outside these affinity sections transfer data through the NoC. The basic ideas upon which dTDMA/NoC is proposed are two following heuristics: 1) Buses supply higher transferring performance than NoCs within less than nine node groups; 2) When data rate increases, the performance of NoCs downgrades is extensively faster than buses. Hence, buses link nodes into affinity groups according to the frequency of nodes' communication. Each group of nodes connects with an NoC's router through a particular component called a bridge. Meanwhile, nodes outside all groups are also attached to routers for transferring data. Experimental simulation results show that the proposed hybrid interconnect improves the systems' performance and energy efficiency. In the worst case, the proposal reduces 15.2% of latency and 8% of power consumption compared to traditional meshes.

Grot et al. introduced MECS [15] (Multidrop Express Channels) that exploits a CMesh NoC, presented in the mixture-topology group and bus-like one-to-many (1-to-m) channels. Although the architecture of the 1-to-m channel is likely a bus, only a primary node can broadcast data to secondary nodes linked through the channel. With the support of 1-to-m channels, the interconnect can handle multicast and broadcast with slightly additional overhead. The authors conducted simulations with many workloads and compared them with CMesh and Flatten Butterfly [21]. Experimental results show that MECS with 64 nodes saves 9% latency compared to the other interconnects.

Manevich et al. presented BENoC (Bus-enhanced NoC) [25] to combine an NoC with a technological bus. The bus with low and predictable latency transfers control signals in the system-wide distribution and issues broadcast and multicast. Hence, buses can help avoid the complexity and overhead of these behaviors for short messages with the NoC. Experimental results with simulations show that the BENoC obtains speedup by 3× compared to traditional NoCs.

Das et al. [7] used buses and a NoC to define hierarchical hybrid interconnects. A bus links every eight nodes to form a local network. In addition, these buses connect to 2D-mesh NoC's routers through adapters to define the entire network. Data transmission in the hybrid network can be performed entirely through the bus or become global transfers through NoC's routers to the destination. Simulation results show that the proposed interconnect is 14% better than traditional meshes in performance.

Avakian et al. presented a reconfigurable hybrid interconnect called RAMS [1] consisting of bus-based subsystems linked to mesh NoC's routers. Based on the heuristic that buses better support a small number of communication nodes (vary from 1 to 8), RAMS exploits scalable bus-based multi/many-core subsystems connected with each NoC's router. Compared to 2D-mesh NoC, the experimental results show that RAMS performs better than the original NoC.

Tsai et al. in [37] introduced a combination of buses and NoC for a hybrid interconnect. Instead of connecting only buses like RÁMS, NoC's routers in this proposal attach both bus-based subsystems and computing cores. Using data communication graphs of applications, the framework in this work classifies more frequent communication cores into affinity groups. Meanwhile, ungrouped cores function as independent computing nodes. Due to the high communication rate, a bus links computing nodes in an affinity group to define a subsystem. Finally, these subsystems attach to routers through network interfaces. Experimental simulation results show that the proposed architecture saves latency by 17.6.

Zarkesh-Ha et al. proposed a similar mixture of buses and 2D-mesh called HNoC [40]. Local buses transfer data for nearest-neighbor communication while the global 2D-mesh NoC is responsible for further communication. In other words, along with the 2D-mesh NoC, nodes of two adjacent routers are linked through a local bus to conduct nearest-neighbor communication. Consequently, global traffic through the NoC is reduced at a higher throughput and lower energy consumption. Simulation results indicate that 4.5× throughput improvement and 58% energy consumption reduction were obtained compared to only 2D-mesh.

Giefers et al. [12] presented a hybrid interconnect with three different architectures, including a reconfigurable mesh transformable to buses, a traditional NoC, and a barrier network. The mesh contains reconfigurable switches linked to computing nodes that can configure the switch dynamically to form buses. Along with switches, nodes also attach to NoC's routers for further communication. Finally, the barrier network is responsible for controlling the synchronization of nodes. Experimental results with an FPGA-based multi/many-cores platform show that the combination of three architectures offers the highest performance compared to any single one.

MORPHEUS [14] is a well-known heterogeneous hardware accelerator with multiple interconnect architectures. Buses transfer control and synchronization signals while a high-throughput NoC handle data communication among computing nodes and external memory like Flash or DDRAM.

Jin et al. introduced the *duo* [19] hybrid interconnect with a conventional 2D-mesh NoC linked with a reconfigurable multidrop channels bus (similar to MECS [15]). Thanks to the reconfiguration, each row or column requires a single channel rather than $2(n-1)$ like MECS. A framework trace communication patterns of applications to classify them. The framework then defines channels for application domains according to the traced patterns. The simulation results indicate that 15% of latency and 27% of energy consumption were obtained compared to 2D-mesh.

Zhao et al. in [41] presented a bus-NoC hybrid interconnect with buses linked to an NoC. Each NoC's router includes an interface for sharing physical channels between the NoC and buses. The interface is programmable, so NoC's routers can be bypassed to form a bus. When buses are defined from links, NoC's routers store data packets inside them to wait to finish bus transactions. The evaluation results prove that 12% of system performance and 37% of energy efficiency were obtained.

Todorov et al. in [36] designed a deterministic synthesis framework to define application-specific interconnects with buses and an NoC. The application use-cases with the bandwidth, latency, and packet size are parameters of the synthesis tool to divide computing nodes into clusters. Low communication clusters link to shared buses while high communication ones attach to NoC's router. The author also proposed a deadlock-free routing algorithm to handle the data flow of the interconnect. Experimental results demonstrate that the interconnect achieves similar latency with traditional NoC with 22.6% of hardware resource reduction compared to a conventional NoC.

Table 3 concludes all the aforementioned architecture-mixture interconnects. We also summarize the goals of each proposal in the last column of the table. According to the goals, most approaches target performance like the mixture topologies interconnects above.

Table 3. Architecture mixture hybrid interconnect

Research	Mixture topology	Input data[a]	Goals
[31]	Bus/NoC	Communication rate	Latency, Power
[15]	Bus-like/NoC	Static	Latency
[25]	Bus/NoC	Static[b]	Performance
[7]	Bus/NoC	Static	Performance
[1]	Bus/NoC	Memory access rate	Performance
[37]	Bus/NoC	Communication bandwidth	Latency
[40]	Bus/NoC	Static	Throughput, Energy
[12]	Bus/NoC/ Barrier	Static	Performance
[14]	Bus/NoC	Static	Throughput
[19]	Bus-like/NoC	Communication rate	Latency, Energy
[41]	Bus/NoC	Static	Performance, Energy
[36]	Bus/NoC routers	Bandwidth and Latency	Area

[a]Parameters determine the topology.
[b]*Static*: fixed design without any parameters taken into account.

4   Conclusion

In this paper, we summarizes on-chip hybrid interconnect architectures for the literature. We classify these hybrid interconnects into two different categories. The first one includes hybrid interconnects that create the interconnects by using different Network-on-Chip topologies. We named this group as *topology-mixture hybrid interconnect*. The second group, named *architecture-mixture hybrid interconnects*, combines different architectures, such as bus and NoC, to form hybrid interconnects. Each of proposals in each class provide different approach with various goals. Researchers can choose the most appropriate one for their multi/many-core systems.

Acknowledgment. We acknowledge Ho Chi Minh City University of Technology (HCMUT), VNU-HCM for supporting this study.

References

1. Avakian, A., et al.: A reconfigurable architecture for multicore systems. In: IPDPSW, pp. 1–8 (2010). https://doi.org/10.1109/IPDPSW.2010.5470753
2. Balfour, J., Dally, W.J.: Design tradeoffs for tiled CMP on-chip networks. In: Proceedings of the 20th Annual International Conference on Supercomputing, ICS 2006, pp. 187–198. ACM, New York (2006). https://doi.org/10.1145/1183401.1183430. http://doi.acm.org/10.1145/1183401.1183430
3. Balkan, A., Qu, G., Vishkin, U.: A mesh-of-trees interconnection network for single-chip parallel processing. In: International Conference on Application-Specific Systems, Architectures and Processors, ASAP 2006, pp. 73–80 (2006). https://doi.org/10.1109/ASAP.2006.6

4. Balkan, A.O., Qu, G., Vishkin, U.: An area-efficient high-throughput hybrid interconnection network for single-chip parallel processing. In: Proceedings of the
45th Annual Design Automation Conference, DAC 2008, pp. 435–440, ACM,
New York (2008). https://doi.org/10.1145/1391469.1391583. http://doi.acm.org/
10.1145/1391469.1391583
5. Bourduas, S., Zilic, Z.: Modeling and evaluation of ring-based interconnects for network-on-chip. J. Syst. Archit. **57**(1), 39–60 (2011). https://doi.
org/10.1016/j.sysarc.2010.07.002. http://www.sciencedirect.com/science/article/
pii/S138376211000069X. Special Issue On-Chip Parallel and Network-Based Systems
6. Camacho, J., Flich, J., Roca, A., Duato, J.: PC-mesh: a dynamic parallel concentrated mesh. In: 2011 International Conference on Parallel Processing (ICPP), pp.
642–651 (2011). https://doi.org/10.1109/ICPP.2011.21
7. Das, R., et al.: Design and evaluation of a hierarchical on-chip interconnect for
next-generation CMPs. In: HPCA 2009, pp. 175–186 (2009). https://doi.org/10.
1109/HPCA.2009.4798252
8. Duato, J., Yalamanchili, S., Lionel, N.: Interconnection Networks: An Engineering
Approach. Morgan Kaufmann Publishers Inc., San Francisco (2002)
9. El-Rewini, H., Abd-El-Barr, M.: Advanced Computer Architecture and Parallel Processing (Wiley Series on Parallel and Distributed Computing). Wiley-
Interscience (2005)
10. Gazettabyte: Altera's 30 billion transistor FPGA (2016). http://www.gazettabyte.
com/home/2015/6/28/alteras-30-billion-transistor-fpga.html
11. Gebali, F.: Interconnection Networks, pp. 83–103. Wiley (2011). https://doi.org/
10.1002/9780470932025.ch5
12. Giefers, H., Platzner, M.: A triple hybrid interconnect for many-cores: reconfigurable mesh, NoC and barrier. In: FPL, pp. 223–228 (2010). https://doi.org/10.
1109/FPL.2010.52
13. Grama, A., Gupta, A., Karypis, G., Kumar, V.: Introduction to Parallel Computing, 2nd edn. Addison-Wesley Longman Publishing Co., Inc., Boston (2002)
14. Grasset, A., et al.: The Morpheus heterogeneous dynamically reconfigurable platform. Int. J. Parallel Program. **39**(3), 328–356 (2011)
15. Grot, B., et al.: Express cube topologies for on-chip interconnects. In: HPCA, pp.
163–174 (2009). https://doi.org/10.1109/HPCA.2009.4798251
16. Guerrier, P., Greiner, A.: A generic architecture for on-chip packet-switched inter-
connections. In: DATE, pp. 250–256 (2000). https://doi.org/10.1109/DATE.2000.
840047
17. Hur, J.: Customizing and hardwiring on-chip interconnects in FPGAs. Ph.D. thesis,
Delft University of Technology, Delft, Netherlands (2011)
18. Jerger, N.E., Peh, L.S.: On-Chip Networks, 1st edn. Morgan and Claypool Publishers (2009)
19. Jin, Y., et al.: Communication-aware globally-coordinated on-chip networks. Parallel Distrib. Syst. **23**(2), 242–254 (2012). https://doi.org/10.1109/TPDS.2011.164
20. Kang, K., Park, S., Lee, J.B., Benini, L., Micheli, G.D.: A power-efficient 3-D on-
chip interconnect for multi-core accelerators with stacked L2 cache. In: 2016 Design,
Automation Test in Europe Conference Exhibition (DATE), pp. 1465–1468 (2016)
21. Kim, J., Balfour, J., Dally, W.: Flattened butterfly topology for on-chip networks.
Comput. Archit. Lett. **6**(2), 37–40 (2007). https://doi.org/10.1109/L-CA.2007.10
22. Kim, W.J., Hwang, S.Y.: Design of an area-efficient and low-power NoC architecture using a hybrid network topology. IEICE Trans. Fundam. Electron. Commun.

Comput. Sci. **E91-A**(11), 3297–3303 (2008). https://doi.org/10.1093/ietfec/e91-a.11.3297

23. Kogel, T., Leupers, R., Meyr, H.: Classification of platform elements. In: Kogel, T., Leupers, R., Meyr, H. (eds.) Integrated System-Level Modeling of Network-on-Chip enabled Multi-Processor Platforms, pp. 15–32. Springer, Dordrecht (2006). https://doi.org/10.1007/1-4020-4826-2_3

24. Kumar, R., et al.: Heterogeneous chip multiprocessors. Computer **38**(11), 32–38 (2005)

25. Manevich, R., et al.: Best of both worlds: a bus enhanced NoC (BENoC). In: Networks-on-Chip, pp. 173–182 (2009). https://doi.org/10.1109/NOCS.2009.5071465

26. Matos, D., Concatto, C., Carro, L.: Reconfigurable intercommunication infrastructure: NoCs. In: Beck, A.C.S., Lang Lisbôa, C.A., Carro, L. (eds.) Adaptable Embedded Systems, pp. 119–161. Springer, New York (2013). https://doi.org/10.1007/978-1-4614-1746-0_5

27. Modarressi, M., Tavakkol, A., Sarbazi-Azad, H.: Virtual point-to-point connections for NoCs. IEEE Trans. Comput.-Aided Des. Integr. Circuits Syst. **29**(6), 855–868 (2010). https://doi.org/10.1109/TCAD.2010.2048402

28. Murali, S., et al.: Designing application-specific networks on chips with floorplan information. In: Proceedings of the 2006 IEEE/ACM International Conference on Computer-Aided Design, ICCAD 2006, pp. 355–362. ACM, New York (2006). https://doi.org/10.1145/1233501.1233573. http://doi.acm.org/10.1145/1233501.1233573

29. Pasricha, S., Dutt, N.: Basic concepts of bus-based communication architectures, chapter 2. In: Pasricha, S., Dutt, N. (eds.) On-Chip Communication Architectures, pp. 17–41. Systems on Silicon, Morgan Kaufmann (2008). https://doi.org/10.1016/B978-0-12-373892-9.00002-5. http://www.sciencedirect.com/science/article/pii/B9780123738929000025

30. Pham, D., Holt, J., Deshpande, S.: Embedded multicore systems: design challenges and opportunities. In: Hübner, M., Becker, J. (eds.) Multiprocessor System-on-Chip, pp. 197–222. Springer, New York (2011). https://doi.org/10.1007/978-1-4419-6460-1_9

31. Richardson, T., et al.: A hybrid SoC interconnect with dynamic TDMA-based transaction-less buses and on-chip networks. In: VLSI Design, p. 8 (2006). https://doi.org/10.1109/VLSID.2006.10

32. Rutzig, M., et al.: Multicore platforms: processors, communication and memories. In: Beck, A., Lang Lisbôa, C., Carro, L. (eds.) Adaptable Embedded Systems, pp. 243–277. Springer, Heidelberg (2013). https://doi.org/10.1007/978-1-4614-1746-0_8

33. Sanchez, D., et al.: An analysis of on-chip interconnection networks for large-scale chip multiprocessors. ACM Trans. Archit. Code Optim. **7**(1), 4:1–4:28 (2010)

34. Stensgaard, M., Sparso, J.: ReNoC: a network-on-chip architecture with reconfigurable topology. In: Second ACM/IEEE International Symposium on Networks-on-Chip, 2008, NoCS 2008, pp. 55–64 (2008). https://doi.org/10.1109/NOCS.2008.4492725

35. Swaminathan, K., Gopi, S., Rajkumar, Lakshminarayanan, G., Ko, S.B.: A novel hybrid topology for network on chip. In: 2014 IEEE 27th Canadian Conference on Electrical and Computer Engineering (CCECE), pp. 1–6 (2014). https://doi.org/10.1109/CCECE.2014.6901083

36. Todorov, V., Mueller-Gritschneder, D., Reinig, H., Schlichtmann, U., et al.: Deterministic synthesis of hybrid application-specific network-on-chip topologies. Comput.-Aided Des. Integr. Circuits Syst. **33**(10), 1503–1516 (2014). https://doi.org/10.1109/TCAD.2014.2331556

37. Tsai, K.L., et al.: Design of low latency on-chip communication based on hybrid NoC architecture. In: NEWCAS, pp. 257–260 (2010). https://doi.org/10.1109/NEWCAS.2010.5603934

38. Wang, C., Hu, W.H., Lee, S.E., Bagherzadeh, N.: Area and power-efficient innovative congestion-aware network-on-chip architecture. J. Syst. Archit. **57**(1), 24–38 (2011). https://doi.org/10.1016/j.sysarc.2010.10.009. http://www.sciencedirect.com/science/article/pii/S1383762110001359. Special Issue On-Chip Parallel And Network-Based Systems

39. Yin, J., Zhou, P., Sapatnekar, S.S., Zhai, A.: Energy-efficient time-division multiplexed hybrid-switched NoC for heterogeneous multicore systems. In: Proceedings of the 2014 IEEE 28th International Parallel and Distributed Processing Symposium, IPDPS 2014, Washington, DC, USA, pp. 293–303. IEEE Computer Society (2014). https://doi.org/10.1109/IPDPS.2014.40

40. Zarkesh-Ha, P., et al.: Hybrid network on chip (HNoC): local buses with a global mesh architecture. In: System Level Interconnect Prediction, pp. 9–14. ACM, New York (2010)

41. Zhao, H., et al.: A hybrid NoC design for cache coherence optimization for chip multiprocessors. In: DAC, pp. 834–842. ACM, New York (2012)

Context-Aware Technologies

A Framework for Brain-Computer Interfaces Closed-Loop Communication Systems

Mina Cu[ID], Gabrielle Peko[ID], Johnny Chan[ID], and David Sundaram[✉][ID]

The University of Auckland, Auckland 1010, New Zealand
{mina.cu,d.sundaram}@auckland.ac.nz

Abstract. This paper is a review of the brain-computer interface technology and its latest applications on human subjects. The brain-computer interface is an emerging technology that utilizes neurophysiological signals produced through the electrode interactions initiated inside the human brain to control external devices. Research on connecting human brains via brain-computer interfaces has been progressing with a lack of details on the technology used in closed-loop communication, which often leads to rumours, scepticism, and misunderstanding. We aim to alleviate these issues and to this end, we first analyze descriptions of brain-computer interface technology. We then explain the operational mechanisms of existing brain-computer interfaces and how they can perform direct brain-to-brain communication between human subjects separated in different locations. Findings from the literature motivate us to present a closed-loop communication framework that enables the combination of brain-computer interfaces and telecommunication channels such as vocal and text messages. Finally, we discuss the implications and limitations underlying the theoretical findings. The contribution of this paper is to provide a better understanding of emerging technology to support communication and innovation.

Keywords: Brain-computer interface · Brain-to-brain interface · Closed-loop communication · Cryptography

1 Brain-Computer Interfaces

Brain-computer interface (BCI) or brain-machine interface (BMI), is a novel technology that uses neurophysiological signals produced through the electrode interactions initiated inside the human brain to control external devices [5]. The awareness of reading the human brain has been mentioned since the early 20th century as a theoretical concept derived from the combination of Electroencephalography (EEG) and mathematical analysis methods [33]. The neurofeedback and operant conditions of neuroelectric activity are the underpinning of the BCI. In most types of BCI, the biofeedback's EEG signals, or event-related potentials brain signals will be collected and analyzed due to our brain giving the distinguished types of brainwaves for each subject received in biofeedback [18].

© ICST Institute for Computer Sciences, Social Informatics and Telecommunications Engineering 2023
Published by Springer Nature Switzerland AG 2023. All Rights Reserved
C. V. Phan and T. D. Nguyen (Eds.): ICCASA 2022, LNICST 475, pp. 79–91, 2023.
https://doi.org/10.1007/978-3-031-28816-6_6

There has been a proliferation of BCI research in the last few decades. Nowadays, both firms and scholars have put forward applications of BCI in various domains to challenge innovation boundaries. Mashat et al. [27] point out that BCI has disruptively changed the way of human interaction to open a new era where empowering human interaction will be lifted to its peak by the BCI technology. Mashat et al.'s [27] argument has several implications. Firstly, with the inauguration of BCI, the way people generally communicate with each other could be significantly disrupted. Secondly, people who have strokes, paralysis, or obstacles with communication ability now can have opportunities to use their brainwaves to express their thoughts. Furthermore, the brain-to-brain interface (BTBI) is a significant breakthrough of the BCI technology when an individual's brainwaves are not only employed to control external devices but to control another one's brain. BCI and its applications thus can open a new era where technology ethics, humanity, and governance need to be seriously reconsideration [1, 29, 42]. These issues are also the challenges of BCI in practice. Communication systems using BCI have been proposed ubiquitously, however, these systems mostly appear in the form of experiments or laboratory tests. Overcoming the barrier of the current legislative framework seems not to be possible for BCI in the near future. Furthermore, as BCI is an advanced technology that has a great potential for both intelligence and commercialization once it is approved to be implemented [23], firms/research teams that develop BCI often keep descriptions of solutions in secret.

In most BCI for closed-loop communication studies, descriptions of experiments and test results are well demonstrated. However, the description of BCI solutions is seldomly seen. This setting raises doubts regarding the reliability of results produced by such nascent technology. Due to these matters, it is often claimed there is not enough scientific evidence on the adverse impact BCI might have on human health in the long term [10]. Considering the numerous obstacles, research on BCI is often attracts rumour and distrust from both industry and academic audiences. Furthermore, studies such as those by Laiwalla and Nurmikko [23], Aggarwal and Chugh [1], and Taschereau-Dumouchel and Roy [44], mostly focus on typical aspects of BCI such as ethics, decoding, and its future. Motivating us to focus our efforts on fulfilling an apparent gap.

With the aim of alleviating the misunderstanding and skepticism of closed-loop communication using brainwaves, this paper is set out as a review of the BCI technology with its latest updates and applications on human objects. To achieve this goal, we will review technical descriptions of a series of relevant studies to illustrate the operational mechanisms of BCI. Specifically, we investigate descriptions of the BCI technology to explain the possibility of direct brain-to-brain communication between human subjects separated in different locations. We then use obtained results to conceptualize a closed-loop communication system that consists of BCI and telecommunication channels such as vocal and text messages.

The rest of the paper proceeds as follows. The next section is a brief discussion of how hypotheses were developed. Next, we will introduce the research methodology in the third section. Theoretical findings will be represented in the fourth sections. We then discuss the implications and limitations underlying theoretical findings in the fifth section before providing the conclusion in the final section.

2 Hypotheses

The aim of this paper is to alleviate the misunderstanding and skepticism of closed-loop communication using brainwaves. We assume that audiences have no prior knowledge of BCI technology. We will focus on the use of brainwaves to conduct closed-loop communication between human subjects. Based on the current achievement of BCI studies and the rapid development of communication technology, we propose two hypotheses: (1) It is possible to conduct communication by the transmission of human brainwaves through a global network between human subjects separated at a great distance; and (2) It is possible to design and implement a telecommunication system that uses human brainwaves to carry on closed-loop communication. From this perspective, we will collect, analyze, evaluate, and represent the review of existing BCI systems used for closed-loop communication to provide proof of concepts. Details of the review method will be provided in the following section.

3 Multidisciplinary Literature Review

While seeking an appropriate review method, we realize that there is a lack of publications regarding BCI system designs due to several restraints such as commercial intelligence, technological protection, and other restrictions. Furthermore, a dominant part of published systems remains in the experiment phases. Because of these issues, it was difficult for us to employ practical approaches such as design science research, action research, field, or case study in investigating the use of the BCI systems. Brewer and Hunter [8] suggest that using one or more approaches would enable the investigation where a single research methodology might not be applicable to analyze the problems. Thus, in this paper we utilize a multidisciplinary literature review method to profoundly analyze the meaning and principle of BCI, brain-to-brain interface (BTBI) as the scientific evidence for the feasibility of establishing a brainwaves telecommunication system. We follow the approach to qualitative research outlined by Mayring [28] in the literature review to develop a search query and analysis framework.

Following the search results, we will carry out in-depth analyses and assessments of the relevant studies on BCI. The article selection is based on the prestigious ranking of published journals and the number of citations. The quality of selected articles thus can be guaranteed. The technical details, operational mechanisms of BCI and closed-loop communication, and how such systems can carry on connections between human subjects via brainwaves will be presented following theoretical findings to provide testing results of the hypotheses.

4 Framework for Brain-Computer Interfaces Closed-Loop Communication Systems

In this section, technical descriptions of BCI, their applications that constitute the breakthrough in direct brain-to-brain communication and BCI and telecommunication systems will be represented through the in-depth analysis of selected literature. Along with the framework for BCI closed-loop communication systems.

4.1 Brain-Computer Interfaces

Theoretical findings indicate that since the 1960s, scholars such as Dewan [14] had identified that, by collecting Electroencephalography (EEG) signals (or simplified as brain signals) recorded from human eye movements and decoding them to become Morse codes, it is possible to conduct commands of turning on and off indoor equipment such as light and television. Following Dewan's [14] perspective, the concept of using observable electrical brain signals to work as carriers of information in human-computer communication has been extended in later research. Vidal [46, 47] implements coloured and patterned visual stimulation to examine a new model of evoked responses in the trichromatic absorbing structure by evaluating the sequential events of short duration in bio-electric potentials and the relation between brain states. This eminent approach subsequently raised the interest in the definitive term BCI throughout the field. Farewell and Donchin [19] shifted the use of BCI to translate the EEG signals into interactive movements in a VRML world. Wolpaw et al. (2000) defined BCI as a communicative system that does not depend on the brain's conventional output pathways of peripheral nerves and muscles. The translational algorithm, which converts the user's brainwaves into output, is the key component of Wolpaw et al.'s BCI. In particular, the user encodes the commands in the electrophysiological input transmitted to the BCI processor that recognizes and translates these commands into the signals then expresses them in external devices. Moreover, the study by Birbaumer [4] proves that multiple types of brain signals have been successfully tested in BCI research. According to Lightbody et al. [25], a BCI system can be constructed basically with five major elements including user, signal acquisition, signal processing, user interface, and application. Based on findings outlined by Lightbody et al. [25], we conceptualize major components of a BCI system in Fig. 1.

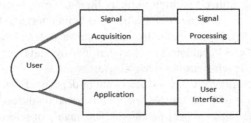

Fig. 1. The major components of a BCI system adapted from lightbody et al. [25]

Nonetheless, a BCI system's components might be varied as it depends on the purposes of the application. Research on BCI used for communication technology has been carried out in recent years. Dewan [15] successfully uses brainwaves to operate a binary digit communication system. In Dewan's system, the user was trained to alter their brain's alpha-wave rhythms – changing the eye movement techniques. The predetermined EEG control signal pattern then corresponded to a Morse code message. In particular, Dewan [15] used a Grass model 7 Polygraph printer to record EEG signals which were transported from the left and right electrodes derivations. These signals then were transferred through a 10c/s bandpass filter to enter the Schmitt stringer which would produce the pulse when the signal's voltage exceeded a threshold to ensure the presence of the pulse for each wave crests when the alpha wave activated. Dewan [15] then injected outputs into a LINC computer which was designed to translate the Morse characters into the alphabet system and displayed the words on the cathode ray tube that was visible to read. Serby et al. [39] proposed a P300-based BCI, which was built on the BCI pattern suggested by Farewell and Donchill [19] regarding a BCI communication system with 36 symbols. The P300-based BCI system uses independent component analysis (ICA) [16] to divide the P300 brainwave source from the ambient sources and filter out the troublesome signals simultaneously. Serby et al.'s [39] BCI system was outstanding for the higher performance of BCI compared with the others at that time. The BCI evaluation indicated that the system delivered reasonable communication effects while maintaining an acceptable level of errors. Similar systems to Serby et al.'s [39] BCI have been applied in subsequent experiments in using brainwaves to conduct virtual commands and robotic controlling [34].

4.2   Brain to Brain Closed-Loop Communication

Closed-loop communication has been well-known as a communication technique that is used to avoid misunderstanding [12]. This technique focuses on repetitive interactions between two objects which establish a loop of communication. Experiments in BCI to allow bidirectional interactions between users were successfully conducted in studies on closed-loop communication over the last decade. O'Doherty et.al [34] employed an invasive method to indicate the competence of the bidirectional communication between a primate brain and an external actuator. It shows the ability to liberate the human brain from physical constraints as both afferent and efferent channels could surpass the subject's body. The study laid a crucial milestone as it opened the new age of brain-machine-brain interfaces which can conduct reciprocal communication between and among neural structures and various external devices. Yoo et al. [52] insist that by using a non-invasive brain-to-brain interface (BTBI), we can establish functional links between two brains. Pais-Vieira et al. [35] develop a BBI to conduct three experiments on real-time sensorimotor information sharing between the brains of two rats. The findings of such experiments indicate that cortical sensorimotor signal patterns, which work as the code of a particular behaviour response, were successfully recorded from the encoder rat and transmitted directly to the brain of the decoder rat to complete a similar behavioural goal. The BTBI was manipulated in three different phases including encoding the detected signals, collecting data of the BCI process, and utilizing the real-time feedback analysis after electrical micro-stimulations. Pais-Vieira et al. [35] implemented the sigmoid function to convert the Z-score value to the number of pulses that were collected in the micro-stimulation pattern. Four distinguished neuron signals were amplified at 20000 to 30000 times and digitized at 40kHz. The data were sorted online afterward in Sort client 2002, Plexon Inc, Dallas, and TX. NEX technologies neuroexplorer version 3.266 was employed to process and analyze data.

One of the pioneer direct BTBI for human objects was presented by Rao et al. [37]. Rao et al. [37] carried out a series of experiments involving connections of two human brains. In these experiments, two users located at two different locations used the BTBI to together complete a virtual task of a computer game in a non-muscle interaction state. Rao et al.'s [37] BTBI system was a combination of an inherent BCI system and transcranial microsimulation (TMS) – an effective non-invasive method for sending commands directly to the user's brain. Specifically, such a BCI system collects EEG signals of the sender and transmits the information via the internet to the receiver's cortex. By using TMS, it allows the sender to conduct a desired motor response in the receiver reflected in the behaviour of the receiver, for example, pressing a button. Rao et al.'s [37] BTBI system was evaluated in three respects including decoding the sender's signals, generating a motor response from the receiver upon stimulation, and achieving a desired goal in the visuomotor task. The findings indicated a possibility of connecting directly human brains for information transmission purposes by a completely non-invasive method.

On the contrary, Grau et al. [21] upgraded the non-invasive stimulation and the BCI to conduct the consciousness transmission between human brains separated at a large distance. Grau et al. [21] extended the distance between two users to be 5000kms to conduct the consciousness transmission from one brain to another appearing as specific flashes of light. The word "hola" and "ciao" were encoded using a 5-bit Bacon cipher and redundancy 7 times to reach a total of 140bits. The signals were transmitted to the receiver's specific occipital cortex site through the transcranial microsimulation (TMS) pulses. The pulses were coded as bit value "1" if the TMS-induced electric field produced phosphenes and bit value "0" if the orthogonal direction did not produce phosphenes. The receiver server confirmed that it was available to receive the sequences of light. Although the messages that the sender and the receiver exchanged were encoded in the phosphenes form [11], the study evidently indicated that there is a possibility of direct mind-to-mind communication between human subjects separated at a great distance. It represents the feasibility of the transformation of traditional language-based communication into a novel type of telepathic communication including emotions and consciousness transmission by a non-invasive method. An upgrade BCI version was suggested to support a bi-directional dialogue between more than two brains or a closed mind-loops, in which the command from one brain is processed and transferred to other brains to conduct the same command. Nevertheless, the study raises concerns about the ethical and legislative responsibilities for this new type of human interrelation.

In another approach, the experiment by Mashat et al. [27] indicate that it is possible to control human muscles by BTBI. As the human brain sends the electrical and chemical messages back and forth, it is believed that the muscle signals can be converted to electromyography signals and transmitted consecutively to the decoder to make the similar muscle movement of the encoder [41, 43]. Mashat et al. [27] examined the approach to the human-to-human closed-loop control by combining the BTBI and muscle-to-muscle interface. Mashat et al. [27] introduce a system in which the artificial elements are connected functionally to the human nerves to control hand motions. Mashat et al. [27] tested such system performance in 6 dyads of healthy subjects with response accuracy results that could indicate the probability of creating a controlled loop by both human and automatic devices. Findings the from above studies have supported our first hypothesis – it is possible to conduct communication by the transmission of human brainwaves through a global network between human subjects separated at a great distance.

4.3   Integration of Brain-Computer Interfaces and Telecommunication Systems

Using the internet to send text messages technology has long been acknowledged as a common high-tech achievement as presented by Vieri, Tomasso, and Vieri [48] and Gabriel [20]. The system developed by Gabriel [20] allows users to send the message to a hardware device through the primary wireless network and subsequently forward it to a host server. This process will transmit the message to the device in the receiving wireless network and to the intended recipient afterward. The connection is conducted via the internet with multidirectional options, for instance, the recipient can send back the messages to the sender's cellular telephone or to a hardware device via email or an HTML-based interface. Vieri, Tomasso, and Vieri [48] propose the design of a communication system that is capable to send and receive text messages through the internet and expressing them in speech form on the recipient's device. A central server combined with software permits users to convert the primary message into vocal form, reach a telephone number, and conduct other commands such as storage, authorization to control, select, check, confirm or identify the website's operational criteria.

Vieri, Tomasso, and Vieri's [48] system for sending and receiving text messages converted into speech consists of the following components:

- A data input device comprised of hardware that allows users to write a text or record a vocal message, access phone numbers, and send to a server.
- An interconnection system consisted of a modem, data transmitting and receiving cards, and apparatus to connect to the satellite. This system works as a connection between the data input device and the server.
- A hardware-server installed a software program to convert text message to voice message, set up for sending out, and link other apps for operation purposes; and common phone to receive the message and give feedback.
- A transmission line to transfer the vocal message such as a telephone line consisting of voice modern or other technological peripherals.

Vocal message communication systems have been used in some research of indirect brain recording regards word pair classification during imagined speech [6, 9, 22, 26, 40]. Pandarinath et al. [36] proposed a high-performance BCI for non-muscle communication which can control the movement of a computer cursor to express the user's thoughts. In addition, Chartier et al. [13] collect articulatory kinetic movements from the human sensorimotor cortex produced when speaking and encode them to track the neural mechanisms underlying articulation. The brain signals of the coordinative movements of the voice producing system such as jaw, tongue, lips, and larynx were recorded while users speak common English sentences. These signals help capture a wide range of articulatory kinematic movement types that can be manifested in movement trajectories with harmonic oscillator dynamics. Chartier et al.'s [13] findings contribute to the understanding of the complex kinematics based on continuous speech production, which has been employed in later studies on neural decoding of spoken sentences [2, 13].

With the aim of removing obstacles in the communication of people with neurological impairments symptoms, Anumanchipalli et al. [2] develop a BCI that translates neural activity into speech (Fig. 2). This upgraded BCI resolves the challenge of decoding speech from neural activity due to the requirements of accuracy and rapid multi-dimensional control of vocal tract articulators when speaking. Such BCI works as a neural decoder that can synthesize the kinematic and sound representations collected from neuron firing activities to become audible speech. The BCI system first decodes the cortical activity into articulatory movement data and converts them into speech acoustics afterward. In Anumanchipalli et al.'s [2] experiments, audiences could hear the synthesized speech properly. Furthermore, it was capable to synthesize the speech when a user mimed the sentence silently proving the possibility of transferring human thoughts into speech.

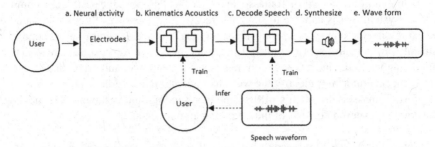

Fig. 2. BCI system to convert brainwaves to speech adapted from anumanchipalli et al. [2]

Assessment results from existing studies have supported our second hypothesis - it is possible that, theoretically, a telecommunication system that uses human brainwaves to carry on closed-loop communication can be established by the combination of BCI and telecommunication methods. In the next section, we will conceptualize findings from the above results to establish a framework for BCI closed-loop communication systems.

4.4 Framework for Brain-Computer Interfaces Closed-loop Communication Systems

Even though studies on vocal message communication systems and BCI have been carried on, extant research has not been clear on the possibility of establishing a telecommunication system. Motivated by such findings from the literature review, we aim to draw a framework that can extend the use of BCI for communication via the integration of a telecommunication system. Anumanchipalli et al. 's [2] BCI system and Vieri, Tomasso, and Vieri's [48] system for sending and converting text messages to speech enables us to conceptualize a framework for sending SMS messages by brainwaves. The system components generally include an EEG headset, EmotivePro Software, internet protocol, and the cellular telephone telecommunication network (Fig. 3). The headset firstly collects users' EEG signals and transfers them to the BCI server via internet. The server then converts neural activities to become kinematics acoustics which can be decoded and synthesized to become speech. The user's speech then will be connected to the smartphone that can recognize sound commands to define the recipient, input content, and conduct the sending out the message to a receiver device.

The proposed framework consists of the below components:

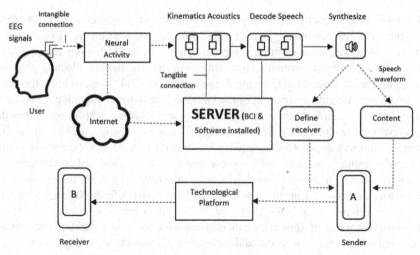

Fig. 3. Framework for sending SMS messages by brainwaves

- The headset that can detect 14 channels (AF3, F7, F3, FC5, T7, P7, O1, O2, P8, T8, FC6, F4, F8, AF4) and 2 references (In the CMS/DRL noise cancellation configuration P3/P4 locations) of EEG signals to ensure the quality of detection process.
- Mobile and computer devices.
- Conditions: All recordings were made in the laboratory condition. All data were recorded directly to the computer and carefully synchronized.
- Languages: English.
- Objects: Two users who voluntarily participate in the experiments.
- Connections: Wi-Fi; Headset connection Bluetooth/ 2.4 GHz band Wi-Fi; Cellular telephone telecommunication network.
- Platform: Voice modem and/or a technological platform make the text completely voice.
- Software: EmotivPro (for signals resolution).
- Data collection: MATLAB, TDT ephys software.
- Data analysis: Python 3.6, Tensorflow 1.4, sklearn 0.20, img-pipe, freesurfer, spm12, Festvox.

The proposed framework in its general form could be seen as an integration of the BCI that is able to translate neural activity into speech while connecting to a telecommunication system that can receive and perform repetitive simple commands.

5 Discussion

Wolpaw et al. [50] figure out that the major factor which interferes with the signal transmission is the noise created by the surrounded environment, i.e., power line electrode activities, and biological noises such as the heartbeat, muscle activity, and eyes movement. Additionally, the progress of BCI performance requires high attention and appreciation of users to achieve the best performance. Furthermore, a BCI connection will fail when the subject is in a paralytic state without eye movements [6, 31]. With the development of BCI technology, signal collection and transmission are more warranted nowadays. However, brain-to-brain communication is even much more complex compared to brain-computer communication, which requires the signal collecting processes to be conducted in strict conditions inside the laboratory [21]. Thus, to bring the brain-to-brain communication system out of the laboratory remains challenging. In addition, the non-invasive brain-to-brain communication system requires complex equipment that only a few organizations can suffice. Overall, BCI research is challenging as it involves an interdisciplinary approach that requires researchers to have a proficiency in mathematics, neurobiology, medical and computer science, engineering, and psychology [30]. The contribution of this paper thus can be seen in delivering a better understanding of emerging technology BCI and the development of a framework for BCI closed-loop communication systems. Notably, the proposed framework is beneficial for both academics and industry in terms of simplifying the presentation complex systems, conceptualizing intangible system connections, and representing a framework to implement BCI to telecommunication systems.

The proliferation of BCI technology has sparked controversies and criticism in recent years. It has been censured for posing a threat to human beings because it constitutes a risk of human mind hacking [49]. Lenca and Andomo [24] believe that the rapid development of neurotechnology applications produces unprecedented feasibility in collecting, accessing, sharing, and processing human brain information. Although several studies have indicated that BCI might evoke brain performance to enhance communication [32, 38]. It raises concerns about the ethical and legislative responses regarding this emerging type of human interaction [29]. Swan [42] introduces the idea of the "cloud mind" or "crowded mind" BCI system which can connect human brains to conduct highly effective interactions to become a network of minds. In this network, individuals' minds (human or machine) could join together in sharing perceptions to achieve a common goal. The study suggests that blockchain technology could be the resolution to warrant the security of cloud-mind collaboration. Yang et al. [51] suggest that we can create an ethical robot based on BCI technology that benefits human beings. Nonetheless, the existing human right might not be sufficient to respond to these new issues, especially in the four key rights such as cognitive liberty, mental privacy, mental integrity, and psychological continuity which would be highly related in the coming decades [24].

In recent years, using the quantum entanglement approach in cryptography for enhancing data security has been implemented in several systems [49], which might be an option for securing BCI data privacy. Einstein [17] indicated that the quantum entanglement process occurs when two particles in different locations can have related properties. The physical phenomenon occurs when the particle groups interact in ways in which the quantum state of each particle cannot be depicted independently of others even between great distances. The quantum state thus must be depicted for the system entirely [7]. Such a process implies a suitable state of occurrence for closed-loop communication via BCI, especially for brain-to-brain communication within a great distance. Research in quantum communication for satellite-to-ground networks has been indicated the possibility of completely secure quantum communication. The communication will be partially entangled in multiple states in which the teleportation was performed only through an end-to-end entangled process [3, 45]. By employing quantum cryptography for information sharing, the human brainwaves data can possibly be secured in a sheer state to avoid the violation of data privacy. The bi-directional signals exchange within more than two brains or the closed mind-loops thus could be secured as an end-to-end information sharing process to protect the information and only can be decoded by recipient systems. This would require further investigations through future research. Our work at this point has provided a theoretical support to the development of advanced technology such as BCI for communication innovation.

6   Conclusion

In summary, utilizing extant literature, we have tested the proposed hypotheses and achieved theoretical findings that indicate the possibility to conduct bidirectional connections between human brains located at a great distance for communication purposes. The telecommunication system that allows sending SMS messages by human brainwaves is also theoretically possible to achieve. The above findings support two proposed hypotheses. Furthermore, this paper uses the theoretical findings to develop a framework BCI closed-loop communication systems that benefits both academics and industry audiences. The limitations of BCI for closed-loop communication are detected as: the noise signals created by the surrounded environment; laboratory requirements; scarcity of equipment and intellectual resources; unknown impacts on mental health; and challenges in ethics, legislation, data privacy, and data security. The primary difference between this paper compared to existing BCI research can be seen in the in-depth review of technical descriptions of BCI and their applications to deliver a better understanding of the complex BCI technology. The findings from this review can help mitigate the scepticism, criticism, and misunderstanding of BCI technology. This paper contributes to common knowledge in terms of supporting communication technology development and innovation. Theoretical findings outlined in this paper can possibly be a foundation for future research towards the development of brain-to-brain telecommunication systems.

References

1. Aggarwal, S., Chugh, N.: Ethical implications of closed loop brain device: 10-year review. Mind. Mach. **30**(1), 145–170 (2020)
2. Anumanchipalli, G.K., Chartier, J., Chang, E.F.: Speech synthesis from neural decoding of spoken sentences. Nature **568**(7753), 493 (2019)
3. Bennett, C.H., Bernstein, H.J., Popescu, S., Schumacher, B.: Concentrating partial entanglement by local operations. Phys. Rev. A **53**(4), 2046 (1996)
4. Birbaumer, N.: Breaking the silence: Brain–computer interfaces (BCI) for communication and motor control. Psychophysiology **43**(6), 517–532 (2006). https://doi.org/10.1111/j.1469-8986.2006.00456.x
5. Birbaumer, N., Cohen, L, G.: Brain computer interfaces: communication and restoration of movement in paralysis. Journal of Physiology, 579 (3), pp621–636 (2007)
6. Birbaumer, N., Strehl, U., Hinterberger, T.: Brain-computer interfaces for verbal communication. In Neuroprosthetics **2**, 1146–1157 (2004)

7. Bowen, W.P., Schnabel, R., Bachor, H.-A., Lam, P.K.: Polarization squeezing of continuous variable stokes parameters. Phy. Rev. Lett. **88**(9), 093601 (2002)
8. Brewer, J., Hunter, A.: Multimethod Research: A Synthesis of Styles. Sage Publications, USA (1989)
9. Brumberg, J.S., Nieto-Castanon, A., Kennedy, P.R., Guenther, F.H.: Brain-Computer Interfaces for speech communication. Speech Commun. **52**(4), 367–379 (2010)
10. Carino-Escobar, R.I., et al.: Longitudinal analysis of stroke patients' brain rhythms during an intervention with a brain-computer interface. Neural Plast. (2019)
11. Carr, S.: Phosphenes: the evidence (1995). http://www.oubliette.org.uk/Three.html
12. Charles, S.: Encyclopedia of Applied Psychology. Academic Press, USA (2004)
13. Chartier, J., Anumanchipalli, G.K., Johnson, K., Chang, E.F.: Encoding of articulatory kinematic trajectories in human speech sensorimotor cortex. Neuron **98**(5), 1042–1054 (2018)
14. Dewan, E.M.: Communication by electroencephalography. Air Force Cambridge Research Labs (1964). http://www.dtic.mil/docs/citations/AD0608970
15. Dewan, E. M.: US6529773 B1, 4 March 2003. http://www.google.com/patents/US6529773
16. Dodge, Y., Commenges, D.: The Oxford Dictionary of Statistical Terms. Oxford University Press, UK (2006)
17. Einstein, A., Podolsky, B., Rosen, N.: Can quantum-mechanical description of physical reality be considered complete? Phys. Rev. **47**(10), 777–780 (1935). https://doi.org/10.1103/PhysRev.47.777
18. Elbert, T., Rockstroh, B., Lutzenberger, W., Birbaumer, N.: Self-Regulation of the Brain and Behavior. Springer Science & Business Media, Cham (2012)
19. Farwell, L.A., Donchin, E.: Talking off the top of your head: toward a mental prosthesisutilizing event-related brain potentials. Electroencephalogr. Clin. Neurophysiol. **70**(6), 510–523 (1988)
20. Gabriel, M., Gabriel, L.: System and method for sending SMS and text messages, 6 May 2008. http://www.google.com/patents/US7369865
21. Grau, C., et al.: Conscious brain-to-brain communication in human using non-invasive technologies. Plos One (2014).https://doi.org/10.1371/journal.pone.0105225
22. Horikawa, T., Kamitani, Y.: Generic decoding of seen and imagined objects using hierarchical visual features. Nat. Commun. **8**, 15037 (2017)
23. Laiwalla, F., Nurmikko, A.: Future of neural interfaces. In: Zheng, X. (ed.) Neural Interface: Frontiers and Applications. AEMB, vol. 1101, pp. 225–241. Springer, Singapore (2019). https://doi.org/10.1007/978-981-13-2050-7_9
24. Ienca, M., Andorno, R.: Towards new human rights in the age of neuroscience and neurotechnology. Life Sci. Soc. Policy **13**(1), 1–27 (2017). https://doi.org/10.1186/s40504-017-0050-1
25. Lightbody, G., et al.: A user centred approach for developing brain-Computer Interfaces. In: 2010 4th International Conference on Pervasive Computing Technologies for Healthcare, pp. 1–8. IEEE, March 2010
26. Martin, S., et al.: Word pair classification during imagined speech using direct brain recordings. Sci. Rep. **6**, 25803 (2016)
27. Mashat, M.E.M., Li, G., Zhang, D.: Human-to-human closed-loop control based on brain-to-brain interface and muscle-to-muscle interface. Sci. Rep. **7**(1), 11001 (2017)
28. Mayring, P.: Qualitative content analysis: theoretical background and procedures. In: Bikner-Ahsbahs, A., Knipping, C., Presmeg, N. (eds.) Approaches to Qualitative Research in Mathematics Education. Advances in Mathematics Education, pp. 365–380. Springer, Dordrecht (2015). https://doi.org/10.1007/978-94-017-9181-6_13
29. McCullagh, P., Lightbody, G., Zygierewicz, J., Kernohan, W.G.: Ethical challenges associated with the development and deployment of brain computer interface technology. Neuroethics **7**(2), 109–122 (2014)

30. McFarland, D.J., Wolpaw, J.R.: Sensorimotor rhythm-based brain–computer interface (BCI): model order selection for autoregressive spectral analysis. J. Neural Eng. **5**(2), 155 (2008)
31. McFarland, D.J., McCane, L.M., David, S.V., Wolpaw, J.R.: Spatial filter selection for EEG-based communication. Electroencephalogr. Clin. Neurophysiol. **103**(3), 386–394 (1997)
32. Millán, J.D.R., et al.: Combining brain–computer interfaces and assistive technologies: state-of-the-art and challenges. Front. Neurosci. **161** (2010)
33. Millett, D.: Hans berger: from psychic energy to the EEG. Perspect. Biol. Med. **44**(4), 522–542 (2001)
34. O'Doherty, J.E., et al.: Active tactile exploration enabled by a brain-machine-brain interface. Nature **479**(7372), 228–231 (2011)
35. Pais-Vieira, M., Lebedev, M., Kunicki, C., Wang, J., Nicolelis, M.A.L.: A brain-to-brain interface for real-time sharing of sensorimotor information. Sci. Rep. **3**, 1319 (2013)
36. Pandarinath, C., et al.: High performance communication by people with paralysis using an intracortical brain-computer interface. Elife **6**, e18554 (2017)
37. Rao, R.P.N., et al.: A direct brain-to-brain interface in humans. PLoS ONE **9**(11), e111332 (2014)
38. Rivet, B., Souloumiac, A., Attina, V., Gibert, G.: xDAWN algorithm to enhance evoked potentials: application to brain–computer interface. IEEE Trans. Biomed. Eng. **56**(8), 2035–2043 (2009)
39. Serby, H., Yom-Tov, E., Inbar, G.F.: An improved P300-based brain-computer interface. IEEE Trans. Neural Syst. Rehabil. Eng. **13**(1), 89–98 (2005)
40. Soman, S., Murthy, B.K.: Using brain computer interface for synthesized speech communication for the physically disabled. Procedia Comput. Sci. **46**, 292–298 (2015)
41. Sunny, T.D., Aparna, T., Neethu, P., Venkateswaran, J., Vishnupriya, V., Vyas, P.S.: Robotic arm with brain – computer interfacing. Procedia Technol. **24**, 1089–1096 (2016)
42. Swan, M.: The future of brain-computer interfaces: blockchaining your way into a cloudmind. J. Evol. Technol. **26**(2), 60–81 (2016)
43. Tabot, G.A., et al.: Restoring the sense of touch with a prosthetic hand through a brain interface. Proc. Natl. Acad. Sci. U.S.A. **110**(45), 18279–18284 (2013)
44. Taschereau-Dumouchel, V., Roy, M.: Could brain decoding machines change our minds? Trends Cogn. Sci. **24**(11), 856–858 (2020)
45. Ursin, R., et al.: Entanglement-based quantum communication over 144 km. Nat. phy. **3**(7), 481–486 (2007)
46. Vidal, J,J.: Toward direct brain-computer communication. Annu. Rev. Biophy. Bioeng. **2**, 157–180 (1973)
47. Vidal, J,J.: Biocybernetic control in man-machine interaction. National Technical Information Service, US Department of Commerce (1974). http://www.dtic.mil/dtic/tr/fulltext/u2/a01 3649.pdf
48. Vieri, R., Tomasso, C., Vieri, F.: System for sending text messages converted into speech throughan internet connection to a telephone and method for running it (2002). https://pat ents.google.com/patent/US7310329B2/en
49. WEF.: scientists have conducted the first ever quantum video call (2017). https://www.wef orum.org/agenda/2017/10/scientists-have-conducted-the-first-ever-quantum-video-call/
50. Wolpaw, J.R., Birbaumer, N., McFarland, D.J., Pfurtscheller, G., Vaughan, T.M.: Brain–computer interfaces for communication and control. Clin. Neurophysiol. **113**(6), 767–791 (2002)
51. Yang, G.Z., et al.: The grand challenges of science robotics. Sci. Robot. **3**(14), eaar7650 (2018)
52. Yoo, S.-S., Kim, H., Filandrianos, E., Taghados, S.J., Park, S.: Non-invasive brain-to-brain interface (BBI): establishing functional links between two brains. PLoS ONE **8**(4), e60410 (2013)

Identification of Abnormal Cucumber Leaves Image Based on Recurrent Residual U-Net and Support Vector Machine Techniques

Nguyen Thanh Binh[1,2]($\boxtimes$) and Nguyen Kim Quyen[3]

[1] Department of Information Systems, Faculty of Computer Science and Engineering, Ho Chi Minh City University of Technology (HCMUT), VNU-HCM, 268 Ly Thuong Kiet Street, District 10, Ho Chi Minh City, Vietnam
ntbinh@hcmut.edu.vn
[2] Vietnam National University Ho Chi Minh City, Linh Trung Ward, Thu Duc City, Ho Chi Minh City, Vietnam
[3] Faculty of Agriculture and Fishery, University of Cuu Long, Vinh Long, Vietnam
nguyenkimquyen@mku.edu.vn

Abstract. Cucumber diseases arise and spread quickly, affecting the yield and quality of cucumbers. The correct diagnosis of diseases on cucumber leaves is an important factor determining the success of control measures. To support accurate identification of cucumber leaf diseases, we proposed a machine learning method to identify powdery mildew diseases, downy mildew diseases, blight diseases, and anthracnose diseases on cucumber leaves. Most of the features of these diseases are similar. Therefore, the automatic identification of these diseases presents many challenges. The proposed method uses the recurrent residual U-Net deep learning model and the traditional support vector machine technique to identify diseases on cucumber leaves with an average accuracy of 96.33%, higher than other methods.

Keywords: Cucumber leaf diseases · Recurrent residual U-Net · SVM · Identify diseases

1 Introduction

Plant disease identification based on computer vision often requires extraction of the shape, ridge, color, and other characteristics of disease spots. This method has low identification efficiency because it depends on farmers' expertise in the field of disease identification in crops [1]. With the rapid development of artificial intelligence technology in recent years, many researchers have conducted related studies based on deep learning technology to improve the accuracy of plant disease identification. The existing methods of plant disease analysis are mainly disease classification.

Amara [2] determined the disease of 60×60 banana leaves based on LeNet. Deep learning also plays an important role in detecting disease severity in plants. Wang [3] created a series of deep convolutional neural networks to diagnose disease severity using

C. V. Phan and T. D. Nguyen (Eds.): ICCASA 2022, LNICST 475, pp. 92–101, 2023.
https://doi.org/10.1007/978-3-031-28816-6_7

black rot images of apples in the Plantvillage dataset. The performance of the shallow learning networks learned from scratch and the deep learning models tuned by transfer learning were also evaluated. The best model is VGG16 learned by transfer learning and the overall accuracy in the test set is 90.4%.

Ferentinos [4] used an open database containing 87,848 images to identify 58 diseases of 25 different plants based on in-depth research. And the best efficiency was 99.53% in accuracy rate. Barbedo [5] investigated the identification of plant diseases from individual lesions and spots using the GoogLeNet architecture, and the obtained accuracy ranged from 75% to 100% for each crop. This variation in accuracy is due to differences in the number of images, the number of diseases, disease states, and degree of difficulty in identification. A CNN neural network usually requires many samples to learn. However, collecting the learning data required by the models is difficult and expensive in many applications [6]. Therefore, the study of data expansion is especially important.

In previous studies, many researchers combined deep learning with transfer learning under the condition of limited dataset [7] to classify plant diseases based on image processing and GPU. Srdjan [8] proposed a method for evaluating deep learning models to identify 14 different classes of plant diseases, including 13 diseases and healthy leaves. He used mixed data with a dataset size of 30,880 images and average accuracy of 96.3% for this method combined with transfer learning method. Liu [9] enhances the training dataset by rotating, mirroring and adding Gaussian noise, adjusting brightness, and adjusting contrast. This method helps to increase the size of the dataset by 12 times and reduce excessive repetition.

In addition to expanding data volumes, improvements in deep learning algorithms are critical to disease recognition outcomes. Through [10] studied the deep network architecture and used images from the PlantVillage dataset to form the data size of 34,727 training set samples, 8702 validation set samples and 10,876 set samples. Experiments show that DenseNets requires fewer parameters and reasonable computation time to achieve the most advanced performance compared to VGG and ResNet. Their accuracy reaches 99.75%.

Picon [11] proposed an improved algorithm based on deep learning neural networks to detect different plant diseases under real acquisition conditions, where different adaptive measures for detection Early disease presentation have been suggested. The obtained results showed that the AuC index of all analyzed diseases was higher than 0.80. Selvaraj [12] relearned three different CNN architectures using transfer learning. By using pre-trained disease recognition models, deep transfer learning was performed to generate networks that could make accurate predictions. Zhong [13] proposes three methods of regression, multi-label classification and focal loss function based on DenseNet-121 CNN to identify diseases on apple leaves. These methods achieved 93.51, 93.31 and 93.71% accuracy on the test dataset.

The disease identification methods in the study cannot automatically locate the disease area from the image and need to extract the disease area manually for identification. Deep learning can also be applied to identify plant diseases. However, at present research in this area is still at an early stage, especially in practical application, due to the continuous improvement of requirements for the identification of plant diseases and diseases.

This paper proposed a method for abnormal cucumber leaves image identification based on modified Recurrent residual U-Net and support vector machine techniques. Main contributions of this study are: (i) the types of abnormal cucumber leaves are explained; (ii) proposed a method for abnormal cucumber leaves image identification based on deep learning model combined on support vector machine techniques traditionally but with high accuracy results. The rest of the paper is organized as follows: Sect. 2 presents the features of abnormal cucumber leaves, and the proposed method for abnormal cucumber leaves identification in Sect. 3. Section 4 and 5 are the experimental results and conclusions, respectively.

2 The Features of Abnormal Cucumber Leaves

Cucumber is growing and increasing in area and production because it is easy to grow and grow in a short time. However, a fundamental cause affecting the area, yield and quality of cucumbers is the serious destruction of some major pests and diseases. There are many types of diseases on cucumber plants. In this section, we only summarize four common diseases such as powdery mildew, downy mildew, blight, and anthracnose. These abnormal presents as Fig. 1.

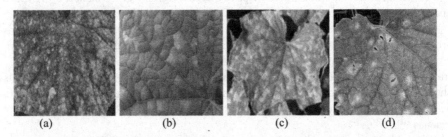

(a)   (b)   (c)   (d)

Fig. 1. Common abnormal on cucumber leaves (a) Powdery mildew disease (b) Downy mildew disease (c) Blight disease (d) Anthracnose disease

Powdery mildew disease appears initially as small, powdery white spots on the leaves. Then the leaves turn yellow, dry, and fall easily and gradually spread to other leaves and parts. The disease is most severe when the powdery mildew spreads down the trunk, branches, and flowers, causing the flowers to dry and fall off, causing the cucumber plant to weaken and then die. It greatly affects the yield and quality of cucumbers. Figure 1a presents a case study for this disease.

Downy mildew disease mainly affects leaves. Spots are small at first, pale green then turn yellow. The diseased spots have an edge-shaped base. When encountering high humidity, right on the underside of the leaf, there is a purple-red chalk layer, which is the spores of the fungus. The lesions coalesce into light brown areas. Severely diseased trees give poor yield and fruit quality, and the tree may die. Figure 1b presents a case study for this disease.

Blight disease appears with small spots of all shapes that may be colorless or green and then gradually turn yellow or light brown scattered throughout the location on cucumber leaves. In particular, the underside of leaves where the disease is located will appear a layer of gray-white mold. When they appear too much, the leaves are deformed, the leaves are torn. Plants cannot perform photosynthesis for a long time, causing the plant to die due to lack of nutrients. Figure 1c presents a case study for this disease.

Anthracnose disease appears initially on leaves with brown lesions forming concentric rings. When the fungal damage is more severe, the black fungal spots are in very prominent circles on the leaves. Figure 1d presents a case study for this disease.

Most of the features of these diseases are similar. Therefore, the automatic identification of these diseases presents many challenges.

3 Identification of Abnormal Cucumber Leaves Image

As present in the above section, most of the features of the abnormal cucumber leaf image are small differences. Therefore, we should choose the identification method that is suitable for this task. The identification method in this case study must ensure accurate feature extraction, avoiding loss information in image. This section clearly presents the proposed method for abnormal identification. To identify cucumber leaves images, the proposed method presented as Fig. 2, includes the stages as: features extraction by Recurrent residual U-Net (R2U-Net) combined on a support vector machine (SVM) for identification.

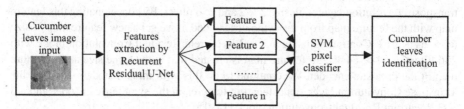

Fig. 2. The proposed method for identification of abnormal cucumber leaves image.

The R2U-Net model is improved from the U-net model. The R2U-Net model is improved by replacing Convolution layers with Recurrent Convolution layers and applying extra block residuals in each of its blocks. The R2U-Net model has two main parts: encoder and decoder. The task of the encoder in the R2U-Net model is to extract features of the image, and the decoder is to restore the image to its original size. Image recovery is done by concatenating feature maps from encoder to decoder. Both the encoder and decoder are built from the Recurrent Residual Convolution block [14].

The Recurrent Residual Convolution block is made up of two identical Recurrent Convolutional layers and a path to combine the results obtained when performing calculations over the two Recurrent Convolutional layers and the input of the block itself. Figure 3 illustrates the structure of the Recurrent Residual Convolution block.

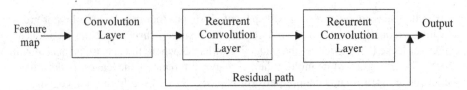

Fig. 3. The structure of the Recurrent Residual Convolution block

In the Recurrent Convolutional layer, it contains the Convolution layer. So, the size and number of filters of the Recurrent Convolutional layer is the size and number of filters of the Convolution layer within it. The architecture of the R2U-Net model is built as follows:

Assume that the cucumber leaf image of size $512 \times 512 \times 1$ is the input image of the R2U-Net model. The image passes through the Recurrent Residual Convolution block of size 3×3, 32 filters and generates a feature map of size $512 \times 512 \times 32$. This feature is passed through the Pooling layer of size 2×2 to obtain a new feature map of size $256 \times 256 \times 32$. We continue to use 3 more sets with each set including 1 Recurrent Residual Convolution block size 3×3 and 1 Pooling layer size 2×2 with the number of filters of Recurrent Residual Convolution block is 64, 128, 256, respectively. The output of one feature map is $32 \times 32 \times 256$. This feature map goes through a Recurrent Residual Convolution block of size 3×3 and the number of filters is 512 to obtain a new feature map of size $32 \times 32 \times 512$. After that, this feature map will be included in the image resizing phase.

When executed on the first decoder, the above feature map is passed through a transpose convolution layer with size 2×2 and 256 filters. By concatenating this feature map with the feature map from the symmetric encoder, we get a new feature map of size $64 \times 64 \times 512$. Continuing using a 3×3 Recurrent Residual Convolution block with 256 filters, a $64 \times 64 \times 256$ feature map is created that is the same size as the feature map in the opposite encoder. We continue to do this with three decoders: through the Transpose Convolution layer, concatenating features in the symmetric encoder and a 3 $\times$ 3 Recurrent Residual Convolution block [14, 15].

The Transpose Convolution layer and the Recurrent Residual Convolution block have the same number of filters as 128, 64, and 32, respectively. At the end of this process, we get a feature map of size $512 \times 512 \times 32$. The segmented image is the result of the feature map just obtained when passing through a 1×1 Convolution layer with a filter number of 1. And this image has a size of $512 \times 512 \times 1$. All Convolution layers are followed by Batch normalization layer and ReLU activation function. Only the last Convolution layer uses Sigmoid function as function activated.

Support vector machines (SVM) can be used for disease identification on cucumber leaves. In the SVM algorithm, the data is as a point in n-dimensional space (where n is some number of objects there are) with the value of each object being the value of a particular coordinate. We do the identification by finding the hyperplane that distinguishes the two classes very well. In the SVM classifier, the SVM kernel is a function that takes a low-dimensional input space and transforms it into a higher-dimensional space. It converts an indivisible problem into a separable problem. It is mainly useful in non-linear decomposition problems. Specifically, it separates data based on labels or outputs that it validates. The features have been identified, extracted from the feature extraction in the above step, they are put into the SVM classifier to identify anomalies in the leaf image.

4 Experimental Results

The dataset, which is collected by us, used to perform the experiments. This dataset contains images taken under different lighting conditions. These images have different colors and orientations. The dataset has 154 images including: 32 powdery mildew images, 31 downy mildew images, 24 blight images and 67 anthracnose images. The size of all images is 512×512 pixels resolution with Portable Network Graphics (.png) file format. Some images are presented in Fig. 4.

Fig. 4. Some images in dataset

The experimentation used 70% dataset for data training and 30% for data testing to evaluate the results. These images augmented the dataset by scaling, clipping, rotation, etc. as in the Table 1. So, the size of the training dataset is expanded to 1000 images.

Table 1. Data augmentation parameters.

Transformation type	Description
Rotation	Randomly rotate image between $(-10°, 10°)$
Clipping	Randomly clip images with angle between $-15°$ and $15°$
Flipping	Horizontal and vertical flip images
Translation	Randomly shift between -10% and 10% of pixels

The experimental programs were developed by the python language. The configuration hardware is on a computer of Intel core i7, 3.2 GHz CPU and 16 GB DDR3 memory. The diagram for cucumber diseases is presented as Fig. 5.

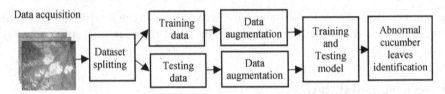

Fig. 5. The diagram for cucumber diseases identification.

To evaluate the identification result, the accuracy metrics are used. Sensitivity (Se) is defined as the ability to detect abnormal images, ranges from 0 to 1 and calculated as Eq. (1). TP (true positives) is the number of true positives. FN (false negatives) is the number of false negatives.

$$Se = \frac{TP}{TP + FN} \tag{1}$$

Specificity (Sp) is defined as the ability to distinguish images that have abnormal or not, ranges from 0 to 1 and is calculated as in the Eq. (2). TN (true negatives) is the number of true negatives. FP (false positives) is the number of false positives.

$$Sp = \frac{TN}{TN + FP} \tag{2}$$

Accuracy (Acc) is defined as the result accuracy of the proposed method in the test dataset, ranging from 0 to 1 (equivalent from 0% to 100%). The accuracy values are calculated as Eq. (3).

$$Acc = \frac{TP + TN}{TP + FN + TN + FP} \tag{3}$$

The experimentations are implemented in all images of above the datasets. Table 2 presented the evaluation of the abnormal leaf images identification between machine learning models, such as: SVM, VGG-16, VGG-19, U-Net and SVM method with the proposed method. The combination of the R2U-Net and SVM method is better than others.

Table 2. The evaluation of the abnormal leaf images identification (%) between machine learning models.

Disease leaf	Accuracy (%)				
	SVM method	VGG-16 method	VGG-19 method	U-Net + SVM method	Proposed method
Powdery mildew	78.124	87.342	91.119	91.981	94.163

(continued)

Table 2. (*continued*)

Disease leaf	Accuracy (%)				
	SVM method	VGG-16 method	VGG-19 method	U-Net + SVM method	Proposed method
Downy mildew	82.568	88.692	91.347	92.953	97.642
Blight	79.656	89.173	93.670	94.679	95.761
Anthracnose	78.359	86.228	89.181	91.267	96.751

Table 3. The results of identification average accuracy between the proposed method with the recent methods.

Method	Year	Dataset collection		
		Sensitivity	Specificity	Accuracy
Shanwen method [16]	2017	0.8252	0.9521	0.8783
Abdul method [17]	2021	0.8690	0.9696	0.9133
Nazar method [18]	2022	0.9221	0.9856	0.9516
Proposed method	2022	0.9398	0.894	0.9633

Table 3 presents the average accuracy of the proposed method is 96.33% while the average accuracy of Shanwen method [16], Abdul method [17] and Nazar method [18] are 87.83%, 91.33% and 95.16%, respectively.

As presented in the above, the R2U-Net architecture is improved by replacing Convolution layers with Recurrent Convolution layers and applying extra block residuals in each of its blocks. So, we get more features to improve the identification task. While Shanwen [16] proposed a method to recognize the rate of cucumber disease based on the Global-Local singular value decomposition. They used the watershed algorithm to segment from each cucumber disease leaf image and used a SVM classifier. Abdul [17] used LAB color space and region of interest to extract through K-mean clustering and SVM for identification. Nazar [18] used methods involving the fusion and selection of the features combined on VGG and Inception V3 deep learning models to be considered and fine-tuned. These methods have low accuracy.

5   Conclusions and Future Works

The correct diagnosis of diseases on cucumber leaves is an important factor determining the success of control measures. However, many diseases have similar symptoms, making local disease identification difficult, sometimes impossible. The application of machine learning in identification and classification of diseases on images of cucumber leaves is an inevitable trend. This paper proposed a method for abnormal cucumber leaves image identification based on modified Recurrent residual U-Net combined on support vector machine techniques. The results of the proposed method compare with other methods and are better than others. To crease the accuracy of the proposed method, improving deep learning architecture is necessary and experimenting on other datasets in future work.

Acknowledgement. We acknowledge the support of time and facilities from Ho Chi Minh City University of Technology (HCMUT), VNU-HCM and University of Cuu Long for this study.

References

1. Mohanty, S.P., Hughes, D.P., Salathé, M.: Using deep learning for image-based plant disease detection. Front. Plant Sci. **7**, 1419 (2016)
2. Amara, J., Bouaziz, B., Algergawy, A.: A deep learning based approach for banana leaf diseases classification. Lecture Notes in Informatics (LNI). Gesellschaft Für Informatik, Bonn, pp. 79–88 (2017)
3. Wang, G., Sun, Y., Wang, J.: Automatic image-based plant disease severity estimation using deep learning. Comput. Intell. Neurosci. 1–8 (2017). https://doi.org/10.1155/2017/2917536
4. Ferentinos, K.P.: Deep learning models for plant disease detection and diagnosis. Comput. Electron. Agric. **145**, 311–318 (2018)
5. Arnal, B., Jayme, G.: Plant disease identification from individual lesions and spots using deep learning. Biosyst. Eng. **180**, 96–107 (2019)
6. Lee, S.H., Chan, C.S., Wilkin, P., et al.: Deep-plant: plant identification with convolutional neural networks. In: IEEE International Conference on Image Processing, pp. 452–456. IEEE (2015)
7. Pan, S.J., Yang, Q.: A survey on transfer learning. IEEE Trans. Knowl. Data Eng. **22**(10), 1345–1359 (2010)
8. Srdjan, S., Marko, A., Andras, A.: Deep neural networks based recognition of plant diseases by leaf image classification. Comput. Intell. Neurosci. **6**, 1–11 (2016)
9. Liu, B., Zhang, Y., He, D.J.: Identification of apple leaf diseases based on deep convolutional neural networks. Symmetry **10**(1), 11 (2016). https://doi.org/10.3390/sym10010011
10. Too, E.C., Li, Y., Njuki, S.: A comparative study of fine-tuning deep learning models for plant disease identification. Comput. Electron. Agric. **161**, 272–279 (2016)
11. Picon, A., Alvarez-Gila, A., Seitz, M., Ortiz-Barredo, A., Echazarra, J., Johannes, A.: Deep convolutional neural networks for mobile capture devicebased crop disease classification in the wild. Comput. Electron. Agric. **1**(161), 280–290 (2019)
12. Selvaraj, M.G., Vergara, A., Ruiz, H., et al.: AI-powered banana diseases and pest detection. Plant Methods **15**, 92 (2019). https://doi.org/10.1186/s13007-019-0475-z
13. Zhong, Y., Zhao, M.: Research on deep learning in apple leaf disease recognition. Comput. Electron. Agric. **168**, 1–6 (2020). https://doi.org/10.1016/j.compag.2019.105146
14. Mubashar, M., Ali, H., Grönlund, C., Azmat, S.: R2U++: a multiscale recurrent residual U-Net with dense skip connections for medical image segmentation. Neural Comput. Appl. 1–17 (2022). https://doi.org/10.1007/s00521-022-07419-7
15. Muhammad, A.K., et al.: Cucumber leaf diseases recognition using multi level deep Entropy-ELM feature selection. Appl. Sci. **12**(2), 593, 1–19 (2022). https://doi.org/10.3390/app12020593
16. Zhang, S., Xiaowei, W., You, Z., Zhang, L.: Leaf image based cucumber disease recognition using sparse representation classification. Comput. Electron. Agric. **134**, 135–141 (2017)

17. Abdul, R., Zain, T., Shoaib, U.D.M, Ahmed, Z., Muhammad, U.K., Sumair, A.: Cucumber leaf disease classification using local tri-directional patterns and haralick features. In: 2021 International Conference on Artificial Intelligence, pp 258–263 (2021). https://doi.org/10.1109/ICAI52203.2021.9445237

18. Nazar, H., et al.: Multiclass cucumber leaf diseases recognition using best feature selection. CMC-Comput. Mater. Contin. **70**(2), 3281–3294 (2022). https://doi.org/10.32604/cmc.2022.019036

Lung Lesion Images Classification Based on Deep Learning Model and Adaboost Techniques

Nguyen Thanh Binh[1,2(✉)] and Vuong Bao Thy[3]

[1] Department of Information Systems, Faculty of Computer Science and Engineering, Ho Chi Minh City University of Technology (HCMUT), VNU-HCM 268 Ly Thuong Kiet Street, District 10, Ho Chi Minh City, Vietnam
ntbinh@hcmut.edu.vn
[2] Vietnam National University Ho Chi Minh City, Linh Trung Ward Thu Duc City, Ho Chi Minh City, Vietnam
[3] Faculty of Health Sciences, University of Cuu Long, Vinh Long, Vietnam
vuongbaothy@mku.edu.vn

Abstract. Today, the medical industry is promoting the research and application of artificial intelligence in disease diagnosis and treatment. The development of diagnostic methods with the support of electronic devices and information technology can help doctors save time in diagnosing and treating diseases, especially medical images. Diagnosis of lung lesions based on lung images is a case study. This paper proposed a method for lung lesion images classification based on modified U-Net and VGG-19 combined on adaboost techniques. The modified U-Net architecture with 5 pooling and 5 unpooling. It has the unpooling layer with kernels of size 2×2, stride 2×2 to get output consistent with the adaboost. The result of the proposed method is about 97.61% and better results than others in the Covid-19 radiography dataset.

Keywords: Classification · U-Net · Lung lesion images · VGG-19 · Adaboost

1 Introduction

The application of science and technology to the field of health science has been promoted in recent years, especially the application of intelligent processing technology, artificial intelligence to disease diagnosis and treatment. Specifically, the application stages include prediction, screening, analysis and decoding medical image data containing abnormalities.

Covid-19 has been spreading rapidly since the end of 2019. Early detection of people infected with Sars-Cov-2 for treatment is urgent work today. Because infecting subjects that are not detected in time will spread the virus to others [1, 2]. Testing by RT-PCR method is considered as the key to detect Sars-Cov-2 virus [3]. However, this method is time consuming and sometimes test results are misleading.

C. V. Phan and T. D. Nguyen (Eds.): ICCASA 2022, LNICST 475, pp. 102–111, 2023.
https://doi.org/10.1007/978-3-031-28816-6_8

Imaging techniques, such as chest X-ray and chest CT, have been widely used to evaluate lung lesions. Although the X-Ray scanner showed a higher accessibility, most of the Sars-Cov-2 infected subjects showed a bilaterally blurred parenchymal background and the lung shape fused into a circular morphology [6], making it difficult to distinguish Sars-Cov-2 infection when viewing radiographs. In contrast, 3D chest CT is effective in soft tissue differentiation and morphological imaging of lung parenchyma. This image has been widely used for the diagnosis of Covid-19 and is considered an important adjunct to RT-PCR tests [3–5]. Medical image processing using deep learning plays an important role due to its high accuracy and efficiency [7]. The deep learning-based approach has proven highly accurate in detecting Covid-19.

Li [8] used 2D U-Net to segment the lung ROI on CT slices, and then developed COV-Net incorporating ResNet-50 as the backbone to perform Covid-19 detection. Objects are extracted locally from each slice, and an aggregate layer is used to detect global features from a set of local features. The [9] proposed method to improve the CNNs for lung diseases image classification to detect pneumonia images. Javaheri [10] proposes the CovidCTNet method, which uses BCDU-Net for lung segmentation and a convolutional neural network (CNN) to distinguish Covid-19 from other pneumonia. BCDU-Net was pre-trained using data from a Kaggle lung segmentation contest [11].

Prasad [12] used U-Net with ResNet-50 pre-learned weights to detect Covid-19 infection. Hien [13] proposed a method using fuzzy C means for edge detection. Hemdan [14] proposed a method to diagnose Covid-19 by the COVIDX-Net model consisting of seven convolutional neural networks (CNNs). Chest X-ray images and breast cancer diagnosis on mammograms. Although those studies have yielded many good results. However, at present, the research results have the disadvantage that the proposed method is complicated, and the accuracy is not high. To overcome the above drawback, we propose a method of applying deep learning networks to classify images containing lung lesions of patients infected with Sars-Cov-2 virus with high accuracy and comparable with other methods of recently available legislation.

This paper proposed a method for lung lesion images classification based on modified U-net and VGG-19 combined on adaboost techniques. Main contributions of this study are: (i) the types of lung lesions are explained; (ii) proposed a method for lung lesion images classification based on deep learning model combined on adaboost techniques traditionally but with high accuracy results. The rest of the paper is organized as follows: Sect. 2 presents the U-net architectures, VGG-19 architectures, and the proposed method for classification. Section 3 and 4 are the experimental results and conclusions, respectively.

2 Lung Lesion Images Classification Based on Modify U-Net and VGG-19 Combined on Adaboost Techniques

2.1 U-Net and VGG-19 Architectures

The U-Net network consists of two main parts similar to the auto encoder model such as: encoder and decoder. However, they have an additional skip connection (similar to ResNet's) between layers and have the same size in the encoder – decoder. Since in image translation, there is a lot of low-level information that needs to be shared between input and output, passing the information across these networks is necessary. It provides sufficient information to limit the loss of information during feature extraction [15].

U-Net architecture also reduces the phenomenon of vanishing derivatives when training. This phenomenon occurs when the derivative of the error function is too small and approaches 0. Therefore, it is almost impossible for the model to update the parameters based on the derivative of the error function, leading to the model not being able to converge. This phenomenon appears quite commonly in CNN models. Thanks to skip-connection, U-Net has overcome the above phenomenon during training, making it more efficient to update the derivative parameter of the error function. Because it is possible to update the derivative parameter of the error function more efficiently and avoid data loss at the feature extraction stage, U-Net can still ensure high accuracy without too much data training.

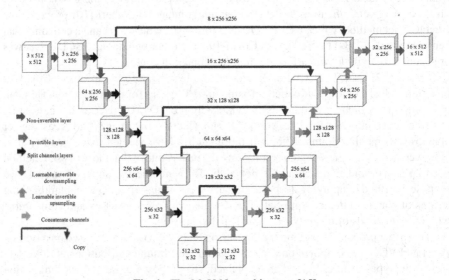

Fig. 1. The MoU-Net architecture [15]

The structure of the U-Net network: the first half of the U-Net network is a CNN consisting of convolutional, ReLU, and pooling network layers. The size of each layer gradually changes after each pooling. The first half of U-Net extracted features in the image. The second half of U-Net has the same structure as the first half of the network. However, the pooling layers are replaced by inverse convolution layers which increase the size of the layers to restore the features of the previously extracted image.

With the advantage of preserving information, avoiding the phenomenon of disappearing derivatives when training, the system uses U-Net as the generating network in the anomaly detection mode. The size of lung lesions is very small. So, we need to modify the U-Net architecture. We use the encoding path to extract low-level features and the decoding path to extract high-level features [15]. The Fig. 1 presented the modifying U-Net architecture (MoU-Net).

VGG is a convolutional neural network (CNN) architecture which helps to increase the depth of such networks. The only other component being pooling layers and a fully connected layer. The network uses small 3 x 3 filters. VGG-19 used 3 × 3 convolutional layers stacked and alternated with max pooling. It has two 4096 fully-connected layers and a softmax classifier. The VGG-19 architecture is present as Fig. 2.

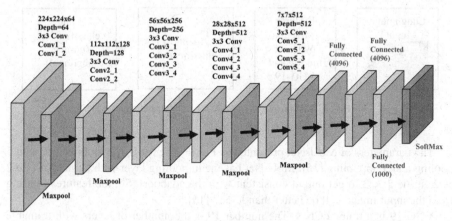

Fig. 2. The VGG-19 architecture

2.2 Lung Lesion Images Classification

This section clearly presents the proposed method for abnormal classifying. Chest X-ray images are valuable in detecting and diagnosing disease. Based on them, we can assess severity, respiratory complications, monitor treatment response and differential diagnosis. However, if only based on X-ray images, it is difficult to differentiate between viral pneumonia and some other etiologies. So, it must be combined with epidemiological characteristics and clinical manifestations to make a diagnosis. Suitable diagnosis. The types of lung lesions caused by Covid-19 that can be seen on X-ray images are: nodules, opacities, multifocal circular opacities, multifocal peripheral pulmonary parenchymal solidification.

Ground glass opacity is an incompletely solidified lesion with a higher density than the surrounding lung parenchyma, the border of blood vessels or bronchi inside the lesion can still be seen. Nodular opacities image are the opacities less than 3cm in diameter, round shape, may be scattered in the lung parenchyma. Pulmonary nodules are often well-demarcated, surrounded by lung parenchyma, and discontinuous with hilar or mediastinum. Bronchial wall thickening are lesions that show thickening of the bronchial wall, due to the accumulation of fluid or mucus around the bronchial wall, in the interstitial tissue. Thickened interlobular septum image associated with interlobular sulcus, cellular infiltration or fibrosis. In viral pneumonia, thickening of the septum is seen in diffuse lesions in acute respiratory distress syndrome.

In the early stages of the disease, X-ray images may be normal. Lesions are often both in the lung parenchyma and in the interstitium. Lesions are usually diffuse, bilateral lower lobes, in the periphery and with little destruction. When the disease is cured, the lungs may become fibrous.

To classify lung lesion images, the proposed method presented as Fig. 3, includes the stages as: features extraction by U-net modify and VGG-19 combined on adaboost classification.

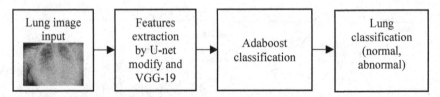

Fig. 3. The proposed method for lung classification

The parameters of MoU-Net presented as Fig. 1. The MoU-Net architecture with 5 pooling and 5 unpooling [15]. MoU-Net has the unpooling layer with kernels of size 2 × 2, stride 2 × 2 to get output consistent with the adaboost. So, the features filtering from the input image will be better than U-Net [15].

VGG-19 is a trained CNN. The number 19 is the number of layers with trainable weights including 16 convolutional layers and 3 fully connected layers. The parameters of VGG-19 presented as Fig. 2 and Table 1.

AdaBoost (Adaptive Boost) is a powerful learning algorithm that accelerates the generation of a strong classifier. It selects good features in a family of weak classifiers and recombines them linearly using weights. Therefore, it gradually improves accuracy by effectively applying a series of weak classifiers.

The adaboost algorithm maintains a normal distribution of weights on each training sample. In the first iteration, the algorithm training a weak classifier using a Haar-like feature performed best to detect the training samples. In the second iteration, the samples used for training, but misclassified by the first weak classifier, are given higher weights such that the Haar-like feature selected this time which must focus the computational ability for these misclassified test pieces. The process iterates and the end results are a cascade of linear combinations of weak classifiers, creating a strong classifier. Therefore, it helps to improve classification accuracy. The algorithm of adaboost as following [16]:

+ Given a set of n samples marked $(x_1, y_1), (x_2, y_2),...., (x_n, y_n)$, where $x_k \in (x_{k1}, x_{k2},..., x_{km})$ is the feature vector and $y_k \in (-1,1)$ is the label of the pattern (1 for object, -1 for background).

+ Initialize the initial weights for all samples, where m is the number of true samples (for object and $y = 1$) and l is the number of false samples (for background and $y = -1$)

$$W_{1,k} = \frac{1}{2m}, \frac{1}{2l} \tag{1}$$

+ Constructing T weak classifiers. Looping $t = 1,..., T$. For each feature in the feature vector, construct a weak classifier h_j with threshold θ_j and error ε_j:

$$\varepsilon_j = \sum_k^n W_{1,k} |h_j(x_k) - y_k| \tag{2}$$

Table 1. The parameters of VGG-19 combined on adaboost for classification

VGG-19 architecture	VGG-19 combined on Adaboost for classification
Conv3 × 3 (64) Conv3 × 3 (64)	Conv3 × 3 (64) Conv3 × 3 (64)
MaxPool	MaxPool
Conv3 × 3 (128) Conv3 × 3 (128)	Conv3 × 3 (128) Conv3 × 3 (128)
MaxPool	MaxPool
Conv3 × 3 (256) Conv3 × 3 (256) Conv3 × 3 (256) Conv3 × 3 (256)	Conv3 × 3 (256) Conv3 × 3 (256) Conv3 × 3 (256) Conv3 × 3 (256)
MaxPool	MaxPool
Conv3 × 3 (512) Conv3 × 3 (512) Conv3 × 3 (512) Conv3 × 3 (512)	Conv3 × 3 (512) Conv3 × 3 (512) Conv3 × 3 (512) Conv3 × 3 (512)
MaxPool	MaxPool
Conv3 × 3 (512) Conv3 × 3 (512) Conv3 × 3 (512) Conv3 × 3 (512)	Conv3 × 3 (512) Conv3 × 3 (512) Conv3 × 3 (512) Conv3 × 3 (512)
MaxPool	MaxPool
Fully connected (4096) Fully connected (4096) Fully connected (1000)	Classification by adaboost
SoftMax	
Lable of image	Lable of image

+ Choosing h_j with the smallest ε_j, we get h_t:
$h_t: X \rightarrow \{1, -1\}$, Update weights:

$$W_{t+1,k} = \frac{w_{t,k}}{z_t} x \begin{cases} e^{-\alpha_t}, h_t(x_k) = y_k \\ e^{\alpha_t}, h_t(x_k) \neq y_k \end{cases} \tag{3}$$

where,

$$\alpha_t = \frac{1}{2} ln(\frac{1 - \varepsilon_j}{\varepsilon_j}) \tag{4}$$

Z_t is the coefficient that used to move W_{t+1} to the range [0, 1]. Strong classifier is built:

$$H(x) = sign(\sum_{t=1}^{T} \propto_t h_t(x)) \tag{5}$$

3   Experimental Results

Our experimental programs were developed by the python language on a computer of Intel core i7, 3.2 GHz CPU and 16 GB DDR3 memory. The lung images in the Covid-19 Radiography dataset [17] are used in our experiments. In this dataset, there are four categories such as: Covid, lung opacity, viral pneumonia, and normal chest X-ray images.

The total of images in this dataset are 21165 images, where 3616 Covid images, 6012 lung opacity images, 1345 viral pneumonia images and 10192 normal images. From the numbers of these images, we see that the numbers of images are not balanced in all above classes. Now, we select the number of images (sub-dataset) in this dataset to create a balanced dataset. In our experiments, we only use two sub-datasets with 1500 covid images and 1500 normal images.

The size of each image is 299 × 299 pixels resolution with Portable Network Graphics (.png) file format. We divided randomly the sub-dataset for 70% training and 30% testing. Some images in this sub-dataset are presented as Fig. 4.

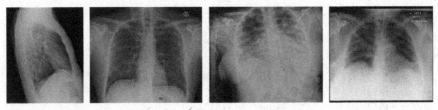

Fig. 4. Some images in sub-dataset

The accuracy is used to evaluate the metrics of the results classification. Sensitivity (Se) defines the ability to detect abnormal images and ranges from 0 to 1. The value of sensitivity range is calculated as Eq. (6).

$$Se = \frac{TP}{TP + FN} \tag{6}$$

where, TP is the number of true positives and FN is the number of false negatives. P and N are the total number of non-responsive and responsive samples in the dataset, respectively.

Specificity (Sp) defines the ability to distinguish images that have abnormal or not and ranges from 0 to 1. The value of specificity ranges is calculated as in the Eq. (7).

$$Sp = \frac{TN}{TN + FP} \tag{7}$$

where, TN is the number of true negatives, FP is the number of false positives.

Accuracy (Acc) represents the result accuracy of the proposed method in the test dataset, and ranges from 0 to 1 (equivalent in the range from 0% to 100%). The accuracy values are calculated as Eq. (8).

$$Acc = \frac{TP + TN}{TP + FN + TN + FP} \tag{8}$$

The experimentations are implemented with all the images in the above datasets. Table 2 presented the evaluation values of adaboost method and some deep learning models: U-Net, MoU-Net, VGG-16, VGG-19 and MoU-Net combined on VGG-19 for lung lesion images classification.

Table 2. The evaluation of the lung lesion images classification (%) between the adaboost and deep learning models.

Method	U-Net + adaboost method	MoU-Net + adaboost method	VGG-16 + adaboost method	VGG-19 + adaboost method	MoU-Net + VGG-19 + adaboost method
Accuracy (%)	93.721	95.582	92.167	93.123	97.598

In Table 2, we apply adaboost for classification. The result of combination of the MoU-Net and VGG-19, and adaboost method is better than others.

Table 3. The classification average evaluation between the proposed method with the recent methods.

Method	Year	The Covid-19 Radiography dataset		
		Sensitivity	Specificity	Accuracy
Vasilis method [18]	2021	0.9302	0.9512	0.9404
Cengil method [19]	2021	0.9574	0.9635	0.9604
Muhammad method [20]	2022	0.9631	0.9711	0.9671
Proposed method	2022	0.9710	0.9807	0.9761

Table 3 presents the results of the proposed method with the recent methods for classification. The average accuracy of the proposed method is 97.61% while the average accuracy of Vasilis method [18], Cengil method [19] and Muhammad method [20] are 94.04%, 96.04% and 96.71%, respectively.

As presented in Sect. 2.2, the MoU-Net architecture with more depth includes 5 pooling and 5 unpooling. The U-Net tradition architecture is only 4 pooling and 4 unpooling. Moreover, we also use VGG-19 and adaboost algorithms to improve the classification task. While Vasilis method [18] used a CNN and added a dense layer on top of a pre-trained baseline CNN (Efficient Net-B0), Cengil method [19] used the CNN architectures such as Alexnet, Xception, NASNETLarge, and Efficient Net-B0 are used as backbones to classify Covid-19 images. And Muhammad method [20] used a hybrid algorithm (Whale-Elephant Herding) for classification. It explains why the proposed method gives the better results versus the other methods.

4 Conclusions and Future Works

The main function of the lungs is to exchange gasses to maintain life, because the capillaries in the alveoli form a dense network. The lungs carry oxygen from the air into the pulmonary veins, and carbon dioxide from the pulmonary arteries out. The lungs are also involved in the metabolism and synthesis of many important substances, filter some toxins in the blood, and are also a place to store blood. Therefore, the factors affecting the lungs that will most damage the lungs are Covid-19. This paper proposed a method to improve U-Net and VGG-19 architectures combined on adaboost techniques for lung lesion images classification. The MoU-Net architecture with 5 pooling and 5 unpooling. MoU-Net has the unpooling layer with kernels of size 2×2, stride 2×2 to get output consistent with the adaboost. So, the features filtering from the input image will be better than U-Net. To evaluate the obtained results, we compare the results of the proposed method with other methods. Our experiment results are better than others in the Covid-19 Radiography dataset. To crease the accuracy of the proposed method, the improving VGG-19 architecture and the time running are necessary and experiment on other datasets in future work.

Acknowledgement. We acknowledge the support of time and facilities from Ho Chi Minh City University of Technology (HCMUT), VNU-HCM and University of Cuu Long for this study.

References

1. Nogrady, B.: What the data say about asymptomatic COVID infections, Nature **587** (7835), 534–535 (2020). https://www.nature.com/articles/d41586-020-03141-3. Accessed 16 May 2022
2. Hong, J.-M., et al.: Epidemiological characteristics and clinical features of patients infected with the COVID-19 virus in Nanchang, Jiangxi China. Front. Med. **7**(571069), 1–9 (2020). https://doi.org/10.3389/fmed.2020.571069
3. Bwire, G.M., Majigo, M.V., Njiro, B.J., Mawazo, A.: Detection profile of SARS-CoV-2 using RT-PCR in different types of clinical specimens: a systematic review and meta-analysis. J. Med. Virol. **2021**(93), 719–725 (2021). https://doi.org/10.1002/jmv.26349
4. Hu, Z., Tang, J., Wang, Z., Zhang, K., Zhang, L., Sun, Q.: Deep learning for image-based cancer detection and diagnosis-a survey. Pattern Recogn. **83**, 134–149 (2018)
5. Paweł, J., Dawid, S., Patryk, O.: Artificial intelligence for COVID-19 detection in medical imaging - diagnostic measures and wasting- a systematic umbrella review. J. Clin. Med. **11**, 1–16 (2022). https://doi.org/10.3390/jcm11072054
6. Chung, M., et al.: CT imaging features of 2019 novel coronavirus (2019-nCoV). Radiology **295**(1), 202–207 (2020)
7. Kroft, L.J.M., van der Velden, L., Girón, I.H., Roelofs, J.J.H., de Roos, A., Geleijns, J.: Added value of ultra–low-dose computed tomography, dose equivalent to chest X-ray radiography, for diagnosing chest pathology. J. Thorac. Imaging **34**(3), 179–186 (2019)
8. Li, L., et al.: Artificial intelligence distinguishes COVID-19 from community acquired pneumonia on chest CT. Radiology **296**(2), 65–71 (2020)
9. The, N.H., Nhung, N.T.H., Binh, N.T.: Adaptive lung diseases images classification technique based on deep learning. In: Van Toi, V., Nguyen, TH., Long, V.B., Huong, H.T.T. (eds.) 8th International Conference on the Development of Biomedical Engineering in Vietnam. BME

2020. IFMBE Proceedings, vol. 85, pp. 803-814. Springer, Cham (2021). https://doi.org/10.1007/978-3-030-75506-5_65

10. Javaheri, T., et al.: CovidCTNet: an open source deep learning approach to diagnose covid-19 using small cohort of CT images. NPJ. Digit. Med. **4**, 1–10 (2021)

11. https://www.kaggle.com/kmader/finding-lungs-in-ct-data. Accessed 16 May 2022

12. Kalane, P., Patil, S., Patil, B.P., Sharma, D.P.: Automatic detection of COVID-19 disease using U-Net architecture based fully convolutional network. Biomed. Sign. Process. Control **67**, 1–9 (2021). https://doi.org/10.1016/j.bspc.2021.102518

13. Hien, N.M., Binh, N.T., Viet, N.Q.: Edge detection based on fuzzy C means in medical image processing system. In: Proceedings of the IEEE International Conference on Systems Science and Engineering, pp. 12–15 (2017). https://doi.org/10.1109/ICSSE.2017.8030827

14. Hemdan, E.E.D., Shouman, M.A., Karar, M.E.: Covidx-net: a framework of deep learning classifiers to diagnose covid-19 in X-ray images, pp 1–4 (2020). arXiv:200311055

15. Binh, N.T., Hien, N.M., Tin, D.T.: Improving U-Net architecture and graph cuts optimization to classify arterioles and venules in retina fundus images. J. Intell. Fuzzy Syst. **42**(4), 4015–4026 (2022). https://doi.org/10.3233/JIFS-212259

16. http://www.robots.ox.ac.uk/~az/lectures/cv/adaboost_matas.pdf. Accessed 16 May 2022

17. https://www.kaggle.com/datasets/tawsifurrahman/covid19-radiography-database. Accessed 16 May 2022

18. Nikolaou, V., Massaro, S., Fakhimi, M., Stergioulas, L., Garn, W.: COVID-19 diagnosis from chest X-rays: developing a simple, fast, and accurate neural network. Health Inf. Sci. Syst. **9**(1), 1–11 (2021). https://doi.org/10.1007/s13755-021-00166-4

19. Cengil, E., Çınar, A.: The effect of deep feature concatenation in the classification problem: an approach on COVID-19 disease detection. Int. J. Imaging Syst. Technol. **32**(1), 26–40 (2021). https://doi.org/10.1002/ima.22659

20. Muhammad, A.K., et al.: COVID-19 classification from chest X-ray images: a framework of deep explainable artificial intelligence. Comput. Intell. Neurosci. 2022, 1–14 (2022). Article ID 4254631

Balltree Similarity: A Novel Space Partition Approach for Collaborative Recommender Systems

Hiep Xuan Huynh$^{(\boxtimes)}$, Nhung Cam Thi Mai, and Hai Thanh Nguyen

College of Information and Communication Technology,
Can Tho University, Can Tho, Vietnam
hxhiep@ctu.edu.vn

Abstract. The recommender systems have been widely applied in numerous applications that support online retailers, video sharing websites, medical systems, etc. Similar measures are essential in providing valuable recommendations to users in such systems. This work presents a novel approach, namely **Ball-Sim**, with a new similarity metric using a balltree structure for recommender systems. Furthermore, we want to leverage the tree structure to determine the closest k nearby users to improve the recommender systems' efficiency. The work's experimental scenarios outlined the steps of building a balltree and identifying nearby users based on the tree structure. Besides, the work also evaluates the implemented recommender system by comparing the recommender system's results based on the balltree-based spatial partitioning with the recommender system using the default parameters. The data used in the experiments is the Movielens dataset, a web-based film recommender system, and an important data source for evaluating the studies, with 100,000 samples, including ratings from 943 users for 1,664 movies. The results show that the recommender system with a balltree-based similarity metric can improve the accuracy compared to a commonly-used measure such as the cosine metric.

Keywords: Balltree · Similarity measure · Movielens · Recommender systems · Spatial partitioning

1 Introduction

Recommender systems research is a field of machine learning with broad applications in e-commerce, entertainment, and education. The system seeks to predict the "products" for the appropriate "user". In e-commerce, the advisory system helps buyers find suitable goods, helps sellers find potential customers, and boosts sales. The system recommends items according to the user's preferences in entertainment and education. Consulting system opens up research potential to build practical systems to assist users in making decisions. A balltree [19] is a binary tree structure that supports a multidimensional spatial partitioning

C. V. Phan and T. D. Nguyen (Eds.): ICCASA 2022, LNICST 475, pp. 112–128, 2023.
https://doi.org/10.1007/978-3-031-28816-6_9

algorithm, distributing data points to find an efficient separating superspace. In addition, the balltree applies a close neighbor search algorithm to find the required data. Selecting a recommender system model is a problem in building an effective advisory system. The algorithm for finding the nearest user to predict a ranking value for current users' items is also quite complicated. Questions to be addressed: Which recommender system model is used? How do we find the users closest to the user needing advice? How do we evaluate whether the model is being used effectively or not? The work uses a collaborative user-based filtering system with a balltree spatial partitioning algorithm to find the nearest neighbors effectively from the questions raised. The work proposes a new approach: using a balltree structure to store users' lists and then searching for the closest user with the k-neighbor algorithm. Then, after the most recent users are available, use the rating system to calculate the average rating for the current user, suggest items, and finally rate the model.

This study proposes an approach, namely **Ball-Sim**, leveraging the balltree structure and building the balltree-based k nearest neighbors search method to provide a recommender system with a novel similarity measure. We also present detailed examples of using balltree for the recommender system. Our approach performs better than the recommender method with cosine measures on Movielens data, including about 100,000 samples.

2 Related Work

Recommender systems are software and engineering tools that provide product recommendations for users to use [1,2]. In the recommender system, three objects need to be considered: users (users), items (items - collectively called news items, or e-commerce sites such as Amazon, items are recommended products for users). Moreover, user responses to the item (called reviews or ratings). The recommender system is based on many different methods and algorithms but can be divided into three types of approaches [1,3–5]: Content-based Recommender system, Collaborative Filtering Systems, and Knowledge-based recommender systems.

2.1 Content-Based Recommender Systems (CBF)

The systems need to learn to suggest similar items that the user has liked in the past. The emphasis technique analyzes the content (attributes) for prediction. For example, if users often read articles related to Linux operating systems or comment on software engineering-related content, the system will make recommendations based on history and recommend similar content. A content-based advisory system matches one or more characteristics compared to user profiles to determine the relevance of that item to a particular user. Therefore, the advisory process determines which products are most suitable for the user's preferences. A list of product features can be given, such as product name, price, color, etc., and other product-related information that the user can find attractive.

Although the recommender model based on content filtering has been success-fully applied in many areas [6–8], there are some disadvantages to this method [6]. The first one may be expertise Focus, where Content-filtering recommender models tend to recommend products similar to what users previously rated. For example, mothers who breastfeed or buy diaper products for their babies regu-larly review and search for mothers' sites also suggest products about diapers and milk. However, shopping needs may also be related to household gadgets, kitchen utensils, or fashion related by age, but these products are not consulted. The second may be a characteristic citation problem where Content analysis is limited by techniques on the content that require items to be described clearly. This problem will be more difficult when selecting complex content features for multimedia data such as graphics, sound, images, and video. New User Problem [6]: Content filtering recommender models are helpful when users rate or buy a relatively large number of products. However, new users have very few ratings, so the system will not recommend suitable products for users.

2.2   Collaborative Filtering Systems (CF)

Collaborative filtering-based recommender systems recommend products to users based on similar product measurements evaluated by other users. These systems work by building a huge database of information about the user's behavior and preferences (user-item matrix) and predicting what the user will like based on the similarities and comparisons. Collaborative filtering is considered the most common technique in the suggestion system. Collaborative filtering techniques work well when there is enough assessment information. Therefore, the recom-mender model based on collaborative filtering depends entirely on user rating data for products. For example, in the collaborative filtering recommender model to introduce movies to viewers, the model finds groups of viewers with similar interests as viewers who need previous advice. Then the model introduces movies that this group of viewers appreciates to those who need advice. The collabora-tive filtering methods [6,7,9] are divided into two main branches: memory-based and model-based. The authors usually use Memory-based approaches to utilize all assessments, products, and users stored in the system, to base these evalua-tions to render private lists.

2.3   Knowledge-Based Recommender Systems

Knowledge-based recommender systems are helpful in case items are not fre-quently used, for example, in e-commerce, real estate-related products, and car tourism-related products. However, the user's rating matrix is not informative enough to suggest since most users only buy the product once with different detailed requirements. Therefore, it is not easy for the model to collect enough evaluation information about a product. On the other hand, the user's pref-erences about the product may change over time. Therefore, the system may combine user ratings, product attributes, and historical knowledge of the simi-larity between user requirements to suggest matches [10–12].

3 The Proposed Recommendation Method Based on Balltree Structure

3.1 Preliminary on Balltree Algorithm

One data structure to speed the finding of neighbors is the balltree structure. Balltree structure is beneficial in cases where the amount of data is considerable. It can be built for data modeling, supporting adding and deleting data, and processing with multidimensional space. This algorithm is also applied in many fields, such as robots, computer vision, speech processing, and graphics. A balltree is a binary tree with a hierarchical structure. Start with 2 clusters (each is a ball) to be created. Since it is a multidimensional space, each ball is called a matching super-sphere. Some points in a multidimensional space will belong to one cluster, not all. The points will belong to the cluster with the shortest distance. Each ball will include two sub-clusters, and each sub-cluster becomes a ball. This sub-cluster is further divided into the next sub-clusters until a certain depth. Each ball in the balltree contains a node-set of points in Euclidean space. Each balltree node can be either the root node (containing all the original data), the intermediate node (containing the set of points), or the leaf node (one data point). Each node consists of 2 components: center and radius. A node can define parent, left, and right child nodes. If it is a root node, there is no parent. If it is a leaf node, there is no child. Each node in the tree identifies the smallest ball containing all the data points in its subtree.

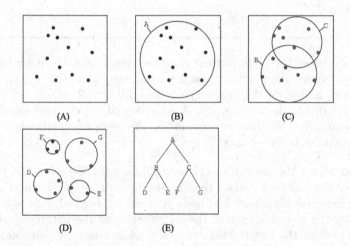

Fig. 1. The steps of building a Balltree.

This study builds the balltree to store user vectors as the recommender system's original data according to a top-down algorithm.

Figure 1 exhibits the steps of building a Balltree where (A) is a set of data, (B) is a root node of the tree, (C) is from the root node divided into two children nodes, (D) is each child node is divided into the underlying child nodes, and (E) is a balltree with the nodes of D, E, F, G considered as the leaf nodes.

The whole top-down algorithm's complexity when building balltree is $O(n * log^2 n)$. The top-down method of balltree construction is a recursive process that starts at the root node, then the intermediate nodes, and finally the leaf nodes. For example, calling pi the initial node, dividing pi into two subnodes consists of four main steps [13] (as shown in Algorithm 1).

Algorithm 1: Create a balltreee structure: create-balltree(D)

Result: A balltree

if *If D only has a point* **then**

    create a leaf node B as a point in D ;

    return B;

else

    Call L, R are two child leaves which will be created from the considering node;

    Create B with 2 children with steps as follows:;

    Calculate the radius r of the circle (the distance from farthest point f to center c) ;

    Center = c (Determine center c);

    B.radius = r (Determine the farthest point f in the data set from center c);

    B.leftchild = create-balltree (L) ;

    B.rightchild =create-balltree (R);

    return B;

end

- Step one: choose the point farthest from the center of pi, the point piL (left).
- Step two: choose the point farthest from piL, the point PIR (right).
- Step three: assign the data points closest to piL or piR.
- Step four: divide the node pi into 2 subnodes viL or viL, and calculate the center and radius for these two subnodes. The algorithm ends when viL and viL are a point in the original data

Figure 2 shows the process of clustering data with Balltree. The blue line is the super-flat line that divides the initial node into two children. The above process is recursive until each leaf node contains an original data point. After constructing the tree structure or the construction of the balltree, perform an efficient search of the constructed structure using k-nearest neighbors (kNN) based on the magnitude and distance between the original data.

3.2   Determining the Closest Neighbors in the Balltree

Defining the query object is complicated and time-consuming from a large amount of data. However, among the algorithms built to query data, k-Nearest neighbor (k-NN - nearest neighbor) is quite efficient and straightforward. The

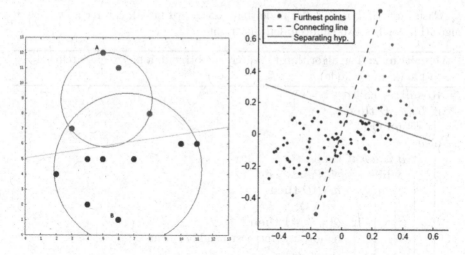

Fig. 2. An illustration of clustering data with Balltree [13].

data structures are applied to k-NN, such as balltree, k-d tree, Principal Axis
Tree (PAT), Orthogonal Structure Tree (OST), Nearest Feature Line (NFL),
and Center Line (CL). The balltree structure is chosen because it is efficient in
multidimensional space. In the multidimensional space, we denote V as a set
of data points (user set is the rows considered in the matrix), Q contains the
neighbor points of query q in V, and K is the latest number of users to search for
a new user. Q contains the k users closest to query q if and only if the maximum
distance from the query point q to the points in Q.

The maximum possible distance from the query point q to the points in B is
calculated by the formula 1.

$$D = \begin{cases} \infty & if |Q| < k \\ max_{x \in Q}|x - q| & if |Q| \le k \end{cases} \quad (1)$$

Likewise, the maximum possible distance from the query point q to the points
in B is calculated by the following formula 2:

$$D_T = \begin{cases} max(|q - T.centroid| - T.radius, D_{B.parent}) & T \neq root \\ max(|q - T.centroid| - T.radius, 0) & T = root \end{cases} \quad (2)$$

The algorithm starts the search from the root node. During the search process, the algorithm recalculates Q. At each node B, the algorithm performs one
of three cases and returns Q containing k positions with the same closest query
condition of query q (detailed in Algorithm 2). Case one: if the distance from
the query point q to the considered node T is more significant than D, ignore B
and return Q. Case two: if T is a leaf node, go through all the points and update

Q. Case three: if T is an inner node (ball, not a leaf node), call recursive search algorithm for B's two children: left and right.

Algorithm 2: The algorithm to search a subtree in a balltree: searchBall-Subtree (k, q, Q, node)

Result: A balltree
if $D_B < D$ then
| return Q ;
else
| if *B is a leaf* then
| | while *x in B.Points()* do
| | | if $|x - q| < D$ then
| | | | add x to Q;
| | | | if $|Q| = k + 1$ then
| | | | | remove the furthest neighbor from Q;
| | | | | Update D;
| | | | end
| | | end
| | end
| else
| | let child1 be the child node closest to q ;
| | let child2 be the child node furthest from q ;
| | searchBallSubtree (k, q, Q, child1) ;
| | searchBallSubtree(k, q, Q, child2) ;
| end
end

We consider an example, including the proposed steps to illustrate the Ball-tree structure's use to determine k-neighbors and similar users. To illustrate the balltree structure, we assume that we have 8 points in the set M: M = $\{X_j\}, j = 1..8$, with each point having coordinates (x, y). We have a matrix M with eight rows and two columns, as shown in Fig. 3.

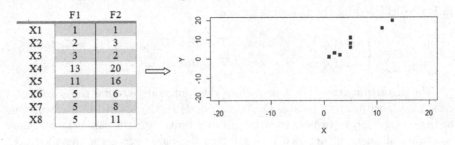

	F1	F2
X1	1	1
X2	2	3
X3	3	2
X4	13	20
X5	11	16
X6	5	6
X7	5	8
X8	5	11

Fig. 3. An example including 8 points, their coordinates, and their visualization.

Building the Balltree from the Given Points. We need to identify the center and radius of nodes from the center in this stage.

Step 1: Determine the center and radius of the parent node of 8 given points: The center $= (\frac{1+2+3+13+11+5+5+5}{8}, \frac{1+3+2+20+16+6+8+11}{8}) \approx (6,8)$. X4 is the farthest point in set A relative to the center (using the formula for calculating the distance between 2 points in the coordinate system). From X4 to the center, we have the radius computed by $\sqrt{(13-6)^2 + (20-8)^2} \approx 13.5$.

Step 2: The algorithm expands the root node A to two child nodes, B and C. In set A, X4 is the farthest point from the center of root node A, while X1 is the farthest from X4. We consider X1 and X4 as two points of two sub-circles, B and C, where B=Node(A).child1 = X1, X2, X3, X6, X7, X8 and C = Node(A).child2 = X4, X5. At this time, the center and radius of the circle B are computed by the Center of B is A.child1 $= (\frac{21}{6}, \frac{31}{6}) \approx (3.5,5)$, X8 as the farthest point in set B. Center of C = A.child2 = (24/2, 36/2) = (12, 18), determine X4 as the farthest point in set C with the radius C = A.child2=2.23.

Step 3: We continue to divide node B and C into their child leaves of D, E, F, G with C.child1 = F = X4, C.child2 = G = X5, B.child1 = D = X1, X2, X3, and B.child2 = E = X6, X7, X8

Step 4: We continue to divide nodes D and E into their child leaves of H, I, K, and L, respectively. At the node D: the Center of D = ((1 + 2 + 3)/3, (1 + 3 + 2)/3) = (2, 2). Determine the point X2 or X3 is the farthest point in D. The radius of a circle D = 1. At the node E: The center of E = ((5 + 5 + 5)/3, (6 + 8 + 11)/3) $\approx$ (5, 8.3). Determine the point X8, which is farthest from the center in D, and the Radius of the circle D = 2.7. We have D.child1 = H = X1, D.child2 = I = X2, X3, E.child1 = K = X8 and E.child2 = L = X6, X7

At this step, I and L can be divided into child nodes, but we only consider k=2 nearest neighbors in this example. It should be considered that the algorithm ends. After splitting the nodes, the model shows the binary tree as Fig. 4.

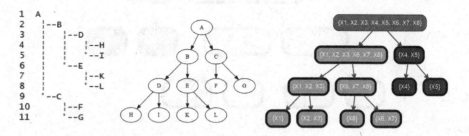

Fig. 4. The Balltree structure illustration to represent the 8 given points.

Determining Neighbours on the Balltree. Suppose that we have a new point, q(7,4). Based on the tree structure constructed in the above steps, we search for the k=2 nearest points to q. The process includes steps as follows.

Step 1: Initialize the values: $K = 2$, determine the 2 nearest neighbours for q with V = X1, X2, X3, X4, X5, X6, X7, X8 and $Q = \emptyset$ (the set of nearest neighbors of q is initially empty), $D_T=0$, since at the beginning, T is initially as the root node.

Step 2: T is the root node, so $D_T = 0, Q = \emptyset$. Continue to consider 2 child nodes, B and C.

Step 3: Calculate the distance from q(7, 4) to the center of B (3.5, 5) and C (12, 18), we obtain $D_{qB} = \overline{qB} = D_{qC} = \sqrt{13.25}$, so B is the closest one to q while C is the farthest from q. B is the intermediate node. The recursion can be applied to the left and right child nodes D and E, and update Q = X1, X2, X3, X6, X7, X8.

Step 4: Consider 2 child nodes of B: D = X1, X2, X3 and E = X6, X7, X8. We calculate the distance from q to center D and E: $D_{qD} = \overline{qD} = \sqrt{29}$ and $D_{qE} = \overline{qE} = \sqrt{22.4}$, so E is closest to q, and D is farthest from q. E is the intermediate node, the recursion is applied to E, and update Q = X6, X7, X8.

Step 5: Consider 2 child nodes of E: K = X8 and L = X6, X7 and calculate the distance from q to center K and L. The Center of K: X8 = (5,11). The center of L: $((5 + 5)/2, (6 + 8)/2) = (5,7)$, and distances between q and K, L is computed by $D_{qK} = \overline{qK} = \sqrt{53}$ and $D_{qL} = \overline{qL} = \sqrt{13}$. From the obtained results, we determine that L is the nearest point to q while K is the farthest from q. L is the intermediate node. We perform the recursion on L's left and right children and update Q = X6, X7. With k = 2 nearest neighbors, the algorithm stops with the return values, including X6 and X7 (Fig. 5).

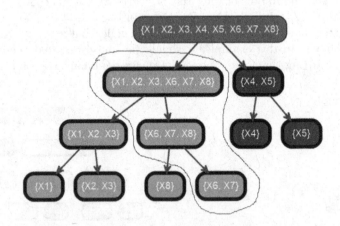

Fig. 5. The red curve covers the branch which is included to exhibit how to determine k = 2 nearest neighbors (X6, X7) of q. (Color figure online)

3.3   Modeling the Problem of Measuring the Similarity of Users in a Recommender System Based on Balltree Structure

Collaborative filtering techniques can be divided into memory-based and model-based approaches. Memory-based techniques include user-based and item-based techniques based on the user's historical or past items' data. This technique consists of three main steps: representing the ranking matrix, Calculating similarity between users or between items, predicting ratings, and making suggestions. We use data mining and machine learning techniques for Model-based techniques to build predictive models based on data collected in the past. These techniques analyze user-item matrices to identify the relationships between items; These relationships are used to compare the list of top-N suggestions. This technique also includes three main steps: Form the ranking matrix, Build models by machine learning method (training phase), and Predict actual data based on the learned model (predictive period). Based on the model, the proposed recommendation method based on balltree spatial partitions is classified into a collaborative filtering group. This study leverages the balltree spatial partition to store the user vectors, calculate their similarity, and predict the result.

Balltree is a complete binary tree data structure built for data modeling, instrumental in multidimensional spatial processing. Balltree is applied in numerous different fields. In this study, the balltree is considered a method to determine the similarity of the user list. Based on a built-in balltree structure, the recommender system determine the closest neighbor to a particular user and ultimately finds advisory values for a new user. Based on the theory of balltree structure, we propose a novel approach in the recommender system with balltree spatial partitions as follows: input data is a matrix, and here is a rating matrix of the user set $U = u_1, u_2, u_3, ..., u_n$ for the set of products - items $I = i_1, i_2, i_3, ..., i_m$. Users are considered a dataset in m-dimensional space, proceeding to build a balltree structure based on that data set. During building a balltree, the two parameters of a node are stored as the node's center and radius (exhibited in Fig. 6). After the balltree has been built, we determine the closest user with the closest k-neighbor algorithm for a given user. At this point, the node's center and radius parameters are used to identify a list of nodes close to the new node using the distance formula.

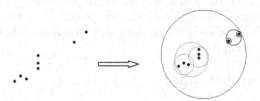

Fig. 6. An illustration of solving the problem with the clusters generated by the balltree approach.

Information Matrix. In a recommender system (RS), the function r is written as follows (Formula 3):

$$r : U \times I \to R \tag{3}$$

The goal of RS is to find a function $r* : U \times I \to R*$ such that $\alpha(r, r*)$ satisfies a certain condition. For example, α is a function that estimates the Mean Absolute Error (MAE) (Formula 4). It must be minimal.

$$MAE = \frac{1}{|T|} \sum |r_{i,j} - r*_{i,j}| \tag{4}$$

where $|T|$ is the total rating of the original data set, $r_{i,j}$ is the rating of user u_i for item i_j while $r*_{i,j}$ is the rating predictions of user u_i for item i_j. Creating recommendations using user-based collaborative filtering can be done as shown in Fig. 7.

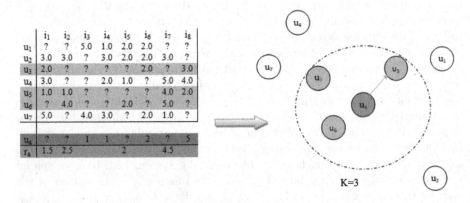

Fig. 7. Suggesting recommendations from the informational function matrix with the k = 3 nearest neighbors.

Providing Recommendations. When a list of users is similar to a user needing to predict, we combine their ratings to generate predictive value. Usually, the predicted results are the average of the values of similar users.

For users who need u_a advice, we determine the results in places that have not yet been validated (question marks are positions that need to be valid). Recommendation results using the predictive function calculate the average value from users similar to u_a.

4   Experimental Results

4.1   Movielens Dataset and Settings for the Experiments

Our method is evaluated on the movielens dataset proposed by grouplens[1]. The dataset includes about 100,000 samples with movies rated by 943 users for 1,664

---

[1] https://grouplens.org.

movies (with 99,392 samples, including ratings of values ranging from 1 to 5). It is organized in a matrix format of 943 rows, 1,664 columns, and 1,569,152 cells containing users' ratings for movies. However, as we know, not all users watch all movies. In the rating matrix, there are only 99,392 user ratings for the category of movies, including 19 genres of movies (action, adventure, animation, children's, comedy, crime, documentary, drama, fantasy, film-noir, horror, musical, mystery, romance, scifi, thriller, war, western).

We assume that each node stores one user vector (one row of data in the initial evaluation matrix). After the tree has been built, the leaf nodes' similarity to a new node is calculated as the data to be predicted. The next step is to find k neighbors to find n users closest to the new user. Finally, calculate the advisory results for this new user.

The performances in Mean Absolute Error (MAE), Root Mean Square Error (RMSE), and Mean Square Error (MSE) are measured by the average results on 5-fold-cross validation.

To build a recommender system based on Balltree, we use recommendarlab[2] tool package and install additional functions to build a recommender system based on balltree structure: build balltree in recommendarlab package and compute user similarity according to balltree structure combining some functions of sklearn [18] (sklearn. neighbors.BallTree) in python.

Taking examples for scenarios in the following sections, we randomly extract a small 10×10 dataset in the Movielens set after the normalization process (exhibited in Table 1). Then, we divide it into a training set and a test set. For samples used in the examples, we assume that at the i-th repetition of a 5-cross evaluation, there are u_5 and u_6 in the training set, and the remaining is in the test set.

4.2   Scenarios

Three scenarios are presented to show how the proposed method works. In the first one, the system receives input data and defines nodes in the balltree structure. Then, we calculate the similarity of the user vectors by finding neighbors through the balltree tree to determine a list of users similar to new users. The last one identifies the value of reviews and advises new users.

Scenario 1. The system receives the data and defines nodes in the balltree. The considered nodes include root, intermediate, and leaf nodes. Next, we transform the dataset into user vectors where each user is one vector from the original dataset. Finally, the NA values are replaced by the value 0.

---

[2] https://cran.r-project.org/web/packages/recommenderlab/index.html.

Table 1. Experimental samples for scenarios presented in a matrix of 10×10 where each column represents movies i_n (n = 1..10) and each row represents ratings of the user u_m (m = 1..10) corresponding to the movie.

	i_1	i_2	i_3	i_4	i_5	i_6	i_7	i_8	i_9	i_{10}
u_1	5	3	3	4	1	5	2	5	5	5
u_2	4	NA	NA	NA	NA	NA	NA	NA	4	4
u_3	NA	NA	NA	NA	NA	NA	NA	NA	NA	NA
u_4	4	3	NA	NA	NA	NA	NA	NA	NA	NA
u_5	4	NA	NA	2	4	4	NA	4	2	5
u_6	NA	NA	5	5	5	5	3	5	NA	NA
u_7	NA	NA	NA	3	NA	NA	3	NA	NA	NA
u_8	4	NA	4	4	NA	4	4	5	3	NA
u_9	NA	NA	NA	NA	4	5	2	2	NA	NA
u_{10}	NA	NA	5	NA	NA	NA	NA	NA	NA	NA

The training set is illustrated as:
$$
\begin{pmatrix} \vec{u_1} \\ \vec{u_2} \\ \vec{u_3} \\ \vec{u_4} \\ \vec{u_7} \\ \vec{u_8} \\ \vec{u_9} \\ \vec{u_{10}} \end{pmatrix} = \begin{pmatrix} 5\,3\,3\,4\,1\,5\,2\,5\,5\,5 \\ 4\,0\,0\,0\,0\,0\,0\,0\,4\,4 \\ 0\,0\,0\,0\,0\,0\,0\,0\,0\,0 \\ 4\,3\,0\,0\,0\,0\,0\,0\,0\,0 \\ 0\,0\,0\,3\,0\,0\,3\,0\,0\,0 \\ 4\,0\,4\,4\,0\,4\,4\,5\,3\,0 \\ 0\,0\,0\,0\,4\,5\,2\,2\,0\,0 \\ 0\,0\,5\,0\,0\,0\,0\,0\,0\,0 \end{pmatrix}
$$

The test set is illustrated as: $\begin{pmatrix} \vec{u_5} \\ \vec{u_6} \end{pmatrix} = \begin{pmatrix} 4\,0\,0\,2\,4\,4\,0\,4\,2\,5 \\ 0\,0\,5\,5\,5\,5\,3\,5\,0\,0 \end{pmatrix}$

Step 1: Determine the center and radius of the parent node. From the training set with $A = u_1, u_2, u_3, u_4, u_7, u_8, u_9, u_{10}$, we determine the center by:

(2.125 0.75 1.5 1.375 0.625 1.75 1.375 1.5 1.5 1.125)

Determine the farthest point in set A to the center from the result obtained above, and using the formula to calculate the distance between n points in the n-dimensional coordinate system, we obtain u_1.

Step 2: We have root node A as the first step. We divide the root node A into two child nodes of B and C. In set A, u_1 is the farthest node from the center of root node A. We obtain u_3, which is the farthest one from u_1. We consider u_3 and u_1 as the center of two sub-circles, B and C where B = Node(A).child1 = $u_2, u_3, u_4, u_7, u_9, u_{10}$ and C = Node(A).child2 = u_1, u_8. At this time, the center of child node B is identified as follows. The center of B = A.child1 is computed with the result:

(1.34 0.5 0.83 0.5 0.67 0.83 0.83 0.34 0.67 0.67)

u_9 is found as the farthest point in set B. The same way is applied to B as C. However, since C only has two children and suppose to determine two neighbors, there is no need to decompose C. In the balltree structure, we draw the root node A and its two child nodes of B and C.

Step 3: We continue to divide the node B into the child nodes where $B.child1 = D = u_2, u_3, u_4$ (u_2 is the farthest point from the center of D) and $B.child2 = E = u_7, u_9, u_{10}$ (u_9 is the point farthest from the center of E).

Step 4: We continue to divide node D and E into the child nodes where $D.child1 = F = u_2$, $D.child2 = G = u_3, u_4$, $E.child1 = H = u_9$, $E.child2 = I = u_7, u_{10}$. The balltree is structured after 4 steps, as exhibited in Fig. 8.

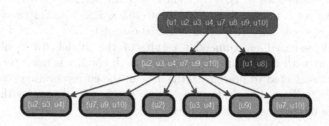

Fig. 8. The structured balltree as an example.

Scenario 2. In this scenario, we calculate the similarity of the user vectors and display a list of the most similar users for the given user.

Taking u_5 as an example, with $u_5 = (4\ 0\ 0\ 2\ 4\ 4\ 0\ 4\ 25)$, the list of users who has the similarity to u_5 as determined as follows.

Step 1: Initialize the values: K = 2, determine 2 neighbors which is the closest to u5 with initialized values of $V = A = u_1, u_2, u_3, u_4, u_7, u_8, u_9, u_{10}$, $Q = \emptyset$, the set of neighbors closest to u5, and $D_T = 0$, since T is initially the root node.

Step 2: Consider T is the root node, so we have $D_T = 0, Q = \emptyset$. Continue with the two child nodes of B and C.

Step 3: To calculate the distance from u_5 to the center of $B = u_2, u_3, u_4, u_7, u_9, u_{10}$ and $C = u_1, u_8$, we compute the distance from u_5 to center of 2 child nodes B (u3) and C(u1) where $D_{u(5)B} = (u(5)B) = 9.85$ and $D_{u(5)C} = (u(5)C) = 6.8$. From the obtained results, we see that $C = u_1, u_8$ is closest to u5, $B = u_2, u_3, u_4, u_7, u_9, u_{10}$ is the farthest node from u5. Since C has only 2 children u_1, u_8 and we set the neighbors $K = 2$, the algorithm stops. The needed list includes u_1 and u_8.

Scenario 3. In this scenario, we calculate the usage of the recommendation and provide suggestions to the new users. We suggest items for the new users from the pre-stored list of user vectors.

Provide ratings for items for the u_5 based on its 2 closest neighbors, u_1 and u_8. The results obtained from scenario 2 for this Scenario include u_1 and u_8. $u_1 = (5\ 3\ 3\ 4\ 1\ 5\ 2\ 5\ 55)$, $u_8 = (4\ 0\ 4\ 4\ 0\ 4\ 4\ 5\ 30)$. u_5 is determined by calculating the mean of u_1 and u_3, the values of 0 are not included in the evaluation formula $u_5 = (4.5\ 3\ 3.5\ 4\ 1\ 4.5\ 3\ 5\ 4\ 5)$.

4.3   The Experimental Results on 100,000 Samples of Movielens Dataset

The work processed the Movielens matrix before being put into the recommender model. First, data are filtering advancement: each user watches at least 50 movies, and each movie has at least 100 users viewing and rating. After filtering data, the matrix result consists of 560 rows and 332 columns. Data representation using a Heat chart in R shows the user's rating in the Movielens set after filtering the data. Proceed to divide into the training data set and test data set. If dividing the data by 80% division is training set, and 20% is test set, the training data set results include 463 users ($463 \times 332 = 45248$ reviews) and a test set of 97 people used ($97 \times 332 = 10050$ ratings).

The balltree-based recommender results of the model are exhibited in a matrix format with a structure of 10×111 (each column is one user, and each cell is a movie selected to present to the user in the corresponding column). For example, Fig. 9 shows consultation results for the first four users, with each user choosing the ten highest-ranked movies.

```
      2                                              11
[1,]  "Blade Runner (1982)"                    [1,]  "Star Wars (1977)"
[2,]  "Silence of the Lambs, The (1991)"       [2,]  "Godfather, The (1972)"
[3,]  "Schindler's List (1993)"                [3,]  "L.A. Confidential (1997)"
[4,]  "Casablanca (1942)"                       [4,]  "Secrets & Lies (1996)"
[5,]  "Raiders of the Lost Ark (1981)"          [5,]  "Leaving Las Vegas (1995)"
[6,]  "Monty Python and the Holy Grail (1974)"  [6,]  "Titanic (1997)"
[7,]  "Big Night (1996)"                        [7,]  "Trainspotting (1996)"
[8,]  "Boot, Das (1981)"                        [8,]  "Good Will Hunting (1997)"
[9,]  "Amadeus (1984)"                          [9,]  "Raiders of the Lost Ark (1981)"
[10,] "Twelve Monkeys (1995)"                   [10,] "Apt Pupil (1998)"

      38                                             49
[1,]  "Star Wars (1977)"                        [1,]  "Godfather, The (1972)"
[2,]  "Fargo (1996)"                            [2,]  "Graduate, The (1967)"
[3,]  "Good Will Hunting (1997)"                [3,]  "Big Night (1996)"
[4,]  "Silence of the Lambs, The (1991)"        [4,]  "Leaving Las Vegas (1995)"
[5,]  "Shawshank Redemption, The (1994)"        [5,]  "Alien (1979)"
[6,]  "Postino, Il (1994)"                      [6,]  "Boot, Das (1981)"
[7,]  "Leaving Las Vegas (1995)"                [7,]  "Taxi Driver (1976)"
[8,]  "Secrets & Lies (1996)"                   [8,]  "Dr. Strangelove or: How I Learned ..."
[9,]  "Boot, Das (1981)"                        [9,]  "Rear Window (1954)"
[10,] "Usual Suspects, The (1995)"              [10,] "Secrets & Lies (1996)"
```

Fig. 9. An illustration of suggesting 10 movies for the first 4 users.

We compare the accuracy of the proposed model with the balltree to the cosine measure (the similarity between 2 users of u and v is computed by Formula 5), a widely-used method in recommender systems [15–17]. The results in Table 2 show that applying a tree structure to a collaborative human-based filter model can improve the model's accuracy.

$$sim(u,v) = cos(\overrightarrow{v}, \overrightarrow{u}) = \frac{\overrightarrow{v} * \overrightarrow{u}}{||\overrightarrow{v}|| * ||\overrightarrow{u}||} \qquad (5)$$

Table 2. Performance comparison in average RMSE, MSE and MAE on 5-fold-cross validation between two approaches

	RMSE	MSE	MAE
UBCF_Balltree	0.9625551	0.9774664	0.7708005
UBCF_Cosine	0.9693691	0.9863076	0.7727980

The figure below shows results comparing the two models' accuracy. The results show that RMSE, MSE, and MAE of User-based collaborative filtering with the Balltree (UBCF_BALLTREE) model are better than these indicators on the User-based collaborative filtering method using Cosine Similarity (UBCF_Cosine).

5   Conclusion

The work focuses on proposing a novel measure that can improve the recommender system's efficiency by combining the recommender system under the user collaborative filtering model based on the balltree binary tree structure. Experiments with **Ball-Sim** on Movielens dataset have achieved a promising performance compared to a commonly-used similarity measurement as cosine. The work also introduced numerous scenarios with detailed steps.

Besides the achieved results, the study's next development direction is to build a recommender system based on numerous different datasets to compare results. Also, there are many algorithms for building balltree trees; the article is expected to begin further studies on balltree-based recommender systems with more diverse algorithms.

Acknowledgment. We want to express our great appreciation to Dr. Nghia Trung Duong, Can Tho University of Technology, and Dr. Lan Phuong Phan, Can Tho University, for their valuable and constructive suggestions during the planning development of this research work.

References

1. Aggarwal, C.C.: Knowledge-based recommender system. In: Recommender Systems, pp. 15–19. Springer, Heidelberg (2016)
2. Adomavicius, G., Tuzhilin, A.: Context-aware recommender systems. In: Ricci, F., Rokach, L., Shapira, B. (eds.) Recommender Systems Handbook, pp. 191–226. Springer, Boston (2015). https://doi.org/10.1007/978-1-4899-7637-6_6
3. Felfernig, A., Jeran, M., Ninaus, G., Reinfrank, F., Reiterer, S., Stettinger, M.: Basic approaches in recommender systems. In: Robillard, M., Maalej, W., Walker, R., Zimmermann, T. (eds.) Recommendation Systems in Software Engineering, pp. 15–37. Springer, Heidelberg (2014). https://doi.org/10.1007/978-3-642-45135-5_2
4. Bauman, K., Tuzhilin, A.: Location-based recommender systems. In: Encyclopedia of GIS, pp. 43–92. Springer, Heidelberg (2017)

5. Ekstrand, M.D., Riedl, J.T., Konstan, J.A.: Collaborative filtering recommender systems, Foundations and Trends in Human-Computer Interaction, SIR Ranking of United States, pp. 1–94 (2011)
6. Aggarwal, C.: Recommender Systems: The Textbook. Springer, Cham (2016). https://doi.org/10.1007/978-3-319-29659-31
7. Isinkaye, F.O., Folajimi, Y.O., Ojokoh, B.A.: Recommender systems: principles, methods, and evaluation. Egypt. Inform. J. **16**, 261–273 (2015)
8. Adomavicius, G., Tuzhilin, A.: Toward the next generation of recommender systems: a survey of the state-of-the-art and possible extensions. IEEE Trans. Knowl. Data Eng. **17**, 734–749 (2005)
9. Herlocker, J.L., Konstan, J.A., Terveen, L.G., Riedl, J.T.: Evaluating collaborative filtering recommender systems. ACM Trans. Inf. Syst. **22**(1), 5–53 (2004). ISSN 1046–8188
10. Felfernig, A., Teppan, E., Gula, B.: Knowledge-based recommender technologies for marketing and sales. Int. J. Pattern Recognit. Artif. Intell. **21**(02), 333–354 (2007)
11. Burke, R.: Knowledge-based recommender systems. Encycl. Libr. Inf. Syst. **69**, 175–186 (2000)
12. Bobadilla, J., Ortega, F., Hernando, A., Gutiérrez, A.: Recommender systems survey. Knowl.-Based Syst. **46**, 109–132 (2013)
13. Dolatshah, M., Hadian, A., Minaei-Bidgoli, B.: Ball*-tree: efficient spatial indexing for constrained nearest-neighbor search in metric spaces. Iran University of Science and Technology (2015)
14. Hua, J., Lianga, J., Kuang, Y., Honavar, V.: A user similarity-based top-N recommendation approach for mobile in-application advertising. School of Computer Science and Engineering, South China University of Technology, Guangzhou 510006, China (2018)
15. Singh, R.H., Maurya, S., Tripathi, T., Narula, T., Srivastav, G.: Movie recommendation system using cosine similarity and KNN. Int. J. Eng. Adv. Technol. (IJEAT) **9**(5), 556–559 (2020). ISSN 2249-8958
16. Gupta, M., Thakkar, A., Aashish, Gupta, V., Rathore, D.P.S.: Movie recommender system using collaborative filtering. In: 2020 International Conference on Electronics and Sustainable Communication Systems (ICESC), Coimbatore, India, pp. 415–420 (2020). https://doi.org/10.1109/ICESC48915.2020.9155879
17. Periyasamy, K., Jaiganesh, J., Ponnambalam, K., Rajasekar, J., Arputharaj, K.: Soft cosine gradient and gaussian mixture joint probability recommender system for online social networks. Analysis and performance evaluation of cosine neighbourhood recommender system. Int. Arab J. Inf. Technol. (IAJIT) **14**(5), 747–754 (2017)
18. Pedregosa, F., et al.: Scikit-learn: machine learning in Python. JMLR **12**, 2825–2830 (2011)
19. Omohundro, S.M.: Five balltree construction algorithms. ICSI Technical Report TR-89-063 (1989)

Fault Diagnosis of Large-Scale Railway Maintenance Equipment Based on GA-RBF Neural Network

Hairui Wang[1], Yuanbo Li[1] (ID), Wenqi Zhang[1] (ID), Yusu Duan[1,2],
and Guifu Zhu[2] (✉)

[1] Faculty of Information Engineering and Automation,
Kunming University of Science and Technology, Kunming, China
{liyuanbo,zhangwenqixxx,duanyusu76}@kust.edu.cn
[2] Information Technology Construction Management Center,
Kunming University of Science and Technology, Kunming, China
zhuguifu@kust.edu.cn

Abstract. At present, the large-scale railway maintenance equipment adopts a diesel engine as the main power plant. Therefore the diesel engine in the event of failure, will seriously affect the large-scale railway maintenance equipment of the normal work. Exploring advanced diesel engine condition monitoring and fault diagnosis technology and looking for practical and effective diesel engine fault diagnosis method, which has already become a research subject widely concerned by many experts at home and abroad. In this paper, genetic algorithm (GA) is used to optimize the parameters of radial basis function (RBF) neural network for diesel engine fault diagnosis, experimental results show the validity of this prediction method, and the accuracy of the proposed algorithm was verified by comparative.

Keywords: Large-scale railway maintenance equipment · Fault diagnosis · RBF neural network optimized by genetic

1 Introduction

Diesel engine's structure is complex, and there are many parts. The relationship between each subsystem is complex, so the fault diagnosis is complex. Typically, a source of the problem may lead to a failure, it may lead to multiple failures. Of course, a fault may be caused by a fault source or multiple fault sources. Therefore, we need to find fault diagnosis method which can scientifically and accurately collect the fault information.

With the continuous development of fault diagnosis, A novel fault detection and diagnostic method of diesel engine by combining rule-based algorithm and Bayesian networks (BNs) or Back Propagation neural networks (BPNNs) is proposed [1]. Wang presents a Bayesian network-based approach for fault isolation

C. V. Phan and T. D. Nguyen (Eds.): ICCASA 2022, LNICST 475, pp. 129–140, 2023.
https://doi.org/10.1007/978-3-031-28816-6_10

in the presence of the uncertainties [2]. Wang presents an adaptive fuzzy PID control method for the diesel engine speed control system that is accompanied by the uncertainty and time variability. [3] dedicated to the optimization of the runner dimensions determined by the numerical calculation [4]. Wang puts forward a bat algorithm based on improved optimization engine fuel system fault diagnosis model of extreme learning machine [5]. However, the neural network still has some disadvantages, such as slow convergence speed, local minimum value, lack of explicit expression between levels, and difficult to determine the network structure, which limits the application and development of neural network in diesel engine fault diagnosis. Based on RBF network, this paper uses genetic algorithm to optimize its network parameters, which makes RBF neural network algorithm have strong global search ability.

Finally, with Germany DEUTZ F12L413F type V-cylinder diesel engine simulation, the fault diagnosis experiments show that the effectiveness of the prediction method, and the accuracy of the algorithm is verified by comparison.

2   Diesel Typical Failure Modes and Failure Characteristics

When the diesel engine is working, it is possible to produce a wide variety of failures, the data was provided by the UK diesel Engineers and user downtime reports Press Association analysis of the results [6]. Injection equipment and fuel supply system fault(27.00%), Water leakage(17.30%), Valve and valve seat failure(11.90%), Bearing fault(7.00%), Piston component failure(6.60%), Leakage and lubrication system failure(5.20%), Turbo system failure(4.40%), Gears and drives fault(3.90%), Governor gear fault(3.90%), Fuel leak(3.50%), Other rupture(2.50%), Other faults(2.50%), Pedestal failure(0.90%), Crankshaft fault(0.20%), Air leakage(3.20%).

Through the analysis of above, it can be seen due to the interaction between diesel engine subsystems, complex relationships, and therefore presents a complex diversity of diesel engine fault, the fault of the main characteristics of the diesel engine: the failure of complexity; fault correlation and relativity; the coexistence of multiple faults.

3   RBF Neural Network

3.1   RBF Network and RBF Element Model

RBF element model having R-dimensional inputs shown in Fig. 1. In Fig. 1, $\|dist\|$ module represents obtaining input vector and weight vector distance. This model uses a Gaussian function as shown in Fig. 2 *radbas* as a radial basis function neural transfer function [7], which n is a distance between the input vector p and the weight vector w and then multiplied by the threshold b. Gaussian function as shown in Fig. 2 is a typical radial basis function, the expression is:

$$f(x) = e^{-x^2} \tag{1}$$

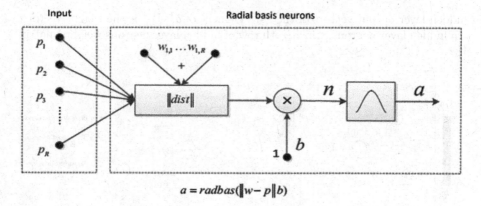

$$a = radbas(\|w - p\|b)$$

Fig. 1. Radial base function artificial neural.

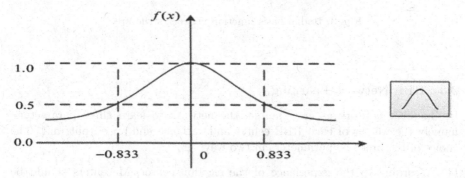

Fig. 2. Gaussian curve.

Center and width are two important parameters radial basis function neurons. Right neurons value vector w radial basis function determines the center, when the input vector p and w coincide, the output of radial basis function neurons reaches a maximum when the input vector p farther distance w, neuron output smaller. Neurons threshold F determines the width of the radial basis function, b is larger, the input vector p while away from the w, the amplitude attenuation function will be.

3.2   RBF Neural Network Model

A typical radial basis function network comprises two layers [8], hidden layer and output layer. Figure 3 shows a radial basis function network diagram, network input dimension for R, number of neurons in the hidden layer is s^1, the output number is s^2, the hidden layer neurons using Gaussian function as a transfer function, output the transfer function layer is a linear function, a_i^1 represents the hidden layer output vectors of the i-th element of a_i^1, W_i^1 is the weight vector i -th hidden layer neurons, which j -th row of hidden layer neurons weights matrix W^1.

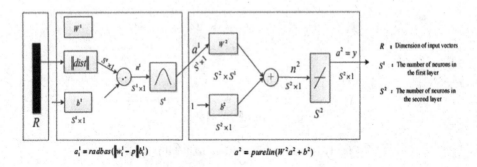

$$a_i^1 = radbas(\|w_i^1 - p\|b_i^1)\qquad\qquad a^2 = purelin(W^2a^1 + b^2)$$

Fig. 3. Radial basis function network structure.

3.3 RBF Network Learning

In Gaussian network as an example, the network to learn three parameters, namely the weight of each RBF center and variance and an output unit. The choice of the first two parameters in two ways [9].

(1) According to the experience of the election center, M centers should be representative. Density of sample points where the center also more appropriate, if the data itself is uniformly distributed, uniform distribution of the centers, the distance between the centers of each set is d, optional variance $\sigma = d/\sqrt{2M}$.

(2) By clustering the sample clustered into M Class, the center is at the center of RBF, the most commonly used is K-means clustering, selforganizing method can also be used in the future to discuss.

If the RBF network classifier seen Parzen window or bit density function method recovery, Fukunagen noted that the usual clustering method given center and a variance is not representative, he proposed the reduction of Parzen algorithm that from N samples, choose r as a standard center should make Kullback distance between two distributions $p_r(X)$ and $p_N(X)$ minimum,

$$K = \int \ln \left[\frac{p_r(X)}{p_N(X)}\right] p_r(X)\,dX = E \times \ln \left[\frac{p_r(X)}{p_N(X)}\right] \qquad (2)$$

wherein, $p_r(X)$ and $p_N(X)$, respectively, by r points or N points of the estimated density function.

After the center and variance RBF function is selected, the output unit weights are available directly calculated from the least squares method. The most common situation is that the above three parameters are used to supervised learning approach to training, such as the use of error correction based on the gradient descent algorithm, an objective function is defined as:

$$E = \frac{1}{2} \sum_{j=1}^{N} e_j^2 \qquad (3)$$

where: N is the number of samples; M is a selected number of hidden units. $e_j = d - F^*(x_j) = d_j - \sum_{i=1}^{m} \omega_i G(\|x_j - t_j\| c_i)$ has three parameters to be learning, $\omega_i, t_j, \sum_i^{-1} \square$, and (with the transformation matrix C_j related).

Given directly below its learning rule (N is the number of iterations).

(1) The weight of the output unit:

$$\frac{\partial E(n)}{\partial \omega_i(n)} = \sum_{j=1}^{N} e_j(n) G(\|x_j - t_j\| c_i)$$

$$\omega_i(n+1) = \omega_i(n) - \eta_1 \frac{\partial E(n)}{\partial \omega_i(n)}, i = 1, 2, \ldots, m. \qquad (4)$$

(2) The center of the hidden unit t_i:

$$\frac{\partial E(n)}{\partial \partial_i(n)} = 2\omega_i(n)$$

$$\sum_{j=1}^{N} e_j(n) G\left(\|x_j - t_i(n)\| c_i \sum^{-1}(n) [x_i - t_i(n)] \right) \qquad (5)$$

$$t_i(n+1) = t_i(n) - \eta_2 \frac{\partial E(n)}{\partial t_i(n)}, i = 1, 2, \ldots, m.$$

(3) Function Width:

$$\frac{\partial E(n)}{\partial \sum_i^{-1} n} = -\omega_i(n) G'(\|x_j - t_j(n)\| c_i) Q_{ji}(n)$$

$$Q_{ji}(n) = [x_j - t_j(n)]^T \qquad (6)$$

$$\sum_i^{-1}(n+1) = \sum_i^{-1}(n) - \eta_3 \frac{\partial E(n)}{\partial \sum_i^{-1} n}$$

In the formula: $e_j(n)$ is the error of the j-th sample time n; $G'(\cdot)$ is derivative of Gaussian function $G(\cdot)$.

4 Fault Diagnosis Method Based on Genetic Algorithm Optimization of RBFNN

4.1 RBFNN Optimized by Genetic Algorithm

Using RBF Neural networks to solve practical problems and generally including three stages [10]:

(1) First creates a RBF Neural network on research issues, and the number of nodes, each layer of the network structure, processing units and hidden connections between base design function;
(2) Combined with the research questions, selecting an appropriate method to determine the topology of the network structure and connection weights between the nodes;
(3) Target performance that can be measured to evaluate the training network. In order to achieve the desired results, you can repeat the process.

Currently, there is a learning algorithm of RBF neural network some short-comings: clustering methods exist must be pre-specified number of categories, and select number of categories would affect the performance of clustering; super-vised learning algorithm is affected by the initial value of the set, and it is difficult to achieve global optimization; some methods and regression-related although to some extent can better solve the problem of the hidden layer number and the value of the centers, but the regression coefficients of selected parameters and width, you need to try or cross-validation, therefore, some limitations exist in the actual application process.

4.2 Fault Diagnosis of Diesel Engines Based on Genetic Algorithm Optimization of RBFNN

Combined with the above, the establishment of an experimental model of vibra-tion signal acquisition and pressure signal analysis system based on the detection system shown in Fig. 4 Working principle of the piezoelectric vibration sensor signal acquisition, while the point sensor signal collection point dead stop after processing the charge amplifier into DASP data acquisition system, and then through the computer signal analysis system data processing, fault diagnosis of diesel engines [11].

In order to improve the reliability of diagnosis, should reflect as much as possible to extract fault feature info extracted dynamic index signal timedomain waveform as the characteristic parameter.

We mainly on the following 5 kinds of diesel engine fault diagnosis: more oil f_1, fuel supply advance angle nights f_2, supply advance angle early f_3, the oil valve wear f_4, injector needle stuck f_5.

The 5 kinds of common faults of diesel engine fault, there is a certain degree of representativeness. Vibration Fault sample collected data and pressure fault sample data shown in Table 1 and Table 2. We use the formula: $x_i' = \frac{x_i - x_{min}}{x_{max} - x_{min}}$, the above data is normalized, but the results are omitted.

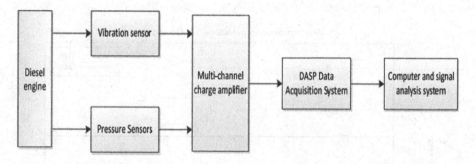

Fig. 4. The working principle diagram of the diesel engine signal detection system.

4.3 RBF Network Training Results

RBF network with the substance of troubleshooting is to conduct sample learning and pattern recognition. RBF network in the creation process, can automatically increase the number of neurons in the hidden layer unit until MSE meeting the objectives set up, so the process of creating a network that is network training process.

Setting training network error precision $goal = 0.00001$, after several tests, will be extended to the constant $spread = 0.9$, will each increase the number of hidden layer neurons is set to 1, the maximum is set to 40 the number of

Table 1. Pressure fault sample data

Fault types		Sample data							
		x_p	$\mu_{|x|}$	ψ_x	x_r	K	I	G	L
f_1	1	6.9323	10.0512	1.5023	0.3128	44.2460	105.8000	7.8742	10.4347
	2	6.9234	10.0635	1.5078	0.3089	44.3450	105.6000	7.8734	10.4456
	3	6.9345	10.0546	1.5067	0.3123	44.2340	105.9000	7.8656	10.4235
f_2	1	3.7209	12.6345	2.1245	0.3482	63.1502	100.0000	4.5352	7.9300
	2	3.7322	12.6234	1.1380	0.3545	61.1345	101.1000	4.5245	7.9289
	3	3.7255	12.6123	1.1325	0.3493	63.5678	100.8000	4.5453	7.9168
f_3	1	3.9520	14.3550	1.5330	0.3265	61.1076	94.1000	4.5010	6.5479
	2	3.9450	14.3443	1.5439	0.3267	63.9999	94.0000	4.4956	6.5372
	3	3.9534	14.3654	1.5346	0.3124	64.1234	94.2000	4.5012	6.5234
f_4	1	2.9580	8.0384	1.5854	0.3937	30.9800	43.1000	3.5345	5.3542
	2	2.9577	8.0478	1.5860	0.3910	30.9756	43.4000	3.5678	5.3467
	3	2.9430	8.0345	1.5862	0.4000	30.9876	43.5000	3.5467	15.3098
f_5	1	4.4000	22.9567	2.9856	0.2090	248.3011	276.0000	5.3567	12.0712
	2	4.3450	21.9870	3.1089	0.2089	249.0000	278.0000	5.3876	12.0876
	3	4.4900	23.0000	2.9767	0.2100	248.9000	279.0000	5.3767	12.1123

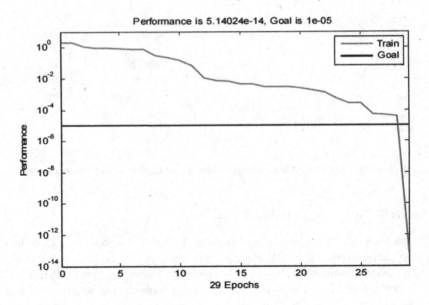

Fig. 5. The training results of RBFNN.

Table 2. Vibration fault sample data

Fault types	Sample data	x_p	$\mu_{|x|}$	ψ_x	x_r	K	I	G	L
f_1	1	6.9323	10.0512	1.5023	0.3128	44.2460	105.8000	7.8742	10.4347
	2	6.9234	10.0635	1.5078	0.3089	44.3450	105.6000	7.8734	10.4456
	3	6.9345	10.0546	1.5067	0.3123	44.2340	105.9000	7.8656	10.4235
f_2	1	3.7209	12.6345	2.1245	0.3482	63.1502	100.0000	4.5352	7.9300
	2	3.7322	12.6234	1.1380	0.3545	61.1345	101.1000	4.5245	7.9289
	3	3.7255	12.6123	1.1325	0.3493	63.5678	100.8000	4.5453	7.9168
f_3	1	3.9520	14.3550	1.5330	0.3265	61.1076	94.1000	4.5010	6.5479
	2	3.9450	14.3443	1.5439	0.3267	63.9999	94.0000	4.4956	6.5372
	3	3.9534	14.3654	1.5346	0.3124	64.1234	94.2000	4.5012	6.5234
f_4	1	2.9580	8.0384	1.5854	0.3937	30.9800	43.1000	3.5345	5.3542
	2	2.9577	8.0478	1.5860	0.3910	30.9756	43.4000	3.5678	5.3467
	3	2.9430	8.0345	1.5862	0.4000	30.9876	43.5000	3.5467	15.3098
f_5	1	4.4000	22.9567	2.9856	0.2090	248.3011	276.0000	5.3567	12.0712
	2	4.3450	21.9870	3.1089	0.2089	249.0000	278.0000	5.3876	12.0876
	3	4.4900	23.0000	2.9767	0.2100	248.9000	279.0000	5.3767	12.1123

neurons. As can be seen from Fig. 5, when training to 13 steps, error precision to meet the requirements. The corresponding input samples, RBF neural network output mode, the failed node close to 1, the non-faulty nodes close to 0.

Table 3. Vibration testing data

Fault types	Sample data							
	x_p	$\mu_{|x|}$	ψ_x	x_r	K	I	G	L
f_1	0.1042	0.0188	0.0063	0.0000	0.0410	1.0000	0.1472	0.1906
f_2	0.0985	0.0181	0.0057	0.0000	0.0410	1.0000	0.1196	0.1613
f_3	0.0791	0.0160	0.0049	0.0000	0.0379	1.0000	0.0975	0.1371
f_4	0.1539	0.0184	0.0056	0.0397	0.0000	1.0000	0.1817	0.2313
f_5	0.1384	0.0218	0.0041	0.0000	0.0611	1.0000	0.1551	0.1859

4.4 Network Training Results of Genetic Algorithm Optimization

Control lead using binary code, parameter uses a decimal encoding genes. Accuracy of approximation error objective function indicated by

$$MSE = \frac{1}{2} \sum_{k}^{N} (\text{yout}(k) - \text{ymout}(k))^2 \qquad (7)$$

where N is the number of samples, *yout* expected output values, ymout of actual output values for RBF Neural network. Choosing roulette method is used to choose. Cross way uses the word cross. In mutation, with some probability negate the control gene; the uniform variation method for parameter real-value variation of the gene. Identify hidden nodes of RBF nerve number, hidden layer node centers, base width and linear output power value, taking the maximum number of optimization as 150 generations, hidden layer node number is 5. Training results are shown in Fig. 6.

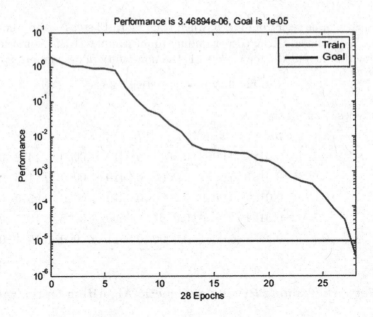

Fig. 6. The training results of genetic RBFNN.

4.5   System Test

To test network troubleshooting capabilities and accuracy of network simulation follows. The vibration test data and the pressure test data (Table 3, Table 4) into which the neural network has been trained, the training results as shown in Table 5.

Table 4. The results of fault diagnosis by different neural network

Types of neural network	Fault types	Actual output				
RBF neural network	f_1	1.0097	−0.0043	−0.0012	−0.0036	−0.0006
	f_2	−0.0325	1.0147	0.0025	0.0060	0.0094
	f_3	−0.0204	0.0394	0.9732	0.0093	−0.0015
	f_4	0.0097	−0.0010	−0.0040	0.9972	−0.0020
	f_5	0.1488	−0.0529	−0.0486	−0.0390	0.9917
GA-RBF neural network	f_1	0.9984	−0.0001	0.0002	0.0012	0.0003
	f_2	−0.0170	1.0060	0.0034	−0.0020	0.0097
	f_3	−0.0187	0.0190	0.9734	−0.0067	−0.0044
	f_4	−0.0022	0.0052	−0.0041	1.0026	−0.0015
	f_5	0.0442	0.0026	−0.0510	0.0112	0.9931

Table 5. Pressure testing data

Fault types	Sample data							
	x_p	$\mu_{|x|}$	ψ_x	x_r	K	I	G	L
f_1	0.0602	0.0930	0.0114	0.0000	0.4196	1.0000	0.0715	0.0960
f_2	0.0323	0.1230	0.0179	0.0000	0.6312	1.0000	0.0420	0.0760
f_3	0.0364	0.1499	0.0129	0.0000	0.6908	1.0000	0.0445	0.0664
f_4	0.0622	0.1694	0.0280	0.0000	0.7278	1.0000	0.0735	0.1163
f_5	0.0152	0.0821	0.0100	0.0000	0.8863	1.0000	0.0186	0.0429

5 Conclusions

The genetic algorithm is a global parallel and capable of random search method for optimizing the function to be substantially unrestricted, do not meet the conditions of continuous or differentiable, just solution to meet the requirements under the Solution Function self- restraint, with global convergence and robustness can be. Thus, genetic algorithms to optimize the RBF neural network, RBFneural algorithm can make a powerful global search capability.

Acknowledgements. This work was supported by the National Natural Science Foundation of China (Grant Nos. 61263023 and 61863016).

References

1. Cai, B., Sun, X., Wang, J., Yang, C., Liu, Y.: Fault detection and diagnostic method of diesel engine by combining rule-based algorithm and BNs/BPNNs. J. Manuf. Syst. **57**(7), 148–157 (2020)
2. Jw, A., Zw, A., Vs, B., Xm, A., Fg, B., Wl, A.: Exploiting Bayesian networks for fault isolation: a diagnostic case study of diesel fuel injection system. ISA Trans. **75**, 276–286 (2018)
3. Wang, H., Wang, L., Liao, Y., Yang, H.: Research on engine speed control system based on fuzzy adaptive PID controller. Manuf. Technol. **19**(6), 1080–1087 (2019)
4. Majerník, J., Gapár, T., Podail, M., Kolínsk, J.: Optimization of the runner numerical design dimensions using the simulation program. Manuf. Technol. **19**(2), 273–279 (2019)
5. Wang, H., Jing, W., Li, Y., Yang, H.: Fault diagnosis of fuel system based on improved extreme learning machine. Neural Process. Lett. **53**(4), 2553–2565 (2020). https://doi.org/10.1007/s11063-019-10186-7
6. Parikh, C.R., Pont, M.J., Jones, N.B.: Application of Dempster–Shafer theory in condition monitoring applications: a case study. Pattern Recogn. Lett. **22**(6–7), 777–785 (2001)
7. Samanta, B., Al-Balushi, K.R., Al-Araimi, S.A.: Artificial neural networks and support vector machines with genetic algorithm for bearing fault detection. Eng. Appl. Artif. Intell. **16**(7–8), 657–665 (2003)

8. Orozco, J., Cruz, J., Besada, E., Ruipérez, P.: An asynchronous, robust, and distributed multisensor fusion system for mobile robots. Int. J. Robot. Res. **19**(10), 914–932 (2000)
9. Coello, C.C., Lechuga, M.S.: MOPSO: a proposal for multiple objective particle swarm optimization. In: Proceedings of the 2002 Congress on Evolutionary Computation (CEC 2002) (Cat. No. 02TH8600), vol. 2, pp. 1051–1056. IEEE (2002)
10. Sun, H., Zhang, Q., Song, X.T.: Fault diagnosis of diesel engines based on RBF neural network. Small Internal Combustion Engine and Motorcycle (2009)
11. Goumas, S.K., Zervakis, M.E., Stavrakakis, G.S.: Classification of washing machines vibration signals using discrete wavelet analysis for feature extraction. IEEE Trans. Instrum. Meas. **51**(3), 497–508 (2002)

Prediction of Chaotic Time Series Based on LSTM, Autoencoder and Chaos Theory

Nguyen Duc Huy[2]([✉]) and Duong Tuan Anh[1,2]

[1] Department of Information Technology, HCMC University of Foreign Languages and
Information Technology, Ho Chi Minh City, Vietnam
anh.dt@huflit.edu.vn
[2] Faculty of Computer Science and Engineering, Ho Chi Minh City University of Technology,
Ho Chi Minh City, Vietnam
ndhuy13@gmail.com

Abstract. Time-series forecasting, especially in a chaotic system, is a critical problem because its application is ubiquitous in several real-world fields, namely finance, environment, traffic, meteorology, industry, etc. In literature, there are many proposed methods for chaotic time series forecasting, but it is still challenging to yield a high predictive accuracy due to the chaotic characteristic which is very sensitive on the initial condition. In this work, we propose a fusion approach that takes advantage of chaos theory to represent time series data into phase space and combines autoencoder (AE) with Long Short-Terms Memory (LSTM) networks. First of all, the task of phase-space reconstruction starts with determining appropriate time lag and embedding dimension for the input time series. Next, autoencoder, which is constructed by LSTM cells, takes responsibility for latent-feature extraction through an unsupervised learning task and feeds the extracted data into LSTM-based forecaster. The experimental results on seven datasets including both synthetic and real-world chaotic time series reveal that our proposed method outperforms other forecasting methods using only stacked autoencoder, LSTM with or without chaos theory.

Keywords: Chaos · Phase space reconstruction · LSTM · Autoencoder · Chaotic time series forecasting

1 Introduction

Chaotic time series prediction is involved in various practical areas such as finance, traffic, environment, meteorology, geology, industry, etc. Chaos is one of the characteristics of time series, indicating the sensitivity of a chaotic system when has a small change of initial condition, as known as the Butterfly Effect. Several studies indicate that chaos theory can be utilized to yield better predictive results in chaotic time series forecasting.

However, it is still challenging to make accurate results in chaotic time series forecasting. The conventional methods using statistical and mathemetical techniques (for

C. V. Phan and T. D. Nguyen (Eds.): ICCASA 2022, LNICST 475, pp. 141–155, 2023.
https://doi.org/10.1007/978-3-031-28816-6_11

instance, moving average, exponential smoothing, ARIMA model), k-nearest- neighbors algorithm, Multi-Layer-Perceptron (MLP) neural networks, Radial-Basis-Function (RBF) Networks and Support Vector Machines (SVMs), do not yield reliable prediction accuracy in case of time series with chaotic characteristics.

Taking advantage of the advances of deep learning in the past decade, several researchers have applied deep neural networks, such as Deep Belief Networks (DBN), Stacked Autoencoder (SAE), Long Short-Term Memory (LSTM) in forecasting chaotic time series. Through experiments in these works it is found out that Deep Neural Networks (DNN) can bring out better predictive performance. Some remarkable studies which apply DNN in chaotic time series forecasting can be listed as follows.

Kuremoto et al., in 2014, introduced a DBN model which stacks several restricted Boltzmann Machines (RBM) and one multi-layer perceptron (MLP) network to forecast chaotic time series [1]. For a specific kind of chaotic time series, namely short-term passenger flow in the China railway system, Zhang et al. [2] proposed a method which incorporates LSTM network and chaos theory in 2018. In 2019, Xu et al. [3] applied Continuous Deep Belief Neural Network combined with chaos theory for daily urban water demand prediction. Yang and Shen, in 2020 [4] proposed a method for chaotic time series forecasting by means of Differencing Long Short Term Memory (D-LSTM) and chaos theory. After that, more generally, the study of Phien et al. [5] in 2021 revealed that LSTM is more effective for chaotic time series prediction than DBN even though both use phase-space reconstruction in chaos theory. Sangiorgio et al. [6] in 2020 also combined chaos theory and LSTM for multi-step ahead forecasting in chaotic time series which brought out good prediction accuracy. Xu et al. in 2022 [7] combined SAE and particle swarm optimization for multivariate chaotic time series forecasting.

Recently, there have been some research works which integrate autoencoder, a kind of deep neural network to LSTM in order to enhance the predictive accuracy of LSTM in time series forecasting. Li et al. in 2018 [8] proposed a fusion approach which utilizes sparse autoencoder to extract features and LSTM-based forecaster to predict water quality. Heryadi in 2018 [9] studied a hybrid method which combines autoencoder and LSTM for short-term weather forecasting. Hoa et al. in 2021 [10] used a hybrid method which combines LSTM-based autoencoder and LSTM-based forecaster to predict foreign exchange rate which provided reliable prediction results.

Inspired by the main ideas from the two forecasting methods ([8–10]), in this work, we aim to apply these ideas in the context of chaotic time series. That means we attempt to combine LSTM-based autoencoder, LSTM and chaos theory to improve one- step-ahead prediction in chaotic time series. The main idea is that the proposed approach first transforms the univariate time series data to phase space and extracts latent features by the encoder from the unsupervised-trained autoencoder. After that, an LSTM-based forecaster is trained to get a one-step-ahead predicted value. To be more general and diverse, our study evaluates the proposed approach on two kinds of chaotic time series datasets including synthetic datasets (Lorenz, Mackey-Glass, and Rossler system) and real-world datasets (daily foreign exchange rate of AUD/USD, EUR/USD, monthly mean total sunspot number, IBM daily stock closed price). We compare the proposed method to three other deep neural network methods, such as LSTM with or without chaos theory, autoencoder with phase space reconstruction. To examine the prediction results, we use Mean Absolute Error (MAE), Root Mean Squared Error (RMSE), and Mean Absolute Percentage Error (MAPE) as performance measures. The experimental results reveal that our proposed approach brings out a better predictive accuracy than the three other methods in terms of the three above mentioned metrics on the seven tested datasets.

The structure of the paper is as follows. In Sect. 2, we provide some basic backgrounds about chaotic theory, LSTM, and autoencoder (AE). In Sect. 3, the approach of combining chaos theory, autoencoder and LSTM forecaster for chaotic time series forecasting is introduced. Section 4 describes the experimental results which compare the proposed method to LSTM without and with chaos theory, and SAE with chaos theory. Finally, the paper in concluded in Sect. 5.

2 Background

2.1 LSTM and Bidirectional LSTM

Long Short-Term Memory (LSTM) was proposed by Hochreiter and Schmidhuber in 1997 [11]. LSTM is an improved variant of Recurrent Neural Network (RNN) designed specifically for sequence data to overcome long-term dependencies and exponential (or vanishing) gradient problem in RNN. The main idea of LSTM is cell state that has ability to keep or forget information from previous steps. The cell state is constructed by three gates named input gate, output gate, and forget gate. Forget gate takes responsibility of remembering the most useful information and forgetting the rest. Both input and output gate control when input signal and output signal should be processed. With this structure, LSTM unit was possible to handle long-term dependencies. Figure 1 depicts the architecture of each LSTM block (cell).

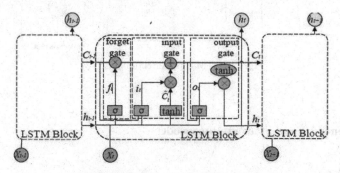

Fig. 1. Long short term memory cell

The activation of each gate is depicted by equations follow:

$$f_t = \sigma(W_f[C_{t-1}, h_{t-1}, x_t] + b_f) \tag{1}$$

$$i_t = \sigma(W_i[C_{t-1}, h_{t-1}, x_t] + b_i) \tag{2}$$

$$\hat{C}_t = \tanh(W_c[h_{t-1}, x_t] + b_c) \tag{3}$$

$$C_t = f_t * C_{t-1} + i_f * \hat{C}_t \tag{4}$$

$$o_t = \sigma(W_o[C_t, h_{t-1}, x_t] + b_o) \tag{5}$$

$$h_t = o_t * \tanh(C_t) \tag{6}$$

where x_t is input vector, h_t is output vector of hidden layer, f_t is forget gate vector, C_t is cell state vector, i_t is input gate vector, o_t is output gate vector, σ is the sigmoid function, W, b respectively denote the weight and bias vector of each gate.

Bidirectional LSTM (Bi-LSTM) [12] is an extension of LSTM model in which two LSTMs are applied to the input data in two diferent directions, forward and backward. Applying the LSTM twice helps to improve learning long-term dependencies and thus consequently will improve the accuracy of the model ([12–14]). Figure 2 presents the structure of Bi-LSTM networks compared to LSTM.

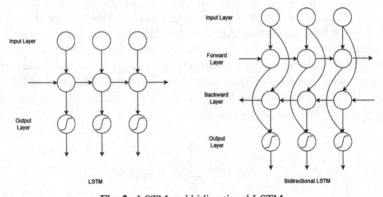

Fig. 2. LSTM and bidirectional LSTM

2.2 Autoencoder and Stacked Autoencoder

Autoencoder
An autoencoder (AE) is a special case of neural networks in which the input is the same as the output. It performs an unsupervised learning task. There are three components in AE including the *encoder*, the *code* and the *decoder*. In AE, the encoder and the decoder may have more than one layer. Firstly, AE compresses an input to a vector representation named code by the encoder. The code is regenerated to the input afterwards. In other words, the output is reconstructed from the code using the decoder. Because of its characteristics, AE is often used to extract latent features, reduce dimensions and

denoise the input data in an unsupervised manner. Figure 3 depicts the architecture of an autoencoder in which both encoder and decoder consist of two layers. The input and output are almost the same, indicating that the code can be represented for input and reconstructed by the decoder. Therefore, after finishing the training step, the encoder is put out separately and used as a feature extractor.

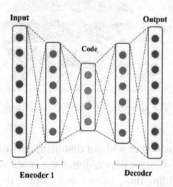

Fig. 3. The structure of an autoencoder model

Stacked Autoencoder

When more than one autoencoder are stacked, a stacked autoencoder (SAE) model is created. In SAE, except input of the first AE, the input of the next AE is taking the output of the previous one. More clearly, considering SAEs with n layers, the first layer is trained as an autoencoder with inputs from training set. After obtaining the first hidden layer, the output of the mth hidden layer is used as the input of the $(m + 1)^{th}$ hidden layer. In this way, multiple autoencoders can be stacked hierarchically. More clearly, considering SAEs with l layers, the first layer is trained as an autoencoder,

Sometimes, SAE architecture can also be applied to forecasting task. In this situation, we need to add a standard predicted layer (for example: fully connected layer) on the top most layer. This is illustrated in Fig. 4.

2.3 Chaos Theory

A chaotic time series is an irregular motion in deterministic system. A common practice in predicting the chaotic time series is to reconstruct the phase space of the system using delay space embedding method described as follows.

Given a single-dimensional time series x_t, where $t = 1, 2,..., N$, the method of time delays can be applied to contruct the phase space [16]. In this method, a corresponding phase space can be formed by assigning an element of the time series xt and its successive delays as coordinates of a multi-dimensional point.

$$X_t = \left\{ x_t, x_{t+\tau}, x_{t+2\tau}, ..., x_{t+(m-1)\tau} \right\} \tag{7}$$

where each X_t is a data point in phase space, τ is referred to the *time lag* while m is termed *embedding dimension*. The dimension of new phase space m is consisdered as the optimal

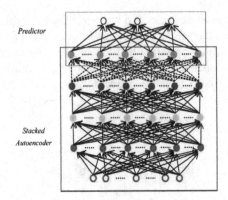

Fig. 4. The structure of SAE for forecasting ([15])

dimension for recovering the object without distorting any of its topological properties, thus it may be different from the true dimension of the space where the object lies. Takens proposed the idea of embedding dimension lower bound, that is $m \geq 2D + 1$, D is the strange attractor dimension ([16]). For each time series, both the τ and m parameters must be estimated.

To select a suitable time delay τ, we can use the *mutual information* method proposed by Fraser and Swinney [17]. To determine the minimum sufficient embedding dimension m we can use the *false nearest neighbor* method proposed by Kennel et al. [18].

Moreover, to check whether a time series has chaotic characteristics or not, we need to compute the largest Lyapunov index. A time series which has a finite positive maximal Lyapunov index is a chaotic time series. There exists a method proposed Rosenstein et al. [19] to calculate the maximal Lyapunov index from a given time series.

3   The Proposed Forecasting Method

Now, we present our proposed approach named AELSTM_C (Auto-Encoder combined with LSTM network and Chaos theory) for chaotic time series forecasting. This approach takes advantage of phase space reconstruction from chaos theory and combines two types of deep neural networks: autoencoder (AE), and LSTM. Specifically, the autoencoder network is constructed simply with an LSTM-based encoder and followed by an LSTM-based decoder. In our proposed model, each encoder layer or decoder layer consists of several LSTM cells.

With the combination of AE and LSTM, the capacity of LSTM to memorize long-term sequence data can be utilized to capture the temporal characteristics and cumulative effects of data. At the same time, autoencoder is used to extract the hidden features in the data and these features are better to overcome the shortcomings of LSTM which is easy to forget recent data, so as to further improve the predictive accuracy of LSTM model.

In training process, the proposed forecasting method performs the following steps.

Step 1: For each input chaotic time series, we determine delay time τ and embedding dimension m by computing Average Mutual Information (AMI) and using False Nearest

Neighbors (FNN) algorithm respectively. Given a one-dimensional time series x_t, where $t = 1, 2, \ldots N$. The vector of m-dimensional phase space is represented as follows, where X is the input data of next step, while the target values are in Y:

$$
X = \begin{bmatrix} x_1 & x_{1+\tau} & \cdots & x_{1+(m-1)\tau} \\ x_2 & x_{2+\tau} & \cdots & x_{2+(m-1)\tau} \\ \vdots & \vdots & & \vdots \\ x_{N-1} & & \cdots & x_{N-1+(m-1)\tau} \end{bmatrix}, Y = \begin{bmatrix} x_{2+(m-1)\tau} \\ x_{3+(m-1)\tau} \\ \vdots \\ x_N \end{bmatrix} \quad (8)
$$

Depending on each dataset, an appropriate data preprocessing method will be chosen afterward. In order to check the chaotic characteristic of a time series, the maximal Lyapunov index would be calculated in this step.

Step 2: The reconstructed data is split into a training part and a testing part with the percentage of 80 and 20, respectively. The unsupervised stage uses an LSTM-based autoencoder to encode and rebuild the input. Each sample in X is both input and target in the autoencoder training process. Then, the encoder is separated and acts like a feature extractor that produces an encoded vector for each input sample from X.

To enhance prediction performance and capture meaningful information, we concatenate the extracted features with the current value and other hand-engineered features like difference, percentage of change.

Step 3: In the supervised stage, the output of the previous step becomes the input which is fed into the forecaster constructed by an LSTM network. The losses are calculated by respectively comparing with the target from Y.

Figure 5. Illustrates the workflow of our proposed method for chaotic time series forecasting.

In testing process, we use the encoder from training process and do not need to retrain. The extracted vector that is generated from each sample by the encoder, concatenates with other features and feed to forecaster afterward to get a prediction result.

We also propose another model for chaotic time series forecasting in which LSTM network is replaced with Bi-Directional LSTM both in autoencoder and forecaster. This model is called AEBiLSTM_C (Auto-Encoder combined with Bi-LSTM network and Chaos theory).

4 Evaluation Experiments

In this evaluation experiment, we compare our two proposed methods (AELSTM_C and AEBiLSTM_C) for chaotic time series forecasting with three other deep neural network methods. As for the test datasets, we use seven univariate chaotic time series datasets including not only synthetic but also real-life datasets.

The Mean Absolute Error (MAE), the Root Mean Square Error (RMSE), the Mean Absolute Percentage Error (MAPE) are used as performance measures in this study. The formulas of the three evaluating measures are given as follows:

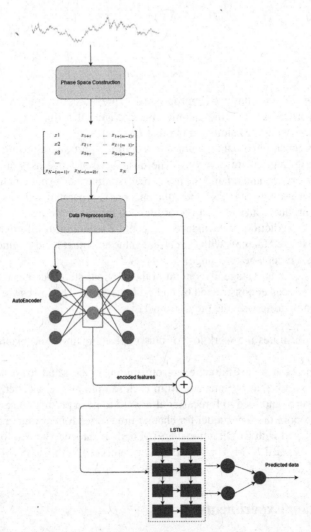

Fig. 5. A block diagram demonstrating the proposed forecasting method

$$MAE = \frac{1}{n} \sum_{t=1}^{n} \left| \hat{y}_t - y_t \right| \qquad (9)$$

$$RMSE = \sqrt{\frac{1}{n} \sum_{t=1}^{n} (\hat{y}_t - y_t)^2} \qquad (10)$$

$$\text{MAPE} = \frac{1}{n} \sum_{t=1}^{n} \frac{|\hat{y}_t - y_t|}{y_t} \qquad (11)$$

in which n is the length of time series, $\hat{y}_t$ is the predicted value at time point t and y_t denotes the actual value in time point t.

The use of these metrics represents various aspects to assess the forecasting models. The first two are absolute evaluation metrics while the last one (MAPE) is a relative metric. The MAPE is a scale-invariant statistic that expresses error as a percentage. The model has higher predictive accuracy when MAE, MSE or MAPE is much closer to 0.

4.1 Datasets and Parameter Estimation

As mentioned before, there are three synthetic and four real life chaotic time series datasets that are used in this experiment. All these datasets have been used in literature as benchmark datasets due to their chaotic characteristics. The detailed description of the datasets is as follows.

1. This dataset is computed from the Lorenz system which is represented by three differential equations as in (12).

$$\begin{cases} \frac{dx}{dt} = a(y - x) \\ \frac{dx}{dt} = xy - cz) \\ \frac{dx}{dt} = x(b - z) - y \end{cases} \qquad (12)$$

   where $a = 10, b = 28, c = 8/3$. In this study, we only use x-axis data containing 1000 points.
2. This dataset is computed from the Mackey-Glass system which is represented by the following differential equation:

$$\frac{dx(t)}{dt} = \frac{ax(t - \tau)}{1 + x^c(t - \tau)} - bx(t) \qquad (13)$$

   where $a = 0.2, b = 0.1, c = 10, r = 17$ and $x0 = 1.2$. This time series dataset consists of 1001 data points.
3. This dataset is computed from the Rossler system, which is represented by the following differential equations:

$$\begin{cases} \frac{dt}{dt} = -z - y \\ \frac{dy}{dt} = x + ay) \\ \frac{dz}{dt} = b + z(x - c) \end{cases} \qquad (14)$$

   where $a = 0.15, b = 0.2$ and $c = 10$. This time series dataset consists of 8192 data points.
4. This dataset consists of the daily closed price of the exchange rate between AUD (Australian Dollar) and USD (US Dollar) from 2nd January 1990 to 31st December 2019. This dataset is denoted as AUDUSD, which contains 7820 data points.

5. This dataset consists of the daily closed price of the exchange rate between EUR (Euro) and USD (US Dollar) from 2nd January 1990 to 31st December 2019. This dataset is denoted as EURUSD, which contains 7820 data points.
6. This dataset consists of monthly smoothed total sunspot numbers from January 1824 to December 2018. It is a widely used benchmark dataset in chaotic time series forecasting. It has 2340 data points.
7. This dataset consists of the daily closed price of IBM stock from 2nd January 2002 to 31st December 2020, which contains 4784 values.

The seven datasets are divided into training-validation and testing parts with the corresponding proportions of 80%, and 20%, respectively. Figure 6 illustrates the plots of seven datasets which the first part (in blue) indicates training-validation part, and the rest is testing part.

In this study, we utilize *nonlinearTseries* [20] and *tseriesChaos* [21] package in R software to determine time lag and embedding dimension for each dataset. Besides, we use Scikit-learn for data preprocessing, and Keras [22] (based on Tensorflow) for training the deep learning models.

Table 1 reports the appropriate parameters that we choose in this work including time lag τ, embedding dimensions m for each dataset, and data preprocessing technique by experiment.

In this work, before feeding to autoencoder (AE), a data preprocessing technique is used depending on each dataset including min-max normalization, zero-mean normalization or just using original data.

Our proposed forecasting methods (AELSTM_C and AEBiLSTM_C) consist of two components, one for each stage: feature extraction and forecasting. Encoder and decoder in AE consist of two layers. LSTM-based forecaster also consists of two layers. The architecture parameters of the two proposed forecasting methods are described in Table 2.

The autoencoder is trained using Backpropagation algorithm with some supporting techniques, such as learning rate scheduler and early stopping. The forecaster is trained using Backpropagation algorithm with some supporting techniques, such as learning rate scheduler, early stopping and dropout.

Table 1. Parameters in phase-space reconstruction for seven datasets.

	Lorenz	Mackey-Glass	Rossler	AUDUSD	EURUSD	Sunspots	IBM
τ	4	4	4	107	59	38	102
m	4	5	4	7	6	6	6

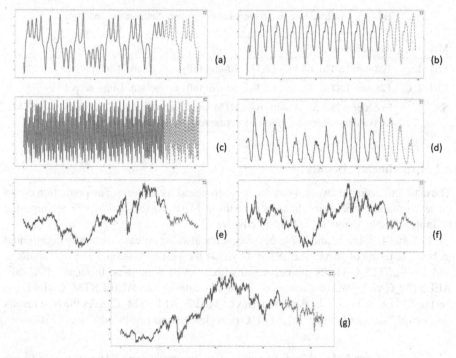

Fig. 6. The plots of seven time series (a) Lorenz, (b) Mackey-Glass, (c) Rossler, (d) Sunspots,(e) AUDUSD, (f) EURUSD and (g) IBM

Table 2. Architecture parameters for two proposed methods

Method	LSTM-based Autoencoder	Forecaster
AELSTM_C	Encoder: 128 LSTM units, 64-LSTM units Decoder: 64 LSTM units, 64 LSTM units	128 LSTM units, 64 LSTM units, 50- units fully connected, 1-unit output
AEBiLSTM_C	Encoder: 128 LSTM units, 64 Bi-LSTM units Decoder: 64 Bi-LSTM units, 64 LSTM units	128 Bi-LSTM units, 64 Bi-LSTM units, 50-units fully connected, 1-unit output

To evaluate the predictive accuracy of our two proposed forecasting methods, we compare these two methods to three other deep neural network methods including LSTM without chaos theory, LSTM with chaos theory, and SAE with chaos theory (denoted as LSTM, LSTM_C, SAE_C, respectively). Notice that SAE_C can be understood as a forecaster contains stacked autoencoder architecture and uses phase space data as input. The architecture parameters of the three comparative methods are shown in Table 3.

Table 3. Architecture parameters for three other comparative methods

Method	Architecture
LSTM	128-unit LSTM, 64-unit LSTM, 50-unit fully connected, 1-unit output
LSTM_C	128-unit LSTM, 64-unit LSTM, 50-unit fully connected, 1-unit output
SAE_C	Encoder: 128-LSTM units, 64- LSTM units, Decoder: 64-LSTM units, 64-LSTM units Followed by: 50-unit fully connected, 1-unit output

4.2 Experimental Results

The experiments in this work focus on one-step-ahead forecasting. The prediction errors on seven chaotic time series datasets in terms of MAE, RMSE and MAPE are reported in Table 4, Table 5, and Table 6, respectively.

In Table 4, Table 5, and Table 6, the best result value on each dataset is highlighted in bold. In terms of MAE, AELSTM_C yields the best results on 5 out of 7 datasets and AEBiLSTM_C yields the best results on 2 out of 7 datasets. In terms of RMSE, AELSTM_C yields the best results on 4 out of 7 datasets and AEBiLSTM_C yields the best results on 3 out of 7 datasets. In terms of MAPE, AELSTM_C gives the best results on 4 out of 7 datasets and AEBiLSTM_C provides the best results on 3 out of 7 datasets.

Table 4. MAE Prediction errors of the five methods on 7 datasets

	AEBiLSTM_C	AELSTM_C	SAE_C	LSTM_C	LSTM
Lorenz	0.002707229	**0.002457134**	0.03475358	0.041782404	1.123163643
Mackey- Glass	**0.000746647**	0.000844273	0.005041643	0.005561022	0.028847694
Rossler	0.003117215	**0.002675147**	0.013910623	0.022279623	0.87368712
AUDUSD	0.003394172	**0.003367457**	0.003457074	0.003466233	0.005352983
EURUSD	**0.004242299**	0.004248584	0.004275216	0.004353091	0.006650565
Sunspots	1.326593694	**1.291807013**	1.365681218	1.844001427	2.648827568
IBM	1.532437417	**1.527935701**	1.547949677	1.547214839	2.318986811

From Table 6, the reduction in the magnitude of MAPE values between AELSTM_C and LSTM_C and between LSTM_C and LSTM can be derived and reported in Table 7. In comparing the AELSTM_C with LSTM_C, the percentage of reduction in MAPE varies from 87.99% to 1.37%. In comparing the LSTM_C with LSTM, the percentage of reduction in MAPE ranges from 96.95% to 32.29%.

Based on the experimental results in Table 4, Table 5, Table 6 and Table 7, we can derive the following findings:

- In all seven tested datasets, the two proposed forecasting methods (AEBiLSTM_C and AELSTM) always bring out the lowest prediction errors and the performance improvement in comparison to the three other deep neural network methods (LSTM_C, SAE_C

Table 5. RMSE prediction errors of the five methods on 7 datasets

	AEBiLSTM_C	AELSTM_C	SAE_C	LSTM_C	LSTM
Lorenz	0.003779549	**0.003233493**	0.051545547	0.064413727	1.365926947
Mackey- Glass	**0.000967249**	0.0010554	0.006046002	0.00676352	0.034668973
Rossler	**0.004590836**	0.00569002	0.026299925	0.04621249	1.045916098
AUDUSD	0.00444350	**0.004426192**	0.004511058	0.004545271	0.006839612
EURUSD	**0.00574289**	0.005749826	0.005796582	0.005851447	0.008764376
Sunspots	1.877174774	**1.830231368**	1.912499436	2.563664491	3.577799998
IBM	2.312525518	**2.30859582**	2.338475677	2.335779534	3.362016134

Table 6. MAPE Prediction errors of the five methods on 7 datasets

	AEBiLSTM_C	AELSTM_C	SAE_C	LSTM_C	LSTM
Lorenz	0.119799658	**0.107294015**	0.67290555	0.824846866	27.04564231
Mackey- Glass	**0.079898069**	0.09816394	0.561337052	0.600053668	3.342857122
Rossler	**0.104063821**	0.126757365	0.646663646	0.948263934	53.52557816
AUDUSD	0.44939974	**0.445757483**	0.458010878	0.457661599	0.700437479
EURUSD	**0.370720357**	0.371291928	0.373560396	0.379574627	0.578685863
Sunspots	2.597493668	**2.559844591**	2.649975593	3.560925701	5.41588127
IBM	1.16278277	**1.159223622**	1.176135408	1.175343294	1.735965376

Table 7. % Reduction of MAPE values between AELSTM_C and LSTM_C and between LSTM_C and LSTM

	% Reduction of AELSTM_C over LSTM_C	% Reduction of LSTM_C over LSTM
Lorenz	87.9923	96.9502
Mackey-Glass	83.6408	82.0497
Rossler	86.6328	98.2384
AUDUSD	02.6013	34.6605
EURUSD	02.1822	34.4073
Sunspots	28.111	34.2500
IBM	01.371	32.2950

and LSTM) are remarkable. This demonstrates that the proposed methods are the best among the five comparative methods over all seven datasets.

– AutoEncoder as a feature extraction unit, phase-space reconstruction for handling chaotic time series and LSTM as a time series forecaster mainly contribute to the improvement of prediction accuracy. It is clear that LSTM_C is much better than LSTM (i.e. LSTM without chaos theory) and SAE_C is better than LSTM_C.
– Compared to AELSTM_C, in some cases, the applying of Bi-LSTM can yield a slight improvement in prediction accuracy.

5   Conclusion and future work

Chaotic time series forecasting is still a challenge because of the extremely complicated characteristics of chaotic time series. Therefore, improving the performance of chaotic time series forecasting is especially important. In this work, we propose a hybrid deep neural network method for the one-step-ahead prediction in chaotic time series which combines chaos theory, latent-feature extraction ability of autoencoder and memorization characteristics of LSTM. Experimental results over three synthetic datasets and four real-life datasets of chaotic time series show that our two proposed approaches (AELSTM_C and AEBiLSTM_C) outperform the three other methods (LSTM_C, SAE_C and LSTM) in terms of forecasting accuracy. Moreover, the experiment results also confirm that chaos theory, AutoEncoder can be combined with LSTM network to improve forecasting performance in chaotic time series.

Deep Neural Network hybrid approach, such as AELSTM_C or AEBiLSTM_C, is a suitable alternative for chaotic time series forecasting. As for future work, we would like to improve our model in some following directions:

– We intend to apply other variants of stacked autoencoder to enhance feature extraction.
– We plan to extend our proposed forecasting methods for multi-step ahead prediction in chaotic time series ([6]).
– We will explore attention mechanism in LSTM ([23]) which can concentrate on influential data points in chaotic time series forecasting.

References

1. Kuremoto, T., Obayashiand, M., Kobayashi, K., Hirata, T. and Mabu, S.: Forecasting chaotic time series data by DBNs. In: 7th International Congress on Image and Signal Processing (2014)
2. Zhang, Y., Zhu, J., Zhang, J.: Short-term passenger flow forecasting based on phase space reconstruction and LSTM. In: Jia, L., Qin, Y., Suo, J., Feng, J., Diao, L., An, M. (eds.) EITRT 2017, LNEE, vol. 482, pp. 679–688. Springer, Singapore (2018). https://doi.org/10.1007/978-981-10-7986-3_69
3. Xu, Y., Zhang, J., Long, Z., Lv, M.: Daily urban water demand forecasting based on chaotic theory and continuous deep belief neural network. Neural Process. Lett. **50**(2), 1173–1189 (2018). https://doi.org/10.1007/s11063-018-9914-5
4. Yang, C.H., Shen, H.Y.: Analysis and prediction of chaotic time series based on deep learning neural networks. In: International Conference on System Science and Engineering (ICSSE), Kagawa, Japan, pp. 1–9 (2020)

5. Phien, N.N., Anh, D.T., Platos, J.: A comparison between deep belief network and LSTM in chaotic time series forecasting. In: Proceedings of International Conference on Machine Learning and Machine Intelligence (MLMI), HangZhou, China, pp. 157–163 (2021)
6. Sangiorgio, M., Dercole, F.: Robustness of LSTM neural networks for multi-step forecasting of chaotic time series. Chaos, Solitons Fractals, vol. 139, p. 110045 (2020)
7. Xu, X., Ren, W.: A hybrid model of stacked autoencoder and modified particle swarm optimization for multivariate chaotic time series forecasting. Appl. Soft Comput. **116**, 108321 (2022)
8. Li, Z., Peng, F., Niu, B., Li, G., Wu, J., Miao, Z.: Water quality prediction model combining sparse auto-encoder and LSTM network. IFAC Pap. Online **51**(17), 831–836 (2018)
9. Heryadi, Y.: Learning hierarchical weather data representtion for short-term weather forecasting using autoencoder and Long Short Term Memory models. In: Proceedings of ACIIDS, pp. 373–384 (2019)
10. Hoa, T.V., Anh, D.T., Hieu, D.N.: Foreign exchange rate forecasting using autoencoder and LSTM networks. In: Proceedings of International Conference on Intelligent Information Technology (ICIIT), pp. 22–28. ACM, Ho Chi Minh City (2021)
11. Hochreiter, S., Schmidhuber, J.: Long short-term memory. Neural Comput. **9**(8), 1735–1780 (1997)
12. Schuster, M., Paliwal, K.K.: Bidirectional recurrent neural networks. IEEE Trans. Signal Process **45**, 2673–2681 (1997)
13. Siami-Namini, S., Tavakoli, N., Namin, A.S.: A comparative analysis of forecasting financial time series using ARIMA, LSTM, and BiLSTM. In: Proceedings of IEEE BigData, Los Angeles, CA, USA (2019)
14. Abduljabbar, R.L., Dia, H, Tsai, P.W.: Unidirectional and bidirectional LSTM models for short term traffic prediction. J. Adv. Transp. 589075, 16 (2021)
15. Lv, Y., Duan, Y., Kang, W., Li, Z., Wang, F.Y.: Traffic flow prediction with big data: a deep learning approach. IEEE Trans. Intell. Transp. Syst. **16**(2), 865–873 (2015)
16. Takens, F.: Detecting strange attractors in turbulence. In: Rand, D., Young, L.-S. (eds.) Dynamical Systems and Turbulence, Warwick 1980. LNM, vol. 898, pp. 366–381. Springer, Heidelberg (1981). https://doi.org/10.1007/BFb0091924
17. Fraser, A.M., Swinney, H.L.: Independent coordinates for strange attractors from mutual information. Phys. Rev. A **33**(2), 1134–1140 (1986)
18. Kennel, M.B., Brown, R., Abarbanel, H.D.I.: Determining embedding dimension for phase-space reconstruction using a geometrical construction. Phys. Rev. A **45**(6), 3403–3411 (1992)
19. Rosenstein, M.T., Collins, J.J., Luca, C.J.D.: Reconstruction expansion as a geometry- based framework for choosing proper delay times. PHYSICA D **73**, 82–98 (1994)
20. NonlinearTseries in R. https://cran.r-project.org/web/packages/nonlinearTseries. Accessed 2021
21. tseriesChaos in R. https://cran.r-project.org/web/packages/tseriesChaos/tseries. Accessed 2021
22. Cholett, F.: Keras. http://keras.io. Accessed 2021
23. Du, S., Li, T., Yang, Y., Horng, S.J.: Multivariate time series forecasting via attention- based encoder-decoder framework. Neuro Comput. **388**, 269–279 (2020)

An Approach to Selecting Students Taking Provincial and National Excellent Student Exams

Cam Ngoc Thi Huynh[2,3], Hiep Van Nguyen[1(✉)], Phuoc Vinh Tran[1,2(✉)],
Diu Ngoc Thi Ngo[1], Trung Vinh Tran[4(✉)], and Hong Thi Nguyen[1]

[1] Thudaumot University (TDMU), Thu Dau Mot, Binhduong, Vietnam
{hiepnv,phuoctv,diuntn,hongnt.ktcn}@tdmu.edu.vn,
Phuoc.gis@gmail.com
[2] Institute of Applied Mechanics and Informatics, Ho Chi Minh City, Vietnam
[3] Graduate University of Science and Technology, Ha Noi, Vietnam
[4] Fayetteville State University, Fayetteville, NC, USA
ttran1@uncfsu.edu

Abstract. The provincial and national excellent student exams reserved for Vietnam high schools are organized every year. These exams are the opportunities of high schools to acquire achievements. The problem to be solved by schools is how to select students for excellent student team in each discipline. This research considers that the students of the performance similar to winners in recent years are more likely to win prize. Mathematically, each student or winner is represented as a vector of performance of which features are influenced by the learning and non-learning factors. The vectors representing winners of earlier exams form winner-domain which is determined by its centroid, limiting distance, and limiting tendency. The students from classes are selected for the team of a discipline when their performance vectors are within the winner-domain of the discipline.

Keywords: Excellent student exam · Student selection · Student performance · Performance features · High school education

1 Introduction

In Vietnam, excellent student exams are organized to award prizes at provincial and national levels every year. Several provincial or gifted high schools founded gifted classes to deeply train selected students in each discipline. Every year, each school selects excellent students to form discipline teams for provincial and national exams. The selection is being created based on students' learning outcomes and teachers' perceptibility. The problem to reveal is how to objectively select students for teams.

The idea is that the students of performance features similar to prize-winners in a discipline are most likely to win prize of the discipline. This research approaches the theory of machine learning to selecting students of competency and academic tendency

C. V. Phan and T. D. Nguyen (Eds.): ICCASA 2022, LNICST 475, pp. 156–161, 2023.
https://doi.org/10.1007/978-3-031-28816-6_12

convenient for excellent student exams. Each student or winner is mathematically represented as a vector of performance. For a discipline of a high school, the students of performance similar to winners' performance are selected for excellent student team.

The paper is structured as follows. The next section refers to the context of the research and the related works. The third section divides the features influencing student performance into learning and non-learning factors and mathematically represent the performance as a vector of features. The fourth section applies the method of supervised machine learning to form winner-domain and select students for teams taking excellent student exams. Finally, the fifth section summarizes the contents of the research as well as the difficulty in fact.

2 Context and Related Works

2.1 Context

The excellent student exams are outstanding events of Vietnamese Education sector, every year. The national and provincial exams are not only interested by gifted high schools, but also by other high schools. The schools' leaders expect to congratulate prize-winners from the teams of their schools because these wins significantly contribute to the achievements of the school. This view results in the strong investment of schools in selecting and training students for teams. The students of good performance in the discipline are more likely to win prizes at the exams.

Just at the beginning of each academic year, high schools select excellent students from 10th, 11th, and 12th grades of the disciplines as Information Technology, English language, Geography, etc. to form teams in each discipline. The teachers of each discipline select students for their teams by feeling based on learning outcomes, skills and attitude in learning of the students. The students of teams are taught with specific curricula to take the exams at the end of academic year. Consequently, the selection of students for teams plays an important role in the win at exams.

2.2 Related Works

In recent year, the educational data exploitation is a topic attracting several authors to research for various purposes, specially for improving teaching quality, organizing classroom, intervening student performance early [1–4]. The works focus on the factors influencing the performance of students. Several authors have tried to identify and find out the factors impacting on student performance [2, 3]. They analyze the factors influencing student performance in classroom learning before and after course commencement [2].

Some authors consider that the features of knowledge, individual skills and attitude in learning are the factors influencing student performance [5, 6]. The student's knowledge concerns the teaching of previous school, neighborhood, and age [2]. The student's skills and attitude as self-motivation [7], self-confidence [8], self-reliance [8], self-finding [9], self-investigation [9], self-analysis [10], critical thinking [11], creative thinking [12], interaction [12] also influence student performance. In addition, the socio-economic and demographic background, the family, and behavior of students also impact on their performance [2, 13].

The data mining and machine learning techniques have been significantly contributing to the discovery of values hide in educational data. Some authors have applied the approaches of classification, clustering, regression, decision trees, neural networks, nearest neighboring to analyze learning, performance, and the correlation between performance and impacting factors [14]. Others have applied the algorithms of supervised, unsupervised, semi-supervised, reinforcement leaning to discover student models, predict student performance [15–17].

3   Modelling Performance

The features influencing the performance are composed of the learning factors and non-learning factors. The learning factors can be estimated by learning history, while the non-learning factors composed of personality, family background, and socio-economic environment can be surveyed by questionnaires and/or the other information sources from family and society. Mathematically, the performance is represented as the vector of features, where the vector representing the performance of a student is called student-vector, symbolled as follows.

$$x_n = [s_{1.n}, .., s_{i.n}, .., s_{I.n}]^T = [s_{1.n}; ..; s_{2.i}; ..; s_{I.n}]$$

where:
   $x_n | n = 1, 2, \ldots$: the student-vector of the student n.
   $s_{i.n} | i = 1, 2, \ldots, I$: the feature i of the student n.

The winners of national or provincial excellent student exams in the same discipline are similar in performance [2]. This idea infers that the students of performance similar to winners are more likely to win prize. In this research, the students of the performance similar to the performance of winners in a discipline are selected to be continuously trained for taking the next exams in the discipline. Mathematically, all winner-vectors representing the performance of the winners in the same discipline form the performance domain of the winners in the discipline, called winner-domain; the students who have their performance vectors within winner-domain are selected for team.

4   Selecting Students for Taking Excellent Student Exams

4.1   The Mathematical Features of Winner-Domain

The winner-domain of a discipline is determined by three mathematical features, including the domain centroid, the limiting distance, and the limiting tendency. The domain centroid is the centroid vector of the winner-domain, the limiting distance is the maximal distance from the domain centroid to all vectors of the domain, the limiting tendency is the maximal angle formed by the domain centroid with all vectors of the domain. The following process determines the mathematical features of a winner-domain.

Input: the winner-domain of a discipline is represented as the set W of the winner-vectors of the discipline.

Output: the centroid vector w_c, the limiting distance $d_{\lim}$, and the limiting tendency $\theta_{\lim}$ of the winner-domain W.

- *Step 1:* Define $W = \{w_1, .., w_n, .., w_N\}$ is the winner-domain, where each winner-vector is represented as $w_n = [s_{1.n}, .., s_{i.n}, .., s_{I.n}]^T = [s_{1.n}; ..; s_{i.n}; ..; s_{I.n}]$ which is the vector of the variables of features $s_{i.n}|i = 1, .., I; n = 1, .., N$
- *Step 2:* Determine the centroid w_c of the vector set W.

  The centroid $w_c = [s_{1.c}; ..; s_{i.c}; ..; s_{I.c}]$ of the vector set W is determined by:

$$s_{i.c} = \frac{\sum_{n=1}^{N} s_{i.n}}{N} | i = 1, 2, .., I$$

- *Step 3:* Determine the limiting distance $d_{\lim} = (d_n)_{\max} = (d(w_c, w_n))_{\max}$ of the vector set W.

  The distance $d_n = d(w_c, w_n)$ from the centroid w_c to the vector $w_n|n = 1, 2, .., N$ is defined by Euclidean distance as follows.

$$d_n = d(w_c, w_n) = \sqrt{(s_{1.c} - s_{1.n})^2 + .. + (s_{i.c} - s_{i.n})^2 + .. + (s_{I.c} - s_{I.n})^2}$$

- *Step 4:* Determine the limiting tendency-angle $\cos \theta_{\lim} = (\cos \theta_n)_{\min} = (\cos(w_c, w_n))_{\min}$ of the vectors in the vector set W.

  The tendency-angle θ_n of a vector w_n, which is the angle formed by the centroid w_c and the vector $w_n|n = 1, 2, .., N$, is determined by:

$$\cos \theta_n = \cos(w_c, w_n) = \frac{w_c.w_n}{|w_c||w_n|} = \frac{s_{1.c}s_{1.n} + .. + s_{i.c}s_{i.n} + .. + s_{I.c}s_{I.n}}{\sqrt{(s_{1.c})^2 + .. + (s_{I.c})^2}\sqrt{(s_{1.n})^2 + .. + (s_{I.n})^2}}$$

4.2 The Selection of Students for Excellent Student Team

All students in a discipline of school may be the candidates for the excellent student team in the discipline. Each candidate is represented as a performance vector of features. The following algorithm indicates the candidates of the performance similar to winners to be selected for the gifted class or the team taking national and provincial excellent student exams.

Input:

- The winner-domain features w_c, $d_{\lim}$, and $\theta_{\lim}$;
- The vector set $X = \{x_1, .., x_j, .., x_J\}$ represents candidates of whom the performance features are collected early.

Output: The vector set $Y = \{y_1, .., y_k, .., y_K\}$ represents the excellent candidates selected from the set X.

- *Step 5:* Calculate the distances d_j from x_j to the centroid w_c of the winner-domain for $j = 1, .., J$.

$$d_j = d(w_c, x_j) = \sqrt{(s_{1.c} - s_{1.j})^2 + .. + (s_{i.c} - s_{i.j})^2 + .. + (s_{I.c} - s_{I.j})^2}$$

- *Step 6:* Calculate the tendency-angle θ_j between the vector x_j and the centroid w_c of the winner-domain for $j = 1, .., J$.

$$\cos \theta_j = \cos(w_c, x_j) = \frac{s_{1.c}s_{1.j} + .. + s_{i.c}s_{i.j} + .. + s_{I.c}s_{I.j}}{\sqrt{(s_{1.c})^2 + .. + (s_{I.c})^2}\sqrt{(s_{1.j})^2 + .. + (s_{I.j})^2}}$$

- *Step 7:* Compare d_j with $d_{\lim}$ and θ_j with $\theta_{\lim}$.

  - If $(d_j - \delta d_{\lim} \leq 0) \wedge (\cos \theta_{\lim} - \delta \cos \theta_j \leq 0)$, then $x_j \mapsto y_k \in Y | j = 1, 2, .., J; k = 1, 2, .., K$
  - If $(d_j - \delta d_{\lim} > 0) \vee (\cos \theta_{\lim} - \delta \cos \theta_j > 0)$, then reject this candidate.

  where δ is an arbitrary number estimated by the number of students of the gifted class or the team.

5   Conclusion

This research approached supervised machine learning techniques to selecting excellent students of a high school for teams taking excellent student exams. The approach represented each student as a performance vector of features. The performance vectors of winners in a discipline are structured as the performance domain of winners defined by the domain-centroid, the limiting distance, and the limiting tendency. The student selected for the team has the performance vector within winner-domain, i.e. the distance from the student-vector to the domain-centroid is less than the limiting distance and the tendency of the student-vector is less than the limiting tendency.

The article presents the process selecting excellent students for the teams taking provincial and national excellent student exams in each discipline. The approach is being experimentally applied at a Gifted High School in Kiengiang province - Vietnam to form the team in the discipline of information technology for the next provincial and national excellent student exams. In fact, the data collection of non-learning factors of winners and students is difficult to completely carry out in the first instance. The methods for collecting the data of non-learning factors will be continuously discussed.

References

1. Romero, C.O., Ventura, S.A.: Educational data mining: a review of the state of the art. IEEE Trans. Syst. Man Cybern. Part C Appl. Rev. **40**(6), 601–618 (2010)
2. Khan, A., Ghosh, S.K.: Student performance analysis and prediction in classroom learning: a review of educational data mining studies. Educ. Inf. Technol. **26**(1), 205–240 (2020). https://doi.org/10.1007/s10639-020-10230-3
3. Alturki, S., Alturki, N.: Using educational data mining to predict students' academic performance for applying early interventions. J. Inf. Technol. Educ.: Innov. Pract. **20**(2021), 121–137 (2021)
4. Şahin, M., Yurdugül, H.: Educational data mining and learning analytics: past, present and future. Bartın Univ. J. Fac. Educ. **9**(1), 121–131 (2020)

5. Nguyen, H.T., Tran, A.V.T., Nguyen, T.A.T., Vo, L.T., Tran, P.V.: Multivariate cube for representing multivariable data in visual analytics. In: Cong Vinh, P., Tuan Anh, L., Loan, N., Vongdoiwang Siricharoen, W. (eds.) Context-Aware Systems and Applications. LNICST, vol. 193, pp. 91–100. Springer, Cham (2016). https://doi.org/10.1007/978-3-319-56357-2_10
6. Nguyen, H.T., Tran, A.V.T., Nguyen, T.A.T., Vo, L.T., Tran, P.V.: Multivariate cube integrated retinal variable to visually represent multivariable data. EAI Endors. Trans. Context-Aware Syst. Appl. **4**(12), 1–8 (2017)
7. Druckman, D., Ebner, N.: Discovery learning in management education: design and case analysis. J. Manage. Educ. 1–28 (2017)
8. Ramdhani, M.R.: Discovery learning with scientific approach on geometry. J. Phys. Conf. Ser. **895** (2017)
9. Suwandari, S., Ibrahim, M., Widodo, W.: Application of discovery learning to train the creative thinking skills of elementary school student. Int. J. Innov. Sci. Res. Technol. **4**(12), 410–417 (2019)
10. Nguyen, H.T.: A model representing visually multivariable spatio-temporal data. Doctor of Philosophy, The faculty of Computer Science, University of Information Technology - Vietnam National University in Hochiminh City (2020)
11. Yuliani, K., Saragih, S.: The development of learning devices based guided discovery model to improve understanding concept and critical thinking mathematically ability of students at Islamic junior high school of medan. J. Educ. Pract. **6**(24), 116–128 (2015)
12. Simamora, R.E., Saragih, S., Hasratuddin: Improving students' mathematical problem solving ability and self-efficacy through guided discovery learning in local culture context. Int. Electron. J. Math. Educ. **14**(1), 61–72 (2019)
13. Zhang, X., Sun, G., Pan, Y., Sun, H., He, Y., Tan, J.: Students performance modeling based on behavior pattern. J. Ambient. Intell. Humaniz. Comput. **9**(5), 1659–1670 (2018). https://doi.org/10.1007/s12652-018-0864-6
14. Patil, J.M., Gupta, D.S.R.: Analytical review on various aspects of educational data mining and learning analytics. In: 2019 International Conference on Innovative Trends and Advances in Engineering and Technology (ICITAET), pp. 170–177. IEEE (2019)
15. Hashim, A.S., Awadh, W.A., Hamoud, A.K.: Student performance prediction model based on supervised machine learning algorithms. In: 2nd International Scientific Conference of Al-Ayen University, vol. 928, p. 032019. IOP Publishing (2020)
16. Li, N., Matsuda, N., Cohen, W.W., Koedinger, K.R.: A machine learning approach for automatic student model discovery. In: The 4th International Conference on Educational Data Mining, Eindhoven (2011)
17. Ayodele, T.O.: Types of machine learning algorithms. New Adv. Mach. Learn. **3**, 19–48 (2010)

Safe Interaction Between Human and Robot Using Vision Technique

Ha Quang Thinh Ngo[1,2](✉) and Dang Quy Phan[1,2]

[1] Department of Mechatronics, Faculty of Mechanical Engineering, Ho Chi Minh City University of Technology (HCMUT), 268 Ly Thuong Kiet Street, District 10, Ho Chi Minh City, Vietnam
nhqthinh@hcmut.edu.vn
[2] Vietnam National University Ho Chi Minh City (VNU-HCM), Linh Trung Ward, Thu Duc City, Ho Chi Minh City, Vietnam

Abstract. In recent years, service robot or assistant robot becomes more and more popular since it appears in most of fields in our lives. Together with the significant development of technology, robot does not only serve the daily requirements but also begin to be a closed partner which could carry the bulky goods for employer, inventory for worker or the heavy luggage for tourists. In this paper, a method to avoid obstacles in the presence of human is introduced. Initially, the idea to autonomously navigate in the crowded environment is based on visual approach. Then, a model of human to reach closely is innovated for autonomous robot. The interactive parameters and the concept of social communication are integrated so that robot could improve its awareness about human. To verify our approach, several experiments are launched in the indoor environment. Three test cases are depicted to imitate the real-world situation. From these results, it could be seen clearly that the proposed scheme is effective, feasible and proper for autonomous robot to avoid obstacles.

Keywords: Safe interaction · Autonomous robot · Motion control · Robotics

1 Introduction

Autonomous robot is a type of mobile robot that is capable of operating on its own, performing tasks without human intervention. With sensors, they have the ability to perceive their surroundings. Autonomous robots are increasingly meaningful in industries, commerce, medicine, scientific applications and serving human life. With the development of robotics, these robots are more and more capable of operating in different environments, depending on the field of applications, they have many different types such as painting robots [1], welding robots [2], lawn mowing robots [3], etc. ocean exploration robot [4], space work robot [5]. Along with the development of requirements in practice, autonomous robots continue to present new challenges for researchers.

The problem of autonomous robots is how they can operate separately, recognize the environment and perform the tasks set out. The first problem is to move, how the

C. V. Phan and T. D. Nguyen (Eds.): ICCASA 2022, LNICST 475, pp. 162–177, 2023.
https://doi.org/10.1007/978-3-031-28816-6_13

autonomous robot should move, and which moving mechanism is the best choice. Navigation [6] is a fundamental issue in research and construction of autonomous robots. In the research association of autonomous robots, there are two different research directions. In the first direction, research on autonomous robots focuses on navigating at high speed due to information obtained from sensors [7]. This is a type of robots which is capable of operating in both indoor and outdoor environments. It requires the greatly computing power, and is equipped with a high-sensitivity sensor and a large measuring range to be able to control the robot to move at high speed, in environments with complex terrain. For the second direction, it is to solve the problems of autonomous robots that are only used to operate in the room environment [8]. They have a simpler structure than the above type, as well as these robots perform simple tasks.

Navigation challenges for autonomous robots are divided into two categories such global problems and local problems. In the global challenges [9], the working environment of the robot is completely determined, the path and obstacles are completely known in advance. In the local challenges [10], the operating environment of the robot is unknown or only partially known. Sensors and positioning devices allow the robot to identify obstacles, its position in the environment, and help it reach the target.

However, navigating problems for autonomous robots are often not the same as for other types of robots [11, 12]. To be able to steer the autonomous robots, decisions in real-time must be based on continuous information about the environment through sensors, either in indoor or outdoor environments, which is the greatest difference compared to with offline scheduling techniques. Autonomous robots must be able to decide on their own about navigation methods and motion orientations to be able to reach the destination to perform certain tasks.

Navigating an autonomous robot is a job [13] that requires a number of different abilities, including: basic mobility, such as going to a given location; the ability to react to events in real time, such as the sudden appearance of an obstruction; the ability to create, use and maintain an operational environment map; the ability to determine the position of the robot in that map; the ability to make plans to reach a destination or avoid undesirable situations and the ability to adapt to changes in the operating environment.

2   Vision-Based Library and Digital Camera

PCL [14] is a support library for n-D Point Cloud and for image processing in 3D space. The library is built with many algorithms such as filtering, surface reconstruction, segmentation, feature estimation, ... PCL can be used on many platforms such as Linux, MacOS, Windows and Android. To simplify the development, PCL is broken down into several smaller libraries that can be compiled individually. PCL is completely free for the research or development of commercial products. It could be said that PCL is a combination of many small modules. These modules are essentially libraries that perform individual functions before being packaged by the PCL. These basic libraries are:

- Eigen: an open library that supports linear operations, used in most of PCL's mathematical calculations.

- FLANN: (Fast Library for Approximate Nearest Neighbors) supports fast search of neighboring points in 3D space.
- Boost: helps to share pointers across all modules and algorithms in PCL to avoid duplicating data that has been retrieved in the system.
- VTK: (Visualization Toolkit) supports many platforms in obtaining 3D data, supporting the display and estimation of object volumes.
- CMinPack: an open library for solving linear and non-linear maths.

Kinect as Fig. 1 is a Microsoft product based on camera technology developed by PrimeSense, the first products sold in North America on November 4, 2010. Kinect is considered as a peripheral for Xbox 360, allowing to communicate with people through gestures, bringing exciting feelings to Xbox gamers. Kinect's ability to understand human gestures is based on two main features: depth map information, the ability to detect and track human body characteristics (body skeleton tracking).

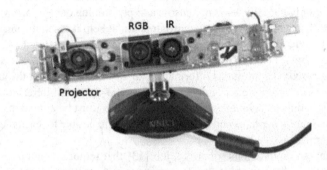

Fig. 1. Inside structure of Kinect camera.

Kinect includes: RGB camera, depth sensor (3D Depth Sensors), microphone array (Multi-array Mic) and motorized tilt angle control (Motorized Tilt).

- RGB Camera: like a normal camera, has a resolution of 640 × 480 at 30 fps.
- Depth sensor: depth is obtained by the combination of two sensors: infrared illuminator (IR Projector) and infrared camera (IR camera).
- Multi-microphone array: includes four microphones arranged along the Kinect as shown in the picture, used for voice control applications.
- Lift angle control motor: is a fairly small DC motor, allowing us to adjust the camera up and down to ensure the camera has the best viewing angle.

Differentiating from the stereo camera technique which uses the same pair of cameras to build a depth map, or the Time-Of-Flight (TOF) technique, that defines the distance by estimating the travel time of the light ray going back and forth, Light Coding technique uses a continuously projected infrared light source combined with an infrared camera to calculate the distance. This computation is done inside the Kinect using PrimeSense's PS1080 SoC chip. This new technology is said to be more accurate and cheaper for usage in indoor environments.

3 Proposed Algorithm

In practice, the working environment of robot is defined by a matrix $M_{m \times n}$. Each component in location (x,y) from origin is performed by 0 or 1. It is assumed that there are N persons who locate around robot, matrix $P = \{p_1, p_2, p_3, \ldots, p_N\}$ with p_i in corresponding to the ith person.

The framework of safety and comfort for human in the social context is launched by 6 functional blocks as Fig. 2 such human states extraction, extended personal space, social interaction detection, social interaction space, dynamic social zone, and approaching humans).

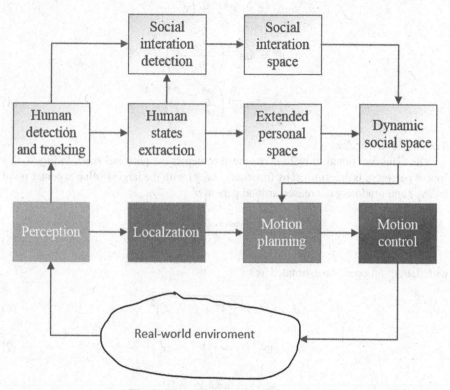

Fig. 2. Block diagram of overall system

A. Comfortable and Safe Zone for Human

Human states play an important role in the framework of human safety and comfort since they provide both spatial and temporal characteristics of the person. Relationship between robot and human illustrates the interactive patterns of the human state including position, gaze direction, velocity, human hand posture, and vision.

The field of view (FoV) from one person is also important to response what human see, where and whom stays in this environment. In this article, it is defined by a vector for field of view H_i for a person p_i which vector H_i has the direction as θ_i^{pv}. FoV for person p_i is 2α which is computed by both left side and right side.

The pose of human is considered as an important source to identify the human's activities. It is essential for robot to improve its awareness. Though, to simplify the input data, the information of human's hand is utilized. The locations of left hand and right hand of human p_i in the xy plane are symbolized by (x_i^{lp}, y_i^{lp}) and (x_i^{rp}, y_i^{rp}). The magnitude (d_i^{lp}, d_i^{rp}) and direction $(\theta_i^{lv}, \theta_i^{rv})$ of vector of hand starting from center point of person p_i to left hand and right hand are illustrated as

$$d_i^{lh} = \sqrt{\left(x_i^p - x_i^{lh}\right)^2 + \left(y_i^p - y_i^{lh}\right)^2} \tag{1}$$

$$d_i^{rh} = \sqrt{\left(x_i^p - x_i^{rh}\right)^2 + \left(y_i^p - y_i^{rh}\right)^2} \tag{2}$$

$$\theta_i^{lh} = tan^{-1}\left(\frac{y_i^{lh} - y_i^p}{x_i^{lh} - x_i^p}\right) \tag{3}$$

$$\theta_i^{rh} = tan^{-1}\left(\frac{y_i^{rh} - y_i^p}{x_i^{rh} - x_i^p}\right) \tag{4}$$

B. Basic Personal Zone

The Gaussian function in 2d is deployed to depict the personal zone. In Fig. 3, this area of person p_i is determined by function $f_i^p(x, y)$ with the largest value at center point (x_i^p, y_i^p) and gradually decreased around person p_i.

$$f_i^p(x, y) = A^p e^{-\left(\frac{dcos\left(\theta - \theta_i^p\right)}{\sqrt{2}\sigma_0^{px}}\right)^2 + \left(\frac{dsin\left(\theta - \theta_i^p\right)}{\sqrt{2}\sigma_0^{px}}\right)^2} \tag{5}$$

with d, θ, θ_i^p, it could be estimated as

$$d = \sqrt{\left(x - x_i^p\right)^2 + \left(y - y_i^p\right)^2} \tag{6}$$

$$\theta = tan^{-1}\left(\left(y - y_i^p\right), \left(x - x_i^p\right)\right) \tag{7}$$

$$\theta_i^p = \{ \begin{matrix} \theta_i^{pv} n\hat{e}'u \, v_i^p > 0 \\ \theta_i^{ph} n\hat{e}'u \, v_i^p = 0 \end{matrix} \tag{8}$$

(x,y) is the location of current point in the matrix $M_{(nxm)}$, (x_i^p, y_i^p) and θ_i^p, θ_i^{pv}, θ_i^{ph} are the position, direction, moving direction, FoV of person p_i. A^p is the selected amplitude. σ_0^{px}, σ_0^{vx} is the standard deviation of the Gaussian function. A set of three main parameters $[A^p, \sigma_0^{px}, \sigma_0^{vx}]$ is utilized in function $f_i^p(x, y)$.

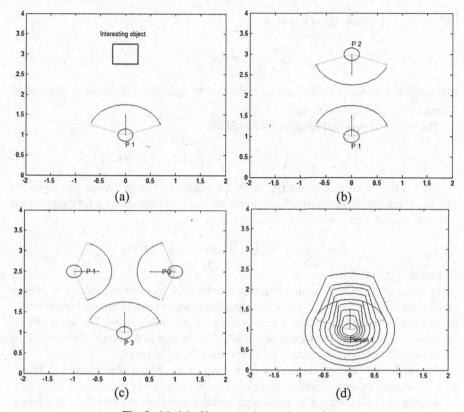

Fig. 3. Model of human and some interactions.

C. Extended Personal Zone

The size and profile of the basic personal zone depends on these parameters A^p, σ_i^{px}, σ_i^{yx}. The environment surrounding a person could be classified into two parts, for example (1) front view including FoV of human and (2) rear view. In the front view, some parameters are well-defined as f_v, f_{front} and f_{fov} consisting of σ_i^{py}.

In order to embed the information from human's hand, the distance is modeled as Eq. (5). $f_i^{lh}(x, y)$ represents the space of left hand, centered at (x_i^p, y_i^p), direction θ_i^{lh} are evaluated as Eq. (3). Then, the parameters are set for a model of left hand $\left[A^p, \sigma_0^{hx}, \sigma_0^{lhy}\right]$ which σ_0^{hx} is determined in advance and σ_0^{lhy} is recognized as

$$\sigma_0^{lhy} = \left(1 + f_h d_i^{lh}\right)\sigma_0^{hy} \tag{9}$$

where d_i^{lh} is a distance from location of human to left hand, f_h is the coefficient of normalization and σ_0^{hy} is known.

Similarly, function $f_i^{rh}(x, y)$ characterizes the space of right hand, centered at (x_i^p, y_i^p), direction θ_i^{rh}. Later, the setting parameters for a model of right hand

$\left[A^p, \sigma_0^{hx}, \sigma_0^{rhy}\right]$ which σ_0^{hx} is known and σ_0^{rhy} is

$$\sigma_0^{lhy} = \left(1 + f_h d_i^{lh}\right)\sigma_0^{hy} \tag{10}$$

where d_i^{rh} is a distance from location of human to right hand, f_h is the coefficient of normalization and σ_0^{hy} is known.

The extended personal space is estimated as

$$f_i^{eps}(x, y) = \max\left(w_1 f_i^p(x, y), w_2 f_i^{lh}(x, y), w_2 f_i^{rh}(x, y)\right) \tag{11}$$

(x,y) is the coordinate in matrix, w_1 is the weight of personal zone and w_2 is the weight of both left hand and right hand. Function $F_{eps}(x, y)$ that denotes for the extended personal zone of every person surrounding robot, is evaluated

$$F_{eps}(x, y) = \max\left(f_1^{eps}(x, y), \ldots, f_N^{eps}(x, y)\right) \tag{12}$$

D. Social Personal Zone

In the social environment, human behavior is influenced by other individuals or objects around, especially the objects with which people are interacting. To ensure human safety, mobile robots need to be aware of the context of social interactions. The space around the robot, social interaction should be classified according to the types of conditions of human-object interaction or interaction between a group of people.

In a real-world environment, it is paid attention to special objects such as televisions, refrigerators and phones in homes, screens in airports or paintings in museums. Depending on the context of human-object social interaction, the robot has to estimate the human-object interaction because that is the key to define the space of human-object interaction.

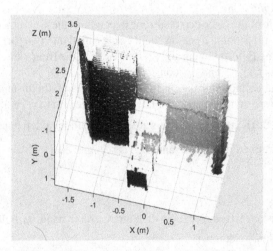

Fig. 4. Modeling of working environment by using PCL library and Kinect.

E. Modeling of Working Environment

To be able to model the operating environment, it must be known the position of objects in the space in front of the robot. As Fig. 4, it should use the depth camera such Kinect which is a pair of infrared transceivers to be able to recognize the position from the robot to the object in space.

(a)   (b)

Fig. 5. Example of depth map obtained from Kinect, (a) practical image, (b) depth map.

Therefore, the usage of Point Cloud Library (PCL) is recommended since it carries out the results with high accuracy, the position of objects on the 3-dimensional coordinate axis is intuitive, making it easy to locate objects. Because of the limited capacity of host computer, it must have to calculate the environment based on Kinect's depth camera as Fig. 5. Kinect's depth map returns a 480×640 matrix with the value of each pixel being the depth value of that point in mm.

The data from depth map (D) is gained and stored into the environmental matrix (M) 480×640. In the x axis, measured values are the depth in cm unit

$$x_M = \frac{x_D}{10} \tag{13}$$

In the same way, these values in the y axis are in cm unit. The unit of size is converted from pixel to cm via the extended angle of depth map

$$y_M = \frac{y_D - 320}{320} * \tan\left(29 * \frac{pi}{180}\right) * x_M \tag{14}$$

In Fig. 6, white color indicates the obstacles which values are 1 while the others are 0. After inserting the estimated values, the environmental matrix M has been shown.

F. Segmentation

Data clustering (or just clustering), also known as cluster analysis, is the segmentation analysis, categorical analysis or unsupervised classification. It is a method of creating groups of objects or clusters. The 2D point cloud in the previous section will require an efficient data clustering method.

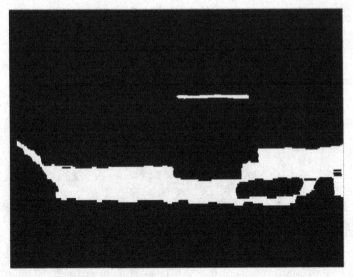

Fig. 6. Result of the image processing data from depth map.

In this stage as Fig. 7, it might use the association of pixel points on the environmental matrix to define separate objects in space in order to create a moving environment for the robot. This process is to filter pixels that have no association with 4 pixels around them to remove noise and get only the object where each pixel is associated with at least 4 pixels around it.

G. Identification of the Bounded Objects

Firstly, it is considered to define some rough contours of objects in space. This contour is derived from the convex vertices of each object and they are joined to form the contour for each object. The contour is a set-in real vector space V such that for two points x, y, hence the line segment [x, y] is also contained in the set. But this contour also includes the concave parts of the object and it occupies quite a large space. So, it must have to find a way to concave this space line to be able to reduce the occupied area thereby increasing the active area. For a given discrete data point, the convex contour can be uniquely determined: find the polygon whose vertices are a subset of the data points and maximize the area while minimizing the circumference. In contrast, the concave shell definition will not define a single polygon: find a polygon whose vertices are a subset of the data points and minimize area and perimeter simultaneously. It is clear that minimizing both area and circumference at the same time is a conflicting goal, and it is therefore possible to define many different concave shells for a given data point.

For the ambient matrix, the algorithm is applied to find the convex contour of the object. To do this, the standard set of Matlab functions was used to return the set of convex polygon vertices in CCW or CW order. Figure 8(left) shows the result of applying the aggregation function to each data cluster presented in Fig. 8(right) to obtain the corresponding convex bodies.

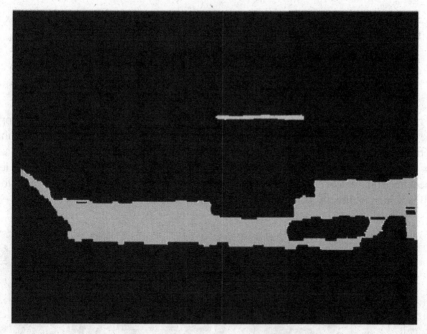

Fig. 7. Segmentation of objects in environment.

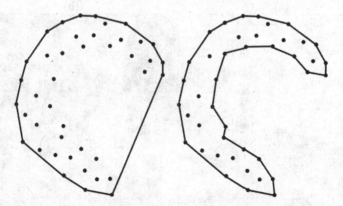

Fig. 8. Differences between convex-hull and concave-hull with 2D points.

The algorithm for calculating the concave shell of a dataset is based on the idea presented by Peter Wasmeier [15], who implemented a function in Matlab called hull-fit. First, it runs the complex function to obtain the vertices of the corresponding convex body and arranges them clockwise. It then performs a distance calculation between all neighboring vertices to find any distance greater than the maximum allowed distance. If it finds any matching distance then it uses the following two conditions to find another suitable point in the data set as the next vertex:

1. Since we know that the contour definition is clockwise, the next selected vertex is the point with the smallest positive angle with which the contour intersects.
2. The distance to a vertex must be less than the length of the line.

4 Results in Experiments

To validate the proposed approach, several experiments have carried out in our laboratory. The type of robot is WDD (Wheeled Differential Drive) which provide the flexible motion and stable movement. It has two side wheels for driving while both front and rear wheel are to balance. Robot turns left or right owing to the differences between left wheel and right wheel correspondingly. The driving actuators are two DC servo motors 100 W which is directly connected to the shaft of wheel.

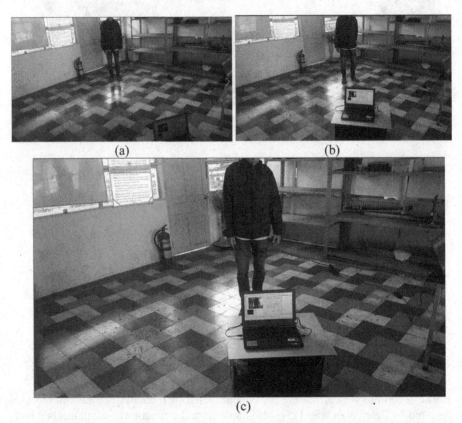

(a)   (b)

(c)

Fig. 9. Experiment in following a human, (a) turn right, (b) turn left and (c) go back and forth.

In this section, there are three test scenarios so that the effectiveness of our method, the feasible application in practice and the popular situation for the assisted mission are proved. Firstly, robot should follow human to support or supervise as Fig. 9. This task might be necessary in the common places such as super market, warehouse, office or lobby of hotel. The wheeled robot could carry the bulky goods for employer, inventory for worker or the heavy luggage for tourists. In order to complete this mission, robot must recognize human via digital camera located on the top. After identifying the target, it could track as soon as possible. However, it always keeps a safe distance from human's position for emergent case.

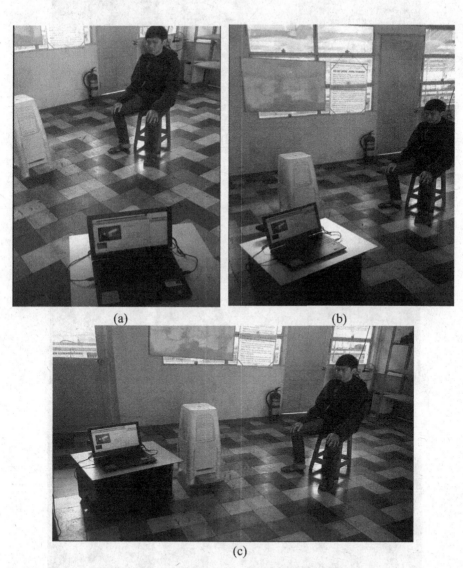

(a)   (b)

(c)

Fig. 10. Experiment in navigating between human and object with the proposed approach.

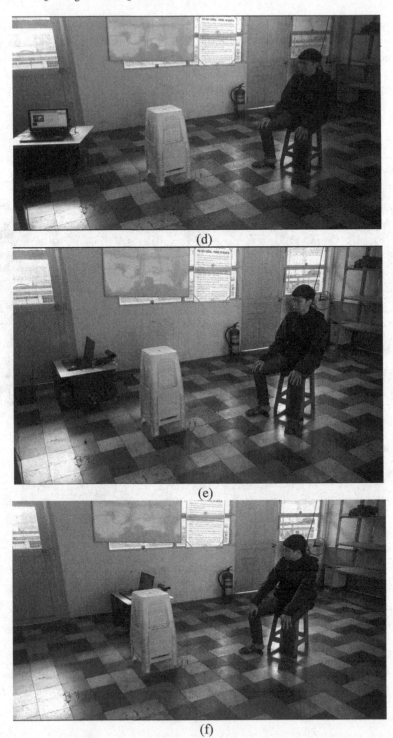

(d)

(e)

(f)

Fig. 10. (*continued*)

In the second test, the proposed method for autonomous navigation is deployed. There are commonly several obstacles, i.e. table, chair or fan in the indoor environment since robot works in the office or warehouse. In Fig. 10, the experimental context consists of some plastic chairs, tables, fan and fire extinguisher. Especially, human stays on the way go to destination. It means that autonomous robot must pass those obstacles and human to reach the target. In this case, it recognizes human and some things through vision technique. It is aware of human presence and adjust the system parameters related to model. Robot must respect the personal zone and does not violate the interactive rules. Also, for ensuring the safety and comfort, it would generate the trajectory to cover both

(a)

(b)

Fig. 11. Experiment in navigating between human and object without the proposed approach.

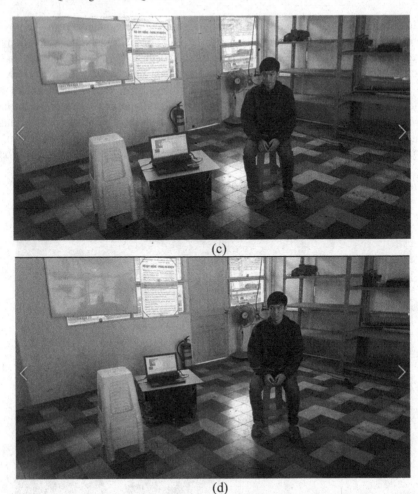

(c)

(d)

Fig. 11. (*continued*)

human and obstacles. The series of images from Fig. 10a to Fig. 10f to demonstrate the entire operation.

To compare with the traditional method, Fig. 11 illustrates the conventional navigation in the front of human. Usually, robot treats human as a regular obstacle. There is no human-aware information in this case. Therefore, this robot moves to destination by coming across human although the comfort or safety could be interrupted.

5   Conclusions

In this paper, a method to autonomously navigate in the presence of human was mentioned. The target control is the robot type of WDD and the target technique is based on vision. The knowledge of human model is embedded into robot so that it could behave socially and safely. The experimental validation on the real hardware has been described in three cases. According to these results, the feasibility, effectiveness and properness of our approach are verified.

Acknowledgements. We acknowledge the support of time and facilities from Ho Chi Minh City University of Technology (HCMUT), VNU-HCM for this study.

References

1. Asadi, E., Li, B., Chen, I.M.: Pictobot: a cooperative painting robot for interior finishing of industrial developments. IEEE Robot. Autom. Mag. **25**(2), 82–94 (2018)
2. Yang, L., et al.: A welding quality detection method for arc welding robot based on 3D reconstruction with SFS algorithm. Int. J. Adv. Manuf. Technol. **94**(1–4), 1209–1220 (2017). https://doi.org/10.1007/s00170-017-0991-9
3. Daniyan, I., Balogun, V., Adeodu, A., Oladapo, B., Peter, J.K., Mpofu, K.: Development and performance evaluation of a robot for lawn mowing. Procedia Manuf. **49**, 42–48 (2020)
4. Bernardi, M., et al.: AURORA, a multi-sensor dataset for robotic ocean exploration. Int. J. Robot. Res. **41**(5), 461–469 (2022)
5. Peng, J., Xu, W., Liang, B., Wu, A.G.: Virtual stereovision pose measurement of noncooperative space targets for a dual-arm space robot. IEEE Trans. Instrum. Meas. **69**(1), 76–88 (2019)
6. Jalali, S.M.J., Ahmadian, S., Khosravi, A., Mirjalili, S., Mahmoudi, M.R., Nahavandi, S.: Neuroevolution-based autonomous robot navigation: a comparative study. Cogn. Syst. Res. **62**, 35–43 (2020)
7. Kalogeiton, V.S., Ioannidis, K., Sirakoulis, G.C., Kosmatopoulos, E.B.: Real-time active SLAM and obstacle avoidance for an autonomous robot based on stereo vision. Cybern. Syst. **50**(3), 239–260 (2019)
8. Wang, J., Luo, C.: Automatic wall defect detection using an autonomous robot: a focus on data collection. In: Computing in Civil Engineering 2019: Data, Sensing, and Analytics, pp. 312–319. American Society of Civil Engineers, Reston, VA (2019)
9. Gharajeh, M.S., Jond, H.B.: Hybrid global positioning system-adaptive neuro-fuzzy inference system based autonomous mobile robot navigation. Robot. Auton. Syst. **134**, 103669 (2020)
10. Gul, F., Rahiman, W., Nazli Alhady, S.S.: A comprehensive study for robot navigation techniques. Cogent Eng. **6**(1), 1632046 (2019)
11. Arrouch, I., Ahmad, N.S., Goh, P., Mohamad-Saleh, J.: Close proximity time-to-collision prediction for autonomous robot navigation: an exponential GPR approach. Alex. Eng. J. **61**(12), 11171–11183 (2022)
12. Malavazi, F.B., Guyonneau, R., Fasquel, J.B., Lagrange, S., Mercier, F.: LiDAR-only based navigation algorithm for an autonomous agricultural robot. Comput. Electron. Agric. **154**, 71–79 (2018)
13. Alatise, M.B., Hancke, G.P.: A review on challenges of autonomous mobile robot and sensor fusion methods. IEEE Access **8**, 39830–39846 (2020)
14. Rusu, R.B., Cousins, S.: 3D is here: point cloud library (PCL). In: 2011 IEEE International Conference on Robotics and Automation, pp. 1–4. IEEE (2011)
15. Thuro, K., et al.: New landslide monitoring techniques–developments and experiences of the alpEWAS project (2010)

Application of the Image Processing Technique for Powerline Robot

Ha Quang Thinh Ngo[1,2]([⊠]) and The Tri Bui[1,2]

[1] Department of Mechatronics, Faculty of Mechanical Engineering, Ho Chi Minh City University of Technology (HCMUT), 268 Ly Thuong Kiet Street, District 10, Ho Chi Minh City, Vietnam
nhqthinh@hcmut.edu.vn
[2] Vietnam National University Ho Chi Minh City (VNU-HCM), Linh Trung Ward, Thu Duc City, Ho Chi Minh City, Vietnam

Abstract. Applying image processing to electromechanical systems is a problem of interest to scientists, in order to serve humans in many fields. To do that, there needs to be a connection between image processing and mechanical construction to create complete mobile cameras. One of the research directions is about mobile cameras, specifically a system consisting of dual cameras that detect and track moving objects, and at the same time calculate the distance from the dual camera system to the target, this system can be application in object tracking robot. In this paper, the research object includes the camera system designed according to the pan-tilt structure, the algorithm used for object detection is YOLO-based on CNN, estimating the distance from the camera system to the object. By means of stereo vision, control the pan-tilt system to automatically track objects.

Keywords: Image processing · Powerline robot · Machine learning

1 Introduction

In the context of the world economy rapidly expanding to promote global competition in all industrial sectors. It leads to optimization of production operations, efficient process management or the integration of multiple functions into a single unit [1–5]. There are various ways to enhance the competition in the market where efficiency in material handling tasks has been given considerable attention. As it increases industrial productivity and reduces labor costs associated with logistics and distribution jobs, most businesses focus on improving various raw material supply technologies. They often use automated guided vehicles (AGVs) for industrial warehouses to overcome the mentioned problems. In [6–8], the authors developed a PID-based algorithm for a wheelless AGV to follow a reference trajectory to prevent oscillations during travel. Some camera apps help the robot track [9–12] - instead of using an infrared sensor - to determine if it should keep moving forward or turn left and right. Compared with simplified models

---

T. T. Bui—Graduate student.

© ICST Institute for Computer Sciences, Social Informatics and Telecommunications Engineering 2023
Published by Springer Nature Switzerland AG 2023. All Rights Reserved
C. V. Phan and T. D. Nguyen (Eds.): ICCASA 2022, LNICST 475, pp. 178–189, 2023.
https://doi.org/10.1007/978-3-031-28816-6_14

and other classical control techniques [13–15], the results show stability at lower speeds. The researchers [16–20] have designed an AGV control system based on the fuzzy PID diagram that helps the AGV trolley to have robustness and stable operation for a long time. Main controller chip like STM32F207 is a powerful microprocessor with high speed, large memory and low cost [21, 22].

The content of this paper proposes an image processing method that is widely applied in all fields today. The technique used is mainly an artificial intelligence algorithm consisting of many layers of neurons. The training sample set is selected in accordance with the actual conditions. After the training process, the algorithm is able to recognize the object within the effective range of the camera. The second part is followed by the presentation of the mechanical design for the camera frame structure. The distance calculation method is described in Sect. 3. Some explanations about neural networks in Sect. 4 are applied in the algorithm. Next, the content of part 5 revolves around object recognition based on some characteristics of the object. Experimental results are presented in Sect. 6. Finally, some conclusions are made after applying the algorithm in practice.

2 Computational Method for Distance

Usually, the method used to extract 3D information is to use multiple images, also known as multiple images method, of which a simple method is stereo vision. This method uses two cameras to reconstruct a 3D scene. To determine distance information, the features of the object in one image (or more) are first matched in another image (simultaneous images of the object from separate cameras). Then, the difference in the features of the object in the two images will be used to calculate the distance.

The stereo vision method requires the two optical axes of the two cameras to be parallel. This method is geometrically illustrated as shown below:

- p and p′ is the intersection of two rays CP and CP′ with the image plane I′I. C,C′ is the center of the lens, P is the object
- f is the focal length of a lens
- b is called the baseline, which is the distance between the 2 lens centers. With the same Z distance, increasing baseline will lead to increased accuracy when determining Z distance because of limited camera resolution
- Disparity D is the horizontal displacement of the same object on 2 images taken from 2 cameras (Fig. 1).

Using similar triangles obtained,

$$\frac{b}{Z} = \frac{b - (d + d')}{Z - f} = \frac{d + d'}{f} \tag{1}$$

We have,

$$Z = \frac{f \cdot b}{D} \tag{2}$$

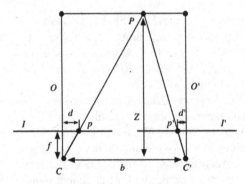

Fig. 1. Geometric description of stereo vision

The parameters D, f, b are calculated through the process of calibrating the camera system, rectification and un-distortion.

In reality, the camera can never be set up perfectly to achieve the frontal parallel as shown in the figure. Instead, we often have to compute, find projections, and correct distortions (rectify). Left and right images so that they align (row-aligned) (Fig. 2).

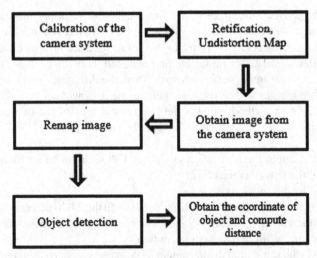

Fig. 2. Block diagram of the image processing method

Stereo calibrate is used to calculate the internal and external parameters of the camera system. These parameters can be measured manually or using the cv::stereoCalibrate function of the OpenCV library. This function returns the internal and external parameter matrices of the camera in which the focal length f and the baseline b are used for the distance calculation step, in addition, the function also returns the matrices used for the rectification, un-distortion process.

Rectification is the step of projecting 2 image planes onto a plane parallel to the line joining the 2 lens centers, each pixel or object in one image can be found on the same row in another image. This process also makes the 2 optical axes of the 2 cameras parallel. Un-distortion is the step that removes radial and tangential distortion.

The functions in OpenCV used for the 2 steps Rectification and Un-Distortion will return the matrices used for the remap process. The remap process uses these matrices on the original pixel matrix to create a rectify and undistorted pixel matrix. The object detection step uses the object detection algorithm to determine the pixel coordinates of the object's position on the 2 images, these coordinates are used to calculate the distance D. Later, the value of f, D and b which are gained, would be substituted into $Z = \frac{f \cdot b}{D}$ to calculate the distance.

3   Convolutional Neural Network - CNN

The CNN network processes the image through a number of layers. Here's an overview of the layers and their purposes:

- Convolutional layer – Used to detect features.
- Non-linearity layer – Use non-linearity in the system.
- Pooling (Down sampling) layer – Reduce the amount of weights and control overfitting.
- Flattening layer – Prepares the data for the Fully-Connected layer.
- Fully-Connected layer – Used for classification.

Basically, in the end, CNN is a neural network used to solve classification problems, but it uses other layers to prepare data and detect certain features beforehand.

Fig. 3. Filter with size 3 × 3

Convolutional layer is the main layer of the CNN network, responsible for detecting features such as straight edges, curves, and simple colors. This is done by using a filter on the image to extract some low- and high-level features on the image. The filter is usually a multidimensional array containing the pixel values. Example: Consider a 5 × 5 image channel where each pixel has a value of 1 or 0. And use the following simple 3 × 3 filter as Fig. 3.

After each convolutional layer there is usually a nonlinear layer. This class uses one of the activation functions. The commonly used function is the rectifier function, so this layer is also called the ReLU (Rectify Linear Units) layer as Fig. 4. This rectifier function $f(x) = \max(0, x)$ will return the values in the image less than 0 to 0. The figure below illustrates the use of this function.

Original Image   Feature Map   Non-Linear

Fig. 4. Application of ReLU technique on image

Pooling layer (composite layer) is the layer inserted between consecutive convolutional layers in the CNN network. The function of this layer is to reduce the spatial size of the array, the number of parameters and computation in the network. There are different types of pooling like L2 pooling, mean pooling, max pooling. Use the filter again. The image below uses a 2×2 max pooling filter onto a 4×4 image. This filter selects the largest number in the part of the image that it covers. In this way, a smaller image is obtained but still contains enough information for the neural network to make an accurate decision. However, many models replace the pooling layer with additional convolutional layers with a larger stride. Also, newer generation models, such as VAEs or GANs, eliminate the Pooling layer altogether.

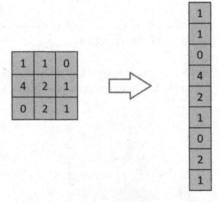

Fig. 5. Example of matrix conversion

The flattening layer is the layer used to prepare the input data of the fully-connected layer. Since neural networks receive data in one dimension as an array of values, this layer uses the data passed from the pooling layer or convolutional layer and compresses the matrices into 1-dimensional arrays as Fig. 5. Below is a visual image of the matrix pressing process.

The fully-connected layer as Fig. 6 is the last layer and the layer that actually performs the classification. This layer basically takes an input, whether it is the output of a convolutional, ReLu, or pool layer, and outputs an N-dimensional vector, where N is the number of classes that the program has to classify. For example, if you want a program that classifies digits from 0 to 9, N would be 10. Each number in this N-dimensional vector represents the probability of a given class. For example, if the resulting vector of a numerical classifier program is [0 .1 .1 .75 0 0 0 0 .05] then 10% chance of image is

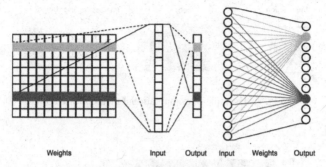

Fig. 6. Example of fully-connected layer

1.10% chance of image is 2.75% the image likelihood is 3 and the image probability is 9. The way the fully-connected layer works is that it looks at the output of the previous layer (this output is the feature map of the high-level features) and determine which feature best corresponds to a particular class. The fully-connected layer can be imagined as a matrix of weights multiplied by the input feature map, resulting in the probabilities of the different classes.

4   An Algorithm for Recognition

The input of the YOLO network is pre-labeled images, the output corresponding to each image is a feature map in the form of a grid of size N × N cells. Corresponding to each cell, the network predicts class probabilities. The input of the YOLO network is pre-labeled images, the output corresponding to each image is a feature map in the form of a grid of size N × N cells. Corresponding to each cell, the network predicts the class probabilities, bounding boxes and confidence scores of each bounding box.

Each cell has B * 5 + C elements. In there:

B is the number of bounding boxes of each cell.
C is the number of class probabilities.
5 is the number of elements of each bounding box (including x,y: coordinates of the center point of the bounding box corresponding to the cell in which the point lies, w - the width of the bounding box corresponding to the original image, h -height of the bounding box relative to the original image, confidence score: the probability that the object is present in the bounding box.

The confidence score is calculated as follows,

$$Pr(Object) * IOU_{pred}^{truth} \qquad (3)$$

The IOU is used to evaluate the detection, the IOU is calculated by dividing the intersection area by the union of the predicted bounding box and the true box (Fig. 7).

The center coordinates, width, and height of the bounding box are converted to segment [0, 1]. The figure below illustrates how these coordinates are calculated (Fig. 8):

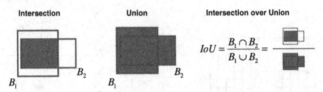

Fig. 7. Example of computational method for IOU

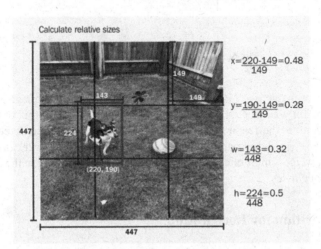

Fig. 8. Example of computational method for coordinates in box

C are class probabilities, Pr(Classi|Object). These probabilities are considered only if the cell contains an object. The network predicts only a unique set of class probabilities for each cell, regardless of the number of bounding boxes B.

At the time of using the images used for the network detection test (time-mem test). Multiply confidence score and class probability,

$$\Pr(Class_i|Object) * \Pr(Object) * IOU_{pred}^{truth} = \Pr(Class_i) * IOU_{pred}^{truth} \qquad (4)$$

Pr(Classi) includes the probability of a class appearing in the bounding box and the confidence score.

5   Results of Research

In the practical application, the proposed scheme is embedded into our powerline robot. From the needs of the power corporation of Vietnam, the power transmission lines are required to be cleaned after a period of time. Otherwise, some unexpected problems could be occurred such decreasing the quality of power line due to the chemical corrosion, short-circuit or discharge phenomenon when the weather condition is bad, and bird nesting avoidance. Since the natural factors would impact on powerline, worker must do the cleaning job once every two or three months. In previous time, those jobs were entirely handled by manual which requires various skills and faces the potential danger. In addition, the power must be cut on the line when the cleaning job is processing. This will cause great economic losses, inconvenience to people's daily lives, and disrupt communications.

The automated solution is introduced as powerline robot that controlled by host computer. Instead of human, robot would reach to power line alone and manipulate the cleaning task. This method has many advantages such as not violating the electrical safety, improving the precision and ensuring the quality of cleaning service. In many

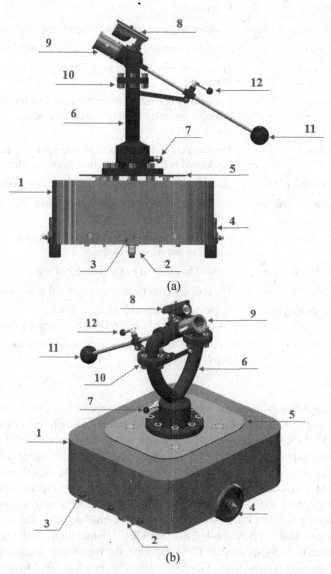

Fig. 9. Computer-based design of the proposed system, (a) front view and (b) 3D view

countries, the powerline robot becomes an indispensable partner when the air condition is unfavorable. As a result, in this paper, the autonomous platform of powerline robot based on the image processing technique is investigated as Fig. 9. List of components in this system is depicted as Table 1. The function of each component and its specification are also explained.

Table 1. List of components for powerline robot.

No.	Specification	Description
1	Body of mobile platform	Its shape might be rectangle or square made by metal material
2	Castor wheel	It moves freely and must be driven by the other wheels
3	Proximity sensor	In the closed distance, this sensing device is to detect any obstacle
4	Driving wheel	It is directly connected with DC motor which manipulate the driving mission by the differences in velocities of left wheel and right wheel
5	Lifting part	The function of this part is to elevate vertically according to the desired height. It is energized by an electric cylinder
6	Body of water gun	Its material is hard enough to suffer the high pressure of water
7	Basement of water gun	It is possibly rotated around z axis in order to provide the wide angle for gun
8	Digital camera	It is used to implement the image processing technique to recognize and measure distance
9	Muzzle of water gun	It could be adjusted by the pressure of water
10	Intermediate coupling	The connection between lower part and upper part
11	Knob of driving hand	In the case of manual control, it is useful for an operator to drive. Additionally, it plays a role as counterweight to balance
12	Navigation lock	Its usage is to fix an angle under the unexpected effect of highly water pressure

With those developments, the application of our approach is clearly stated. Later, the vision-based techniques are implemented. The training for optional object detection will use the YOLOv3-tiny pre-designed network, which has about half the mAP of the YOLOv3 version but has a higher FPS, suitable for training with laptops. no GPU. To increase the mAP to the maximum possible extent of the network, we will use a large and diverse dataset. Detection requires good image information so the input image resolution should be large, be it 416×416 or 608×608. Lowering the resolution will increase the FPS. Training will use Darknet - an open-source neural network framework written in C and CUDA that supports both CPU and GPU computation. Training with GPU will have faster training speed than CPU. Because the thesis uses a computer without a GPU, this training is done using Google Colab. This is a free GPU from Google and we can train YOLO on it. During training, after each iteration, the training program will show the average loss. If this number reaches 0.xxxxx and does not decrease further after many iterations then we will stop the training. After finishing training, we get the weight file.weights which will be used for object detection code.

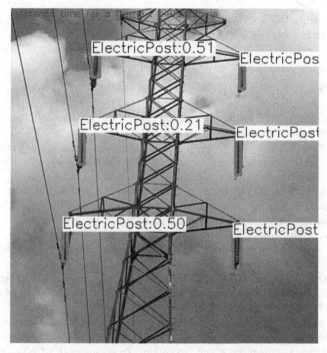

Fig. 10. Experimental result of the proposed method in powerline.

The practical result by using vision approach is shown as Fig. 10. The training process has been trialed in many times so that the weights were as high as possible. There were approximately one thousand of pictures which captured in the outdoor environment. Then, all of them have been labeled and marked in order to feed the machine learning scheme. Along with these results, it also exists some limitations that could affect on the quality of output. One of them is the weather condition or the time of day. Additionally, both terrain and location of powerline are the important factors for the high quality of recognition.

6 Conclusions

In this paper, a novel approach by using vision technique was investigated in the powerline robot. This application is actually essential in the field of electricity transmission due to its advantages such as safe maintenance, high productivity and uniform quality. Initially, a method to estimate distance from robot to powerline was mentioned. It is one of the basis computation to maintain the suitable pressure of water. Later, some definitions of convolutional network were described to provide the knowledge and information. Then, a model of YOLO scheme was recommended to train according to the dataset. The results of both simulation and experiment were clearly shown. It could be seen that our approach is effective, feasible and applicable in this field.

Acknowledgements. We acknowledge the support of time and facilities from Ho Chi Minh City University of Technology (HCMUT), VNU-HCM for this study.

References

1. Chen, R.C.: Automatic license plate recognition via sliding-window darknet-YOLO deep learning. Image Vis. Comput. **87**, 47–56 (2019)
2. Tian, Y., Yang, G., Wang, Z., Wang, H., Li, E., Liang, Z.: Apple detection during different growth stages in orchards using the improved YOLO-V3 model. Comput. Electron. Agric. **157**, 417–426 (2019)
3. Tran, H.A.M., Ngo, H.Q.T., Nguyen, T.P., Nguyen, H.: Implementation of vision-based autonomous mobile platform to control by A∗ algorithm. In: 2018 2nd International Conference on Recent Advances in Signal Processing, Telecommunications & Computing (SigTelCom), pp. 39–44. IEEE (2018)
4. Fang, W., Wang, L., Ren, P.: Tinier-YOLO: a real-time object detection method for constrained environments. IEEE Access **8**, 1935–1944 (2019)
5. Lan, W., Dang, J., Wang, Y., Wang, S.: Pedestrian detection based on YOLO network model. In: 2018 IEEE International Conference on Mechatronics and Automation (ICMA), pp. 1547–1551. IEEE (2018)
6. Bhuiyan, M.R., Khushbu, S.A., Islam, M.S.: A deep learning based assistive system to classify COVID-19 face mask for human safety with YOLOv3. In: 2020 11th International Conference on Computing, Communication and Networking Technologies (ICCCNT), pp. 1–5. IEEE (2020)
7. Laroca, R., et al.: A robust real-time automatic license plate recognition based on the YOLO detector. In: 2018 International Joint Conference on Neural Networks (IJCNN), pp. 1–10. IEEE (2018)
8. Adarsh, P., Rathi, P., Kumar, M.: YOLO v3-Tiny: object detection and recognition using one stage improved model. In: 2020 6th International Conference on Advanced Computing and Communication Systems (ICACCS), pp. 687–694. IEEE (2020)
9. Hurtik, P., Molek, V., Hula, J., Vajgl, M., Vlasanek, P., Nejezchleba, T.: Poly-YOLO: higher speed, more precise detection and instance segmentation for YOLOv3. Neural Comput. Appl. **34**(10), 8275–8290 (2022)
10. Zhang, H., Watanabe, K., Motegi, K., Shiraishi, Y.: ROS based framework for autonomous driving of AGVs. In: Proceedings of the IPS6-04, ICMEMIS, Kiryu, Japan, pp. 4–6 (2019)
11. Linder, T., Pfeiffer, K.Y., Vaskevicius, N., Schirmer, R., Arras, K.O.: Accurate detection and 3D localization of humans using a novel YOLO-based RGB-D fusion approach and synthetic training data. In: 2020 IEEE International Conference on Robotics and Automation (ICRA), pp. 1000–1006. IEEE (2020)
12. Mi, C., Huang, Y., Fu, C., Zhang, Z., Postolache, O.: Vision-based measurement: actualities and developing trends in automated container terminals. IEEE Instrum. Meas. Mag. **24**(4), 65–76 (2021)
13. Cao, Z., Liao, T., Song, W., Chen, Z., Li, C.: Detecting the shuttlecock for a badminton robot: a YOLO based approach. Expert Syst. Appl. **164**, 113833 (2021)

14. Dos Reis, D.H., Welfer, D., De Souza Leite Cuadros, M.A., Gamarra, D.F.T.: Mobile robot navigation using an object recognition software with RGBD images and the YOLO algorithm. Appl. Artif. Intell. **33**(14), 1290–1305 (2019)
15. Yu, Y., Zhang, K., Liu, H., Yang, L., Zhang, D.: Real-time visual localization of the picking points for a ridge-planting strawberry harvesting robot. IEEE Access **8**, 116556–116568 (2020)
16. Kim, H., Kim, H., Lee, S.I., Lee, H.: Autonomous exploration in a cluttered environment for a mobile robot with 2D-map segmentation and object detection. IEEE Robot Autom. Lett. **7**, 6343–6350 (2022)
17. Kulik, S.D., Shtanko, A.N.: Experiments with neural net object detection system YOLO on small training datasets for intelligent robotics. In: Misyurin, S.Y., Arakelian, V., Avetisyan, A.I. (eds.) Advanced Technologies in Robotics and Intelligent Systems. MMS, vol. 80, pp. 157–162. Springer, Cham (2020). https://doi.org/10.1007/978-3-030-33491-8_19
18. Vemula, S., Frye, M.: Real-time powerline detection system for an unmanned aircraft system. In: 2020 IEEE International Conference on Systems, Man, and Cybernetics (SMC), pp. 4493–4497. IEEE (2020)
19. Wang, D., Li, W., Liu, X., Li, N., Zhang, C.: UAV environmental perception and autonomous obstacle avoidance: a deep learning and depth camera combined solution. Comput. Electron. Agric. **175**, 105523 (2020)
20. Ohta, H., Sato, Y., Mori, T., Takaya, K., Kroumov, V.: Image acquisition of power line transmission towers using UAV and deep learning technique for insulators localization and recognition. In: 2019 23rd International Conference on System Theory, Control and Computing (ICSTCC), pp. 125–130. IEEE (2019)
21. Lopez Lopez, R., Batista Sanchez, M.J., Perez Jimenez, M., Arrue, B.C., Ollero, A.: Autonomous UAV system for cleaning insulators in power line inspection and maintenance. Sensors **21**(24), 8488 (2021)
22. Sadykova, D., Pernebayeva, D., Bagheri, M., James, A.: IN-YOLO: real-time detection of outdoor high voltage insulators using UAV imaging. IEEE Trans. Power Delivery **35**(3), 1599–1601 (2019)

Author Index

© ICST Institute for Computer Sciences, Social Informatics and Telecommunications Engineering 2023
Published by Springer Nature Switzerland AG 2023. All Rights Reserved
C. V. Phan and T. D. Nguyen (Eds.): ICCASA 2022, LNICST 475, p. 191, 2023.
https://doi.org/10.1007/978-3-031-28816-6

Printed in the United States
by Baker & Taylor Publisher Services